Y0-BAQ-476

GOOD READING

SIXTH READER

BY

JOHN M. MANLY
PROFESSOR OF ENGLISH, UNIVERSITY OF CHICAGO

EDITH RICKERT
ASSOCIATE PROFESSOR OF ENGLISH, UNIVERSITY OF CHICAGO

NINA LEUBRIE
FORMERLY CRITIC TEACHER, CHICAGO NORMAL SCHOOL

WITH ILLUSTRATIONS BY
BLANCHE GREER

CHARLES SCRIBNER'S SONS
NEW YORK   CHICAGO   BOSTON
          ATLANTA   SAN FRANCISCO

For permission to use selections in this book we are indebted to the following:
Martha P. Bennett for "The Flag Goes By," by Henry Holcomb Bennett; Boni & Liveright for "The Key of Stone," from *The Ancient Man*, by Hendrik Van Loon, and a selection from *Alaska Man's Luck*, by Hjalmar Rutzebek; Brandt & Brandt for "Afternoon on a Hill," from *Renascence*, published by Harper & Brothers, copyright 1917, by Edna St. Vincent Millay; Jonathan Cape for "Nature's Friend" and "When on a Summer's Morn," by W. H. Davies; The Century Company for "The Steeple-Climber" and "The Bridge-Builder," from *Careers of Danger and Daring*, by Cleveland Moffett, and for a selection from "The American Boy," from *The Strenuous Life*, by Theodore Roosevelt; Dodd, Mead & Company for "Work," by Angela Morgan, and for "Loveliest of Trees," by A. E. Housman; George H. Doran Company for "Trees," by Joyce Kilmer, and "A Street Scene," by Lizette Woodworth Reese; Doubleday, Page & Company and A. P. Watt & Son for "The Explorer," by Rudyard Kipling; Doubleday, Page & Company for "Pioneers! O Pioneers!" "I Hear America Singing," and a selection from *Leaves of Grass*, by Walt Whitman; The Macmillan Company and Hamlin Garland for "Do You Hear the Wind?" and a selection from *A Son of the Middle Border*; Harper & Brothers for "The Coyote," from *Roughing It*, by Mark Twain; Henry Holt & Company for "Four Little Foxes," by Lew Sarrett, "Stopping by Woods" and "The Runaway," by Robert Frost, "Primer Lesson," by Carl Sandburg, and "Full Moon" and "Summer Evening," by Walter de la Mare; Houghton, Mifflin Company for "Concord Hymn" and "A Nation's Strength," by Ralph Waldo Emerson, "Old Ironsides," by Oliver Wendell Holmes, "A Rill from the Town Pump," from *Success to the Town Pump*, by Nathaniel Hawthorne, a selection from *My Garden Acquaintance*, by James Russell Lowell, and "A Virginia Plantation," from *George Washington*, by Horace Scudder, "Opportunity," by Edward Rowland Sill; Helen Hoyt for "Ellis Park"; Alfred A. Knopf for "To a Phœbe Bird," by Witter Bynner; Little, Brown & Company for "Autumn," by Emily Dickinson, "Being Neighborly," from *Little Women*, by Louisa M. Alcott, and "A Pawnee Buffalo Hunt," from *The Oregon Trail*, by Francis Parkman; Robert M. McBride & Company for a selection from *The Great White South*, by H. D. Ponting; Macmillan Company for "April," by Sara Teasdale, and "Tewkesbury Road," by John Masefield; Wilbur D. Nesbit for "Who Hath a Book"; Charles Scribner's Sons for "What One Man Did for the Place He Lived In," from *Two Persons*, by Edward W. Bok; selections from *The Adventures of a Grain of Dust*, by Hallam Hawksworth; "The Man Who Crossed the Ranges," from *Some Forgotten Heroes*, by E. Alexander Powell; "The Yellow Mail," from *Held for Orders*, by Frank Spearman; "Wind" and a selection from *Kidnapped*, by Robert Louis Stevenson; "Work," by Henry van Dyke; Small, Maynard & Company for "The Mocking-Bird," by Richard Hovey; Frederick A. Stokes for a selection from *The North Pole*, by Robert Peary; Carolyn Wells for "How to Tell the Wild Animals."

COPYRIGHT, 1928, BY
CHARLES SCRIBNER'S SONS

Printed in the United States of America

This page is like a guide who is about to take you on a wonderful tour and who desires to tell you a few things at the beginning. It is what we call the

PREFACE

This is your book of Good Reading. The aim of the book is

To give you enjoyment in reading;

To take you to many interesting places and introduce you to great persons;

To acquaint you with the best ways of reading so that you will learn to read rapidly and easily get the meaning carried by words;

To extend your reading to many good books, and to help you make them your friends and companions, true and helpful;

To teach you to think clearly, feel rightly, and love deeply the best things in life.

This is the mission of Good Reading!

This part of the book is for you, as well as for your teacher. It is to tell you some points of interest and to guide you into the pleasures to come. We call it

READING AND STUDY HELPS

1. READING

Books are magic windows through which we may see the world and all that is in it from the Beginning to Now.

The Table of Contents will tell you what a magic window you are about to open. You are to enjoy voyages and adventures, visit strange lands and historic places, meet great people, see the heavens in all their glory, and learn how Nature helps man with his work. There are interesting hours ahead.

Have you ever thought how marvelous it is that we can look at a line of queer marks or signs, which we call print, and get thought and feeling from them? Look at these strange signs for a moment

木　　女　　食　　男子　　女子

Do they mean anything to you? They are Chinese words. They mean:
Tree　　Woman　　Food　　Son　　Daughter
But to you they are mysteries. Why?

We know our words because we have learned to recognize them as signs or symbols of meaning. The more quickly and extensively we can recognize them, the better we can read. You will find many suggestions in this book on the best way to read. As you go on, notice the introductions and the many suggestions to aid you in your reading—the Things to Do, Discussions, and Books to Read. All these helps are to aid you in learning the magic and beauty of words.

One thing is of great importance. It is to learn the use of words—their names and meanings. For this purpose, you should make frequent use of the dictionary. For knowing words, it is the greatest book in the world. Learn how to work with it.

Words often have different meanings, or shades of meaning. The real meaning of a word may depend upon the words with which it is used. Then there are words which have nearly the same meaning, like—*silent, still, quiet;* or *dumb, mute, speechless*. There is no more valuable practice in learning to think clearly than to study the different shades of meaning in words.

One of the most helpful things for young readers to do is to keep a Vocabulary Notebook. A common five or ten-cent pocket-size notebook is good enough. In it write down a new word or two each day and learn it—how to pronounce it; how to spell it; and what it means.

To lay up in your mind a store of goodly thoughts in well-wrought words is one of the most important purposes of your reading; for:

> "Books are the keys to wisdom's treasure,
> Books are gates to lands of pleasure;
> Books are paths that upward lead,
> Books are friends; come let us read."

2. Learning How to Read

Learning how to read is an important part of study. Many persons do not know how to read in the best way. Some read slowly, seeing only one or two words at a time. They read words but do not get the meaning. By practice one can learn to take in several words at one glance and a whole line in three or four eye movements. In reading, the eyes should move along the lines of print by quick glances, with very brief pauses at the end of each movement; these movements are called "eye-sweeps." The more words one can take in at a glance or eye-sweep the easier it is for one to read. The mind gets the thought during the brief pauses which occur between these forward eye-sweeps. The pauses are very, very brief.

One should learn to read for ideas and thoughts, and not merely words. Each paragraph usually contains one chief thought. The thing to do is to search for that chief thought as one would look in a crowd for some one he wants to see. When the chief thought is recognized, it is important to grasp it in a friendly manner as one would greet his friend in the crowd.

In any paragraph or lesson, not all facts are of equal worth. Some are much more important than others. It is necessary to learn how to select the important points and to make close friends of them. The next thing to do is to see which is the most important of them all. This kind of reading will make a successful reader.

This book is planned to furnish you with many kinds of

Good Reading. It is intended also to help you learn how to read happily and effectively. As you take up the different parts of this book, notice the suggestions on the points mentioned in these introductory pages. Attention to them will surprise you with your growing ability and power to read rapidly and with understanding.

3. Helps

If you could find a way to help you do your work much more easily and better than ever, would you like it? Many pupils make their reading and work a disagreeable drudgery because they do not know how to do it in the right way. A great deal of time and happiness is therefore wasted.

Here are some helps to aid you in learning how to study. Most persons can increase greatly their ability to study if they will try honestly. Study habits are like all other habits—they must be learned by practice. It has been proved that most students can learn three or four times as much as they do, and learn even in less time, when they know how to make their minds and bodies work together. Try for yourself. It depends largely upon "making up your mind" to do it.

Begin now by reading the following general study helps:

1. Make yourself comfortable.
2. Get the things you need for study.
3. Be sure you understand what you are to do.
4. Think over what you already know about the subject.

5. Get down to business: keep your mind on your work.
6. Do your own work: ask for help only after you have done your best.
7. Be able to tell the important facts in the lesson.
8. Be satisfied only with work well done.

Now learn them "by heart." See how quickly you can memorize them. Tell your teacher how quickly you did it. Ask your teacher to test you on these points.

After you have memorized the eight general study helps, then study the following complete outline. Do not be satisfied with one reading. Study the outline daily until you understand and practice easily every point in it.

STUDY HELPS FOR THE SIXTH GRADE

1. *Keep Fit.* To study well, you must feel well. To do this, sleep at least ten hours each night with windows open. Drink milk; eat vegetables and fruit. Play outdoors all you can. When indoors, take off outdoor wraps.
2. *Make Ready.* All workmen need tools. Good workmen keep them ready and in good condition. Your books, pencils, tablets, and notebooks are your tools. Be a good workman.
3. *Go!* Start promptly, as you would in a game or race. Remember the old saying, "Work while you work and play while you play."
4. *Be Independent.* Ask for help only after you have done your best. Do not be afraid to tackle hard jobs. Make up your mind to master the job.
5. *Ask Questions.* Do not be afraid to ask questions, if you do not understand what to do. Make certain that you know what the work is. Good questions will help you and the teacher also.
6. *Connect Each Lesson with Something You Know.* Ask yourself what you already know about the lesson. Have you learned something about it before? Have you seen something about it in the movies? Have you seen pictures of it or read about it in newspapers and magazines?
7. *Make Up Your Mind to Learn.* Your mind will not do more than you require of it. Make your memory responsible for important points. Write down important things you wish to remember. Learn to make useful outlines. Do not fill them with useless stuff copied from books. Select only important ideas. Try to be original in arrangement. Think out ideas of your own.

8. *Do Good Work.* Do more than just what "will do." Take pride in good work. Make up your mind that you can and will do a good job.
9. *Learn to Do Two Kinds of Reading.* Read rapidly when seeking to find important points or get a general idea of the lesson. Read carefully such things as problems, directions, explanations, and anything else which must be carefully studied. Be careful not to form a bad habit of "skimming" at such times. It is a good thing to stop at the end of a paragraph and try to recall the main point or points which you have read.
10. *Learn How to Use Books.* This is a very important part of your work. It is like the workman learning to use his tools. Here are some of the things to learn how to use: the preface or introduction; table of contents; the index; appendix; footnotes; the glossary; maps and illustrations. Learn how to use reference books; the dictionary; encyclopedias; yearbooks; atlases; magazines, and newspapers.

CONTENTS

READING AND STUDY HELPS
                                                                              PAGE

1. Reading 4
2. Learning How to Read 6
3. Helps 7

VOYAGING AND EXPLORING

1. Some Adventures of Odysseus. *Adapted from "The Odyssey"* . 18
2. The First Voyage Round the World. *Adapted from Antonio Pigafetta* 39
3. The Discovery of the North Pole. *Robert E. Peary* 51
4. First at the North Pole 59
5. The Discovery of the South Pole. *H. D. Ponting* 61

OUR COUNTRY

1. The Man Who Crossed the Ranges. *E. Alexander Powell* . . 70
2. The Explorer. *Rudyard Kipling* 77
3. Three Poems
    Pioneers! O Pioneers! *Walt Whitman* 85
    Song to the Mountains (Pawnee) 91
    Mount Koonak: A Song of Arsut (Eskimaun) 93
4. A Pawnee Buffalo Hunt. *Francis Parkman* 95
5. Homesteading in Alaska. *Hjalmar Rutzebek* 102

SOME FAMOUS PATRIOTIC POEMS

1. Concord Hymn. *Ralph Waldo Emerson* 117
2. Old Ironsides. *Oliver Wendell Holmes* 119
3. An Old-Time Sea Fight. *Walt Whitman* 123
4. The Old Navy. *Frederick Marryat* 126
5. The Star-Spangled Banner. *Francis Scott Key* 128
6. Respect the Flag. *Alvin M. Owsley* 131
7. Pledge to the Flag 132
8. The American's Creed. *William Tyler Page* 133
9. The Flag Goes By. *Henry Holcomb Bennett* 133

Heroes in Everyday Work

		PAGE
1.	The Steeple-Climber. *Cleveland Moffett*	137
2.	Work. *Henry van Dyke*	143
3.	The Bridge-Builder. *Cleveland Moffett*	144
4.	I Hear America Singing. *Walt Whitman*	156
5.	Work. *Angela Morgan*	157

Two Ways of Making the World Better

1. What One Man Did for the Place He Lived In. *Edward Bok* . 161
   (a) Caring for Trees and Birds 161
   (b) Making a True Home 164
2. Trees. *Theodore Roosevelt* 169
3. Loveliest of Trees. *A. E. Housman* 169
4. The American Humane Association. *William O. Stillman* . . 170
5. Poems about Animals
   (1) Four Little Foxes. *Lew Sarrett* 175
   (2) The Runaway. *Robert Frost* 176
   (3) Nature's Friend. *William H. Davies* 178

New Light on Old Heroes

1. Abraham Lincoln
   (1) Lincoln at Gettysburg 183
   (2) The Gettysburg Address. *Abraham Lincoln* 186
   (3) Lincoln's Life as Written by Himself 188
   (4) "He knew to bide his time." *James Russell Lowell* . . . 189
2. The True Story of Hiawatha 190
3. The Autobiography of Benjamin Franklin 197
4. Washington at Home 212
5. A Virginia Plantation. *Horace E. Scudder* 217

The Boy Makes the Man

1. The American Boy. *Theodore Roosevelt* 223
2. Four Poems to Learn
   (1) The Noble Nature. *Ben Jonson* 227
   (2) Do You Fear the Wind? *Hamlin Garland* 228
   (3) A Nation's Strength. *Ralph Waldo Emerson* 229
   (4) Opportunity. *Edward Rowland Sill* 229
3. Three Wild Rides
   (1) Going for the Doctor. *Hamlin Garland* 230
   (2) The Yellow Mail. *Frank Spearman* 238
   (3) An Indian Scare. *Andy Adams* 249

Reading in Real Life

1. Guides for the Story-Teller 256
2. Three Ways of Reading 259
   (1) Reading for Necessary New Information 259
   (2) Reading for Additional Information 260
   (3) Reading for Enjoyment 260
3. The Use of Reference Books 262
   (1) The Encyclopedia 262
   (2) Yearbooks 264
   (3) Using the Dictionary 264
   (4) The Atlas 267
4. Choose a Magazine 267
5. Reading the Newspaper 268
6. Poems
   (1) Treasure. *Old Rhyme* 271
   (2) Who Hath a Book. *Wilbur Dick Nesbit* 272
   (3) No Books. *Stanley E. Crabb* 273
7. The Key of Stone. *Hendrik Van Loon* 274

Fun and Humor in Prose and Verse

1. Limericks 283
2. Rhymes Without Reason 284
   (1) The Camel's Plaint. *Charles Edward Carryl* . . 284
   (2) How to Tell the Wild Animals. *Carolyn Wells* . 286
3. The Coyote. *S. L. Clemens (Mark Twain)* 287
4. Three Poems
   (1) The Akond of Swat. *Edward Lear* 290
   (2) The Blind Men and the Elephant. *J. G. Saxe* . 291
   (3) Their Neighbors' Faults. *J. G. Saxe* 293
5. How Pigs Were First Roasted. *Charles Lamb* . . 295
6. A Rill from the Town Pump. *Nathaniel Hawthorne* 300

Neighbors and Friends

1. Being Neighborly. *Louisa M. Alcott* 308
2. Christmas at Bracebridge Hall. *Washington Irving* . . . 324
3. Kidnapped. *Robert Louis Stevenson* 332

Four Poems

1. Primer Lesson. *Carl Sandburg* 338
2. Wawan Song (Omaha) 338
3. Song to the Pleiades (Pawnee) 339
4. War Song (Dakota) 339

BIRDS AND INSECTS
PAGE

1. How Birds Help Man 339
   (1) Bird Poems
       The Blackbird. *Humbert Wolfe* 340
       Little Trotty Wagtail. *John Clare* 341
       When on a Summer's Morn. *W. H. Davies* 341
   (2) The Economic Value of Birds to Man. *F. M. Chapman* . 342
   (3) $2,105 Spent to Save a Dollar. *C. H. Merriam* . . . 346
   (4) A Reminder: What Birds Do for Us 347
       What We Can Do for Birds 348
   (5) What James Russell Lowell Thought of Animals and Birds . 349
   (6) Chickadee and Titmouse. *Nina Leubrie* 350
   (7) Robins 351
   (8) The Mocking-Bird. *Maurice Thompson* 354
   (9) Bird Poems
       The Mocking-Bird. *Richard Hovey* 356
       The Throstle. *Alfred, Lord Tennyson* 357
       To a Phœbe Bird. *Witter Bynner* 358
       Off the Coast. *George Crabbe* 359
2. Knowing Insects 361
   (1) How a Cricket Makes Its Sound. *Nina Leubrie* . . . 362
   (2) On the Grasshopper and Cricket. *John Keats* . . . 363
   (3) The Voice That Beautifies the Land (Navajo) 364

KNOWING THE PLACE WHERE WE LIVE

1. Some Ways of Studying Flowers
   (1) "Come down to Kew in lilac-time." *Alfred Noyes* . . . 365
   (2) The Goldenrod. *Nina Leubrie* 366
   (3) Fringed Gentians. *Nina Leubrie* 369
   (4) Closed Gentians. *Nina Leubrie* 372
   (5) Jack-in-the-Pulpit 373
2. Flower in the Crannied Wall. *Alfred, Lord Tennyson* . . . 375
3. Sun Printing 376
4. The Town I Live In. *Nina Leubrie*
   (1) Greenbush, a Buried Village 378
   (2) The Living Dune 380
   (3) Indians at Greenbush 382
   (4) Stone Beads 383
5. Outdoors Poems
   (1) Ellis Park. *Helen Hoyt* 385
   (2) Afternoon on a Hill. *Edna St. Vincent Millay* . . . 386

		PAGE
(3) A Street Scene. *Lizette W. Reese*		387
(4) Stopping By Woods on a Snowy Evening. *Robert Frost*		388
(5) Tewkesbury Road. *John Masefield.*		388
(6) April. *Sara Teasdale*		389
(7) Summer Evening. *Walter de la Mare*		390
(8) Autumn. *Emily Dickinson*		390

Nearer Than the Stars

1. The Eighth Psalm 391
2. Nearer Than the Stars 392
3. The Moon 393
4. The Full Moon. *Walter de la Mare* 401
5. The Planets 402
6. The Solar System 404
7. Our Solar System in a Model of the Universe. *Simon B. Newcomb* 405
8. Identifying Planets 407
9. Astronomical Units of Measure 408
10. The Spacious Firmament on High. *Joseph Addison* 409

Nature, Science, and Invention

1. Mr. Ground-Hog and His Shadow. *Hallam Hawksworth* . . . 411
2. The Work of the Winds. *Hallam Hawksworth* 414
   (1) What the Winds Do with Dust 415
   (2) How Dust Helps Make Rain 418
3. Two Poems
   (1) The Wind. *Robert Louis Stevenson* 420
   (2) The Windy Night. *Thomas B. Read* 421
4. How Men Learned to Fly 423
5. How Men Learned to Use Electricity 432
   (1) The Beginning 433
   (2) About Magnets 435
   (3) About Electricity 436
   (4) The Telegraph 436
   (5) The Telephone 439
   (6) The Radio 441

Afterword 442

To L. L. Caldwell, Superintendent of Schools, Hammond, Indiana, and to many teachers in the Hammond schools the authors are especially indebted for constructive suggestions and for the practical trying-out of this material in the classrooms of that city.

"DID YOU EVER DREAM OF EXPLORING?"
Reproduced from a painting, "The Westing Sun," by Gordon Grant.

VOYAGING AND EXPLORING

Did you ever dream of exploring unknown parts of the world? The next best thing to going is reading about such voyages.

The first account printed here is from a Greek story-poem called "The Odyssey," told about three thousand years ago. Even then the Greeks were sailors. Their small sailing ships were not so large as our fishing vessels. In these ships they explored the coasts of the Mediterranean Sea, and some of them even sailed outside into the Atlantic. From their voyages they came home with wild stories of their narrow escapes and the strange things they had seen.

"The Odyssey" was so called from the name of its hero—Odysseus. In the story he was king of Ithaca, an island in the Mediterranean, and he went with the other kings of Greece to fight the Trojans. For ten years, according to "The Iliad," another Greek poem of that time, the Greeks besieged Troy before they conquered the Trojans. They took the city at last by carrying out a plan made by Odysseus. For this reason the gods who favored the Trojans were so angry with Odysseus that they kept him wandering over the seas and living in strange places for ten years before they allowed him to return home. In the parts of "The Odyssey" here quoted, you can read of some of his strange adventures.

SOME ADVENTURES OF ODYSSEUS

THE CHARACTERS IN THE STORY

In reading a story or play, you will find it always helpful to know something about the persons presented and to know how to pronounce their names. The characters in "Some Adventures of Odysseus" are often mentioned in other books; it is therefore important to know them well. Here they are:

Odysseus (ō-dĭs'ūs), king of Ithaca, one of the Greek Islands.
Cyclopes (sī'klō"pēz), a race of one-eyed, giant shepherds.
Poseidon (pō-sī'don), the Greek god of the sea.
Polyphemus (pŏl'ĭ-fē'mŭs), a Cyclops.
Laertes (lȧ-ûr'tēs), father of Odysseus.
Æolus (ē'o-lŭs), god of the winds.
Circe (sûr'sē), an enchantress who changed men into beasts.
Hermes (hûr'mēz), a messenger of the gods; guardian of travelers.
Eurylochus (ū-rĭl'ō-kŭs), a trusted companion of Odysseus.
Sirens (sī'rĕns), sea nymphs said to live on an island off the coast of Italy and to lure sailors to destruction by their beauty and sweet singing.
Scylla (sĭl'ȧ), a rock dangerous to navigation on the Italian side of the Straits of Messina; in mythology a six-headed, twelve-armed monster surrounded by barking dogs, living on the rock Scylla.
Charybdis (kȧ-rĭb'dis), a dangerous whirlpool between Sicily and Italy, near the shore of Sicily; said by the ancients to have been a woman whom Jupiter transformed to a whirlpool.
Phœbus (fē'bŭs), the god of the sun.
Zeus (zūs), the ruler of the Greek gods.
Calypso (kȧ-lĭp'sō), a sea nymph who kept Odysseus seven years on her island.
Phæacians (fė-ā'shŭns), the prosperous seafaring people on the island of Phæacia, supposed to be the same as the island we know as Corfu.

SOME ADVENTURES OF ODYSSEUS

I

The Island of the Cyclopes

Read this story silently. Have you ever thought of making the commas help you to group your words as you read? If you keep your eyes moving until you reach some punctuation mark, then look back to make sure you understand all the words before it, at the end of the sentence you will understand it all. If you form the habit of doing this, you will soon become a good reader and will have much pleasure from books.

In reading Section I, you will find it interesting to follow these directions:

1. In the middle of page 22, stop and write in a few words what you think you would have done to escape.

2. At the bottom of page 24, stop and write what would have happened if Odysseus had not called himself Noman; also, how you think the Greeks escaped.

When Troy had been destroyed, Odysseus and his men set sail for home, hoping to be quickly there. But they soon met great winds and stormy seas, which drove them on for many days and nights, always in fear of death. When they came to land, it was not the shore of their dear country that they saw but the island of the Cyclopes, giant shepherds, who lived in caves among the hills.

In this island there was a good harbor with a smaller island at the mouth of it. There Odysseus told the men of eleven of his ships to wait, while he and the men of his own ship rowed across the harbor to the main island.

They saw above them in the hillside a lofty cave, overgrown with laurels. In front of this was a paved stone court, and in it were growing tall pines and oaks.

To this cave went Odysseus and twelve chosen companions, leaving the others to guard the ship. Odysseus carried a goatskin of wine and a bag of grain, as gifts to whoever lived in the cave.

When the Greeks landed, the courtyard and the cave were empty but for the lambs and kids penned up there. Round about stood baskets of cheeses and bowls of whey.

The companions of Odysseus begged him to let them take away what they could of the cheeses, and to drive before them the lambs and kids down to their ship, and sail away over the salt sea water. But he would not. He was eager to see what kind of man was the owner of the flocks.

Then his men kindled a fire in the cave and made a burnt-offering to their gods. They ate some of the cheeses and sat waiting for the shepherd to return.

It was evening before he came, driving his flocks before him, and carrying a mighty log of wood on his shoulder. He was a huge giant, with only one eye and that set in the middle of his forehead. He entered the cave, dropping his log with a crash. The terrified Greeks ran back and hid in the darkest part of the cavern.

The giant left some of his flock outside in the yard, but those that were to be milked he drove into the cave, and rolled a mighty doorstone against the door so that none might go in or out. So huge and heavy was this stone that twenty-two four-wheeled wagons could not have carried it.

Next, the giant milked the ewes and the bleating goats, all in turn, and gave to each ewe and each mother-goat her young one. Half the milk he curdled at once into cheese, and the other half he set aside in pails for his supper. After he had busily done all this, he made up the fire; and then it was that he spied the Greeks in the far corner, and said to them:

"Who are you, strangers? Where do you come from over the wet ways of the sea? Are you traders or adventurers, who risk your lives wandering about to rob other men?"

Odysseus answered: "Not so. We are Greeks returning home from Troy, but we have been driven out of our course by many winds over the wide seas. It is by chance that we have come to your door. Have mercy on us and honor the gods by giving us the welcome that is due to strangers."

But the giant answered without pity: "Stranger, you are either foolish, or you come from afar, if you think that I care for the will of the gods. We Cyclopes do not worship your gods. We are better than they. But tell me where you have left your well-built ship. Is it at the far end of the island, or near by? Tell me that."

Odysseus was not deceived by him but met his guile[1] with guile, saying: "As for my ship, Poseidon, the earth-shaker, cast it on the rocks of the headland and broke it to pieces. Barely have I and my men escaped destruction."

[1] guile: deceit; cunning; trickery.

The giant said nothing, but he stretched out his great hand and seized two of the sailors. He dashed them to the ground and killed them. Then he cut them up and ate them for his supper, flesh, bones, and all. And the other Greeks in their corner prayed to Zeus, at their wits' end for fear. When the Cyclops had eaten and had drunk his milk, he stretched himself out among his sheep for his night's rest.

At first Odysseus thought to plunge his sword into the giant's heart, but then he remembered that there was none to roll away the great stone from the door. So he and his companions would all perish within the cave. Thus they lay still, mourning for their lost friends, and waited for the day.

How the Greeks Made Ready

When rosy-fingered dawn came into the sky, the giant shepherd rose and kindled his fire and cared for his flock again. When he had busily done all his work, he seized two more of the Greeks and made his meal of them. Afterward, he rolled away the great doorstone, and when he had driven out his flock he set it in place again. With a loud whoop he turned his fat flock toward the hills.

But Odysseus had thought of a plan by which the Greeks might escape. He showed his men a great club of green olive wood lying in the cave. It belonged to the Cyclops and was as tall as the mast of a ship. From it Odysseus cut a piece about a fathom[1] long, and had his companions

---

[1] fathom: a measure of length; six feet.

smooth it while he himself sharpened one end to a point and hardened the point in the fire. When this was done, they hid the piece under rubbish, of which there was much lying about the cave, and cast lots to see which of the men should help Odysseus to put out the giant's eye as he lay asleep. Four of them were thus chosen, the very four that Odysseus would have wished to help him.

In the evening the shepherd came home with his flocks and did his work in orderly fashion as on the night before. Again he seized and ate two of the Greeks for his supper.

Meanwhile, Odysseus had poured into a bowl some of the wine that he had brought with him. This he held up to the Cyclops, saying: "Cyclops, drink the wine that I brought you as a gift, thinking that you would have mercy on us and help us on our homeward way. But so hard-hearted and lawless are you that I wonder whether any other man will ever dare to come to this place."

The giant took the wine and drank it. He was so pleased that he asked for another cup, and still another, saying: "Tell me your name, stranger, and I will give you a gift to make you glad. For this wine of yours is the very drink of the gods."

When Odysseus saw that the wine, to which the giant was unused, was getting about his wits, he said softly: "Cyclops, you ask me my name that you may give me the gift that is the stranger's due. My name is Noman. It is Noman they call me—my father, my mother, and all my friends."

Then out of his pitiless heart the Cyclops answered: "Noman will I eat last of all when the others have been eaten. That shall be your gift."

He sank back and lay on the floor of the cave with upturned face, overcome with sleep from the wine he had been drinking.

Odysseus thrust the sharpened stake deep into the embers of the fire until it glowed and would have burned, had it not been made of green wood. Then he and his comrades suddenly thrust it into the giant's eye. Odysseus sat on the top of it and turned it round and round, as when a man bores a ship timber with a drill. With a terrible cry the Cyclops pulled out the blood-stained stake. The rocks echoed with his cry and the Greeks fled in deadly fear to the recesses of the cavern.

The giant flung the stake from him, and maddened with pain, shouted to his brother Cyclopes, who dwelled near him in the caves along the windy heights. They heard his cry and flocked from all sides, asking him what ailed him: "What has disturbed you, Polyphemus, that you cry out in the night and waken us? Is some one stealing your flocks? Is some one killing you?".

Then the mighty Polyphemus said to them from his cave: "Friends, Noman is killing me!"

They answered: "If no man is killing you, you are surely mad. Pray to your father, Poseidon, that he may help you to recover." With that they went away.

The Cyclops, groaning with pain, felt his way to the mouth of the cave and lifted away the stone. There he sat with his arms outstretched to catch any of them who might try to go out with the sheep.

But again Odysseus had thought of a plan for outwitting him. He had seized the sheep before they began to move out, and bound them together in threes. Under the middle sheep of each three he had bound one of his companions. And he himself seized the thick fleece of a splendid young ram, the best of the flock, and so waited for the dawn.

How They Escaped

In the early morning, as the sheep passed through the door of the cave, Polyphemus felt along their backs, but each time the two sheep on the outside protected the man who was bound under the middle sheep. So they went away to the pasture.

Last of all went the young ram, with Odysseus under him, hanging to his shaggy fleece. On this ram the mighty Polyphemus laid his hands, saying: "Dear ram, why are you the last of the flock to go forth from the cave? You were always the first to the pasture and the first to the streams of the rivers, and the first to return home in the evening. But now you are last. Surely you are sorrowing for your master, who has been blinded by an evil man. Ah, if you could only feel my pain and tell me where he skulks from my wrath, then should his brains be dashed out on the floor of this cave and my heart be somewhat eased." With that he let the ram go.

Outside the cave, Odysseus freed his comrades, and they all ran down to the seaside, driving before them the fat sheep. There they were welcomed with joy by the men whom they had left to guard the ship. There was no time to grieve for those who had been slain. They threw the sheep aboard, took their places on the benches, and, sitting in order, began to row away through the gray sea water.

But before they were out of hearing, Odysseus called back, taunting the Cyclops: "So, then, Cyclops, you did not eat all the friends of a poor, weak fellow like me! Your evil deeds have caught you. Zeus has punished you for eating the guests within your gates!"

At this, Polyphemus was mightily angered. He broke off the peak of a great hill and flung it at the Greeks. It fell in front of the black-prowed ship and made a great wave that drove the ship back on the shore. Odysseus took a pole and pushed her off again, urging his men to row with all their might, to escape this danger.

When they had gone twice as far as before, Odysseus shouted again: "Cyclops, if any one asks you who put out your eye, tell him it was Odysseus, son of Laertes, who lives in Ithaca."

Again the giant hurled a huge rock, far greater than the first. It fell only a little short of the black-prowed ship, and barely missed the rudder. But this time the wave that it made drove the ship outward toward the island at the mouth of the harbor, where the other ships were.

They reached the island safely and there killed some of the sheep of the Cyclops, and offered sacrifice to the gods. All that day they feasted and at night slept on the sea beach.

When early dawn, the rosy-fingered, came into the sky, the sailors climbed aboard and loosed the ropes. Sitting in order on the benches, they struck the gray sea water with their oars. So they went away, glad as men saved from death, yet grieving for their comrades who had been slain by the Cyclops.

QUESTIONS FOR TESTING ACCURACY

Section I—The Island of the Cyclopes

NOTE: One reason why many people fail in life is that they are never accurate. They do not, for instance, pay enough attention to what they read to understand it or to make any use of it. To read in this way is mere waste of time. Here are some questions to test the accuracy of your reading.

1. Why did Odysseus and his men come to the island of the Cyclopes?
2. Who were the Cyclopes? What was peculiar about them?
3. Name the main features of this island.
4. What did the companions of Odysseus want to do? What did they do?
5. Tell in detail what Polyphemus did when he returned that evening before he discovered the Greeks.
6. What conversation did Odysseus have with Polyphemus?
7. What do you imagine were the thoughts and feelings of Odysseus and his companions that night and day in the cave?
8. What were the two main parts in the plan to escape?
9. Did Polyphemus deserve his fate?
10. As you read the other sections of the story, make up some good questions to test your classmates. See who can make the best ones.

When you have read Section II, write an answer to the question: Did Odysseus deserve to be punished for the curiosity of his sailors? Afterwards, discuss your answers in class.

In Section III, does the story of Circe remind you of any other story of persons who were enchanted into animals? It will be fun to see how many stories of this kind you can remember when you come to talk about them.

When you have read Section IV, make drawings of Scylla and Charybdis.

II

THE CAVE OF THE WINDS

Presently the Greeks came to the island where lived Æolus and his twelve children. It was a floating island with unbroken cliffs running up straight from the sea.

They were kindly received by Æolus and his household and remained with them a whole month. As Æolus was eager to hear about all that had happened at Troy, Odysseus told him the whole story and asked him to help them on their homeward way. This he promised to do.

Now Æolus was keeper of the winds. He could either quiet them or stir up storms, as he wished. When the Greeks were leaving, he secretly gave Odysseus a great leather bag of ox-hide, in which he had bound all the violent winds that might otherwise blow and hinder him on his journey. This bag Odysseus made fast in the hold of the ship so that not the least breath of contrary wind should escape. The west wind alone was left out, because this was the one that would blow the ship home.

For nine days and nights they sailed without stopping, and on the tenth day they came so near Ithaca that they could see fires on the shore and people tending them. All this while Odysseus himself had been steering. He would not trust the rudder to any one else for fear their homecoming might be delayed. But at last he was so weary that he fell asleep.

While he slept, some of his men in the hold began to

talk about the strange leather bag that was fastened there. They said to one another: "Look now, how Odysseus is honored by all men wherever he goes. Many are the treasures that he is carrying home from Troy while we go empty-handed. And now Æolus has given him more. Let us see what wealth of gold and silver he has in this bag."

They opened the bag. At once the violent winds burst forth and there came a mighty storm that drove the ship away from home and out upon the high seas.

Odysseus awakened, heartbroken to see what had happened; but there was nothing to do but endure. He muffled his head in his cloak and lay still while the winds drove his ship back to the island of Æolus.

Again he went to Æolus, asking for help; but this time the ruler of the winds said that Odysseus must have angered the gods, to have all these misfortunes. And again he would not help him.

III

The Island of Circe

After being driven about the stormy sea for a long time, the Greeks came at last to an island on which dwelled the goddess Circe, who was also a sorceress.[1]

But the Greeks did not know on whose island they were. Odysseus took his spear and his sharp sword and climbed up from the shore to see whether any one lived on the

[1] sorceress (sôr'sĕr-ĕss): one who works black magic; a witch.

island. On the craggy top of a hill he saw smoke rising from a house that was built in the woods.

He returned, carrying a stag that he had killed for his hungry men.

After they had eaten he divided them into two companies of twenty-two each, with Eurylochus in command of one and himself in command of the other. They drew lots to see which company should go up into the wood and find out who lived in the house he had seen. And the lot fell to the company of Eurylochus.

They went up through the wood until they came to a fair house of polished stone in an open space. All about it were roaming mountain-bred wolves and lions. The Greeks did not know that these were men who had been enchanted by the sorceress Circe; but they were astonished to find that the beasts did not set upon them but romped about, fawning on them and wagging their tails. They acted just as dogs do when their master comes from dinner bringing them pieces of meat.

Standing without the gate, the Greeks heard Circe singing sweetly as she walked back and forth at her loom, weaving splendid tapestries such as only goddesses make.

When the Greeks called to her, at once she came out, the golden-haired goddess, threw wide the shining doors, and bade them enter. In their heedlessness they went— all but Eurylochus, who waited outside, fearing treachery.

Circe led the others in and placed them on chairs and high seats. She made them a meal of cheese and barley and yellow honey, and gave them wine to drink. With the food she mixed drugs that made them utterly forget their own country. And when they had feasted, she touched them with a wand, and at once they were all changed into swine. She shut them up in the styes of swine and gave them nuts and acorns and other things on which wallowing swine feed.

But Eurylochus went back to the ship and told Odysseus what had happened to his companions. Then Odysseus hung from his shoulder his silver-studded sword, and took his bow, and went alone to the house of Circe.

On the way he met Hermes, the messenger of the gods, in the form of a fair young man. Hermes spoke to him and gave him a plant called moly, with a milk-white flower, which would keep him from being enchanted by Circe. Hermes also told him how he could get Circe to help him on his way.

So Odysseus stood at the gate and called to the goddess. She came out as before and led him within and placed him on a carved chair studded with silver nails, with a footstool for his feet. She mixed wine for him in a golden cup, and into it she put her magic drug. And when he had taken the wine, she touched him with her wand, saying, "Go now to the sty and live there with the others of your company."

But Odysseus sprang up and drew his sharp sword as if he would slay her. She fell on her knees with a cry, saying: "Who are you whom I cannot enchant? Where is your city? There is no man but you who could drink unharmed what I have given you. Verily you are Odysseus, who, Hermes told me, would one day come here on his way home from Troy. Put up your sword and be kind to me as I shall be kind to you."

But Odysseus answered, "Nay, Circe, how can you ask me to be kind to you who have turned my companions into swine?"

And although Circe's handmaidens prepared a feast and set it before Odysseus, he would not taste the food, but sat and mourned. When Circe asked him why he sat speechless, he answered: "Oh, Circe, what righteous man would have the heart to taste meat and drink until he had redeemed his friends and seen them face to face? If you in good faith wish me to be your guest, let my men go free."

At this Circe passed out of the hall, with the wand in her hand, and opened the door of the sty. All the swine came out and stood before her. As she anointed each with a charm, the bristles dropped away, and he became a man, younger, taller, and fairer than he had been. They knew Odysseus and took his hands, grieved and ashamed that he should have found them in such a condition. Even the goddess was moved with pity.

After that she was kind to the Greeks. They remained on her island a full year; and when they were about to set out on their homeward journey, she took Odysseus aside and told him what further dangers he would have to face, and how he must meet them.

IV

Scylla and Charybdis

Scarcely was the ship safe past the isle of the Sirens, where Odysseus and his men had narrowly escaped shipwreck, when the air was filled with mist and there came great waves and a terrible roaring of the sea. Odysseus knew that they were approaching Scylla and Charybdis.

They entered a narrow strait. On one side was a rock with a sharp peak that seemed to touch the sky, and above it was a dark cloud. Circe had said that this cloud never passed away, and that there was never clear air in this place, summer or winter. So smooth and so steep was the rock, she had said, that no man could ever climb it, not if he had twenty hands and feet. Half way up the rock, she had said, was the cave of Scylla, a monster with twelve feet, all dangling down, and six necks, exceedingly long. On each neck was a hideous head, and in each head were three rows of teeth, set thick and close. There the monster lived, sunk up to her middle in the hollow cave, yelping terribly and thrusting out her heads as she fished for dolphins, or sea dogs, or whatever larger beast she could reach. No sailors ever boasted, said Circe, that their ship had passed unharmed; for with each of her six heads, Scylla always snatched a man as a ship sped by.

On the other side of the strait was the rock by which lurked Charybdis. It was so near to that of Scylla that a man might shoot an arrow from the one to the other. But this rock was much lower, and on it grew a fig tree, in the shadow of which Charybdis lay in the water. Three times a day she sucked down the dark water, and three times a day she spouted it up again. If a ship was passing when she sucked down the water, no power in the world could save that ship from going down also.

All this Odysseus remembered as his ship entered the strait. He remembered also that Circe had told him to keep nearer to Scylla, for it was better to lose six of his men than to have the ship with all its crew sucked beneath the salt waters.

He bade his men keep well away from Charybdis, and he himself kept a lookout toward the sharp peak of Scylla, but he could not see her anywhere. On the other side, Charybdis most terribly sucked in the salt water and belched it out again like a cauldron on a great fire, and it seethed up until the spray fell even on the tops of the cliffs on both sides. Then as she gulped it down again with a most horrible roaring, the sailors turned pale with fear. But even as they stood watching Charybdis, came Scylla reaching out from the other side and caught in her six mouths six of the best men in the crew. She lifted them high in air, crying aloud and calling Odysseus by name. Just as a fisherman on a headland lets down with a long rod his baits to the little fishes below and as he catches each, flings it writhing ashore, so she caught the sailors and lifted them writhing up to the cliff.

But the ship herself passed on safe through the strait.

V

The Shipwreck

The Greeks sailed onward and landed on an island called Sicily. There they found grazing the famous sacred cattle, which Odysseus knew it was forbidden to touch, because they belonged to Phœbus, the god of the sun. But one day, while the Greeks were waiting for a favorable wind, and when Odysseus himself was not among the sailors, they, nearly starved, cooked and ate some of these cattle.

As soon as they put to sea again, there came a great black cloud, and a wind that broke the mast from its tackle and flung it forward. It fell on the pilot and killed him. Then Zeus struck the ship with lightning and she reeled, and the air was full of the smell of sulphur. When Odysseus was able to look, he found that he was the only man left aboard. He could see his crew floating away among the waves like seagulls. Not one of them ever got back to the ship. They were all drowned as a punishment for stealing the sacred cattle of the sun god.

But Odysseus managed to lash the mast to a piece of the keel, and when the ship fell apart, he was able to float on this. All the night he drifted and in the morning found himself near the dreadful Charybdis. At once she sucked down the mast and keel, but he caught hold of the fig tree that grew on the rock near by and so swung himself high in the air, clinging like a bat until the mast and keel were thrown up again. Then he dropped and swam to them, and so was carried on drifting for nine days.

Odysseus was cast ashore on an island belonging to a goddess named Calypso. He remained with her for seven years; and at last she helped him to build a raft to go home with. But again he was shipwrecked and cast ashore on another island, where a people named the Phæacians lived. When they heard the story of his wanderings, they were sorry for him, and took him home in one of their ships. There, after other adventures, he was able to return to his dear home and the wife and son who had long mourned him as lost.

THINGS TO THINK AND TALK ABOUT

1. In the introduction on page 17, "The Odyssey" is mentioned as a Greek story-poem told about three thousand years ago.

   a. Why is it called a story-poem?
   b. Why is the word *told* used in place of *written?*
   c. Do you know any other story-poems?

2. What trait of character in Odysseus is shown when he taunts the Cyclops?

3. In literature, we sometimes find the figure of speech "between Scylla and Charybdis" to picture a dangerous situation. What does it mean?

4. Which section of the story do you like the best? Why? Would you recommend this story to others?

THINGS TO DO

1. Look up the story of the plan of Odysseus to capture Troy. It shows that curiosity is sometimes dangerous.

2. Would you like to volunteer to learn one section of the story to tell in class? Be sure to use some of the fine phrases of the text. Imagine you are Odysseus or one of his companions telling the story to your friends. Perhaps the pupils in some other room would like to have you tell the story to them.

3. Perhaps you can find in other books some further information about the characters in these stories, and bring it to class. It would be interesting to find the story of Penelope (pê-nĕl′ô-pê), the wife of Odysseus, noted for her faithfulness; also the story of her son Telemachus (tê-lĕm′å-kŭs).

4. Good pictures illustrating the places and events in the story may be found in books of mythology and ancient history.

5. It might prove interesting to ask the English or Latin teacher in High School to come and tell more about these stories.

6. Look up in your geography, or atlas, the probable location of the places.

BOOKS TO READ

If you wish to read the whole story of the wanderings and adventures of Odysseus, you will find the following among the best:

1. "The Adventures of Odysseus," by Padraic Colum. Macmillan.
2. "The Odyssey," by G. H. Palmer. Houghton.
3. "The Odyssey," by Butcher and Lang. Macmillan.

You may like to read also the story of some of the battles fought between the Greeks and the Trojans at Troy, as they are told in the "Iliad." These books will interest you:

4. "The Boy's Iliad," by W. C. Perry. Macmillan.
5. "The Iliad," by Lang, Leaf, and Myers. Macmillan.
6. "The Iliad for Boys and Girls," by A. J. Church. Macmillan.

THE FIRST VOYAGE ROUND THE WORLD

When Columbus reached America he thought, as you know, that the country was Asia. He did not dream that over the ocean there might be another great continent, lying between Europe and Asia.

It was nearly thirty years after America was discovered before any one succeeded in making a voyage round the world. The navigator whose crew did that was a Portuguese nobleman named Ferdinand Magellan. He sailed from Spain, August 10, 1519, with a commission to explore the Molucca Islands[1] and the Spice Islands, and to bring home spices and other precious things. No one dreamed then that South America lay between Magellan and these islands. He had five ships, "very old and patched up," and 237 men. One ship's crew deserted early and took their ship back to Spain; of the other four ships, only one returned, with eighteen men out of the original sixty, nearly all of them sick, after a voyage of about three years, arriving at Seville, September 8, 1522.

Of the many adventures and hardships that the explorers went through, the most interesting account is by an Italian named Antonio Pigafetta, who was on Magellan's ship.

As you read this story silently, see how often you can go on without stopping until you get to a comma or some other punctuation mark. The good reader is always playing a sort of game with himself—to get the exact meaning, the whole meaning, and

---

[1] Molucca (mō-lŭk'á) Islands: a group of islands in the East Indies between Celebes and New Guinea. Look them up in your geography.

THE FIRST VOYAGE ROUND THE WORLD

to get both as fast as he can because he knows that there are so many interesting books to read that he cannot live long enough to read them all.

As you read this account of Magellan, keep in mind two questions so that you can answer them when you have finished:

1. What is there in this story that reminds me of "Robinson Crusoe"? or "The Swiss Family Robinson"?
2. What is there that is like stories of American Indians?

During those three months and twenty days, we ran fully four thousand leagues in the Pacific. This ocean was well named Pacific, for during this time we met with no storm and saw no land except two small uninhabited islands, in which we found only birds and trees [they were near Alexander Selkirk's Island].[1] When we were in the middle of this open sea we saw a cross of five stars, very bright in the west, and they were straight in line with one another.[2]

In the Philippines

Saturday, March 16, 1521, we arrived at daybreak near a high island named Zamal [one of the Philippines]. The next day the captain [Magellan] landed at an uninhabited

[1] Alexander Selkirk's Island: an island off the coast of Chili. Selkirk was a Scottish sailor who joined a privateering expedition to the South Seas in the spring of 1703. He was made master of one of the ships under Captain Stradling. As a result of a quarrel with his commander, he was put ashore on an island off the coast of Chili, and remained there for six years, when he was found and taken off by Captain Woods Rogers, in January, 1709. His experience is the foundation of the story of Robinson Crusoe, by Daniel Defoe.

[2] They are called the Southern Cross: a beautiful group (constellation) of stars visible in the southern hemisphere.

island near it, to be in greater security, to take on water, and to rest a few days. He set up two tents on shore for the sick and had a pig killed for them.

Monday, March 18, after dinner, we saw a boat come toward us with nine men in it; upon which the captain ordered that no one should move or speak without his permission. At once the chief among these people went

toward the captain with signs of being very happy at our arrival. The captain ordered food and drink to be given them, and he gave some of them red caps, looking-glasses, combs, bells, ivory, and other things. They gave us fish and a vessel of palm wine, figs more than a foot long, and smaller ones of a better taste, and two cocoanuts. They made signs with their hands that in four days they would return with rice and more cocoanuts.

The fruit that they call cocoa grows on the palm tree. As we have bread, wine, oil, and vinegar from different kinds of plants, they have all these from the palm tree only. For the wine they make a hole at the top of the palm down to its heart, from which comes a liquor in drops down the tree, which is sweet with a tinge of bitter. They have canes as thick as a man's leg, which they tie to the palm, to draw off this liquor as it drops. The fruit of the palm is the cocoa, which is about as large as a head. Its first husk is green and two fingers thick; under this is another, very hard, and thicker than that of a walnut. Under this rind there is a white marrow as thick as a finger, which they eat fresh with meat and fish, as we do bread. It tastes like almond, and if dried might be used for bread. From the middle of this marrow comes out a clear sweet water, which after a time congeals and becomes as thick as honey. They make their oil from the marrow of this fruit when it is rotten. To make vinegar they let the water in the nut stand in the sun, and it turns to vinegar. From this marrow, milk also can be made, as we found, by scraping the marrow and passing it with its liquid through a cloth; then it was like goat's milk. Two of these trees can keep a family of ten persons; and we were told that trees live as long as a hundred years.

Friday, March 22, the above-mentioned people, who had promised us to return, came about midday, with two boats laden with the said fruit, cocoanuts, sweet oranges, a vessel of palm wine, and a cock to show that they had poultry in their country. We bought all they had. The lord of this people was an old man who had his face painted and gold rings in his ears. The others had many bracelets and rings of gold on their arms, with wrappings of linen round their heads. We remained at this place eight days. The captain went every day to see his sick men; and he gave them every day the liquid of this fruit, the cocoa, which comforted them much.

Monday, March 25, in the afternoon, I went to the side of our ship to fish, and putting my feet on a spar to go down to the storeroom, my feet slipped because it had rained, and I fell into the sea without any one seeing me, and was almost drowned. By luck I found at my left hand the sheet of the large sail, which was in the sea. I seized it and cried out for help until they came and picked me up with the boat.

Thursday, March 28, having seen the night before fire on an island, in the morning we anchored at this island, and eight men came out to our ship in a small boat. The captain, seeing that they were afraid to come on board, tied a red cap and other things to a plank and let the people take them away. About two hours later there came out two long boats, in one of which, under an awning of mats, sat their king. Some of his men came on board and offered our captain a rather large bar of solid gold and a chest full of ginger, which he thanked them for but would not take as presents.

The next morning our captain sent to the king to see whether he could buy provisions for money, saying that he had come to the island as a friend. Then the king came out to the ship with seven or eight of his men carrying china dishes full of fish and rice. The captain gave him a Turkish robe of red and yellow cloth, and a very fine red cap; and gave some of his men knives and others mirrors. Then refreshments were served. The captain told the king, through an interpreter, that he wished to be *cassi, cassi*—brothers—with him; and the king answered that he wished to be the same.

After that the captain showed him cloths of different colors, linen, coral, and much other merchandise, and all the artillery, of which he fired some pieces, to the king's great astonishment. Then the captain had one of his soldiers put on steel armor and placed him in the midst of three comrades, who struck him with swords and daggers. The king thought it very strange that he was not hurt; and the captain told him that a man in steel armor was worth a hundred of his men. He answered that it was true.

At last the captain asked if two of the ship's company might go ashore to the place where they lived, to see some of the things of the country. This the king granted, and I went with another. We went ashore in the boat, and when they saw me write down several names of things as I heard them in their language, the king and others were greatly astonished at this way of speaking. For supper they brought two large china dishes, of which one was full of rice, and the other of pork, with its broth and gravy. After supper we went to the king's palace, which was built like a hay granary, covered with fig and palm leaves. It stood on great timbers high above the ground, so that we had to climb steps and ladders to it. There the king made us sit on a cane mat with our legs doubled, as was the custom. After half an hour there was brought a dish of fish roasted in pieces, and ginger fresh-gathered that moment, and some wine. We slept with the prince on a cane mat with cushions and pillows of leaves. The next morning the king sent a brother of his, the king of another island, to take us back to the ship.

In the island belonging to this king there are mines of gold, which they find in pieces as big as a walnut or an egg, by seeking in the ground. All his dishes are made of it and also some parts of his house. He was the handsomest man that we saw among these nations. He had very black hair coming down to his shoulders, with a silk cloth on his head, and two large gold rings hanging from his ears; he wore a cloth of cotton worked with silk, which covered him from the waist to the knees, and at his side he wore a dagger, with a long handle of gold and a sheath of carved wood. He was tawny and painted all over. Of these kings the painted one is called Raja Calambu, and the other, Raja Siani.

The Death of Magellan

Friday, April 26, one of the chiefs of the island of Matan sent the captain a present, and asked help to subdue another chief who was his enemy and who would not recognize the authority of the king of Spain. The captain decided to go himself with three boats. We entreated him not to go to this enterprise in person; but he as a good shepherd would not abandon his flock.

We set out from Zubu at midnight, sixty men armed with corselets and helmets, and with us the king who had been converted, and many of his followers. We arrived at Matan three hours before daylight.

The captain, before attacking, wished to attempt gentle means, and sent ashore a messenger with words of peace; but the islanders would not make peace.

We waited for daylight. We then leaped into the water up to our thighs, for on account of the shallow water and the rocks the boats could not come close to the beach. We had to walk two good crossbow-shots in the water before reaching land.

There we found the islanders, fifteen hundred in number, drawn up in three squadrons. They came down upon us with terrible shouts, two attacking us on the flanks and the third in front. The captain then divided his men into two bands. Our musketeers and crossbow men fired for half an hour from a distance, but did little damage. The captain shouted not to fire, but he was not listened to. The islanders, seeing that the shots of our guns did them little or no harm, sprang from one side to another, avoiding them, and drew nearer to us, throwing arrows, javelins, spears, stones, and even mud, so that we could hardly defend ourselves.

The captain, in order to disperse them, sent some of our men to fire their houses. This made them more ferocious. The captain had his right leg pierced by a poisoned arrow. On this account he gave orders to retreat by degrees; but almost all our men ran away headlong, so that there were hardly six or eight of us with him. We were so overwhelmed by the lances and stones hurled at us that we could make no more resistance. The bombards[1] in the boat were too far away to help us.

We retreated, little by little, toward the boats, still fighting. We had already got to the distance of a crossbow shot from the shore, with the water up to our knees, but the islanders followed and picked up the spears that they had cast before. They knew our leader, and aimed specially at him, and twice they knocked the helmet from his head. He, with a few of us, like a good knight, remained at his post and would not retreat farther. Thus we fought for more than an hour, until an Indian succeeded in wounding the captain in the face, and in the struggle that followed they all fell upon him, and one gave him a great blow on the left leg, which brought him down on his face. Then they threw themselves upon him, and ran him through with lances and scimitars. Thus they deprived of life our mirror, light, comfort, and true guide. While the Indians were thus overpowering him, several times he turned toward us, to see if we were safe, as if his obstinate fight was all to cover the retreat of his men. We who had fought to extremity, and who were covered with wounds, now seeing that he was dead, proceeded to the boats, which

---

[1] bombards: small cannon.

were on the point of going away. This fatal battle was fought on April 27, 1521.

He died; but I hope Your Illustrious Highness will not allow his memory to be lost. . . . One of his principal virtues was constancy in the most adverse fortune. In the midst of the sea he was able to endure hunger better than we could. Most versed in nautical charts, he knew better than any other the true art of navigation, of which it is a certain proof that he knew by his genius, and his intrepidity, without any one having given him example, how to attempt the circuit of the globe, which he had almost completed.

—*Adapted from Antonio Pigafetta.*

THINGS TO THINK ABOUT

1. Which do you believe required the greater courage and daring: For Magellan to attempt to sail around the world in 1519 or for our airmen to set out to fly around the world in 1925? Arrange your points in good outline form. Perhaps you would like to arrange a debate on this question.

2. Contrast the crossing of the ocean in Magellan's time with passage today.

THINGS TO DO

Find out what you can about the Philippines today. Begin by reading what your geography says about the islands; then read what you find in the encyclopædia or some other book. Compare what you find with Pigafetta's account. You will see that he seems to be telling the truth, and that the islands have not changed greatly since Magellan and his men saw them.

QUESTIONS FOR TESTING YOURSELF

1. How many ships and men did Magellan have? How many returned from the voyage?

2. What happened to the others?

3. What gifts did Magellan give to the chiefs? What did the chiefs give Magellan? Make a list of each in two columns:

Gifts to Magellan	Gifts to the chiefs

5. What customs of the South Sea people are described?

6. Tell how Magellan lost his life.

7. Is there anything in the story which tells whether or not Magellan was a good commander?

8. There is one other important point in this story not mentioned in these questions. What is it?

BOOKS TO READ

1. If you enjoy stories of this kind you may like to read about the voyages of Sir Francis Drake, who sailed round the world in 1579; or about the experiences of Captain Joshua Slocum in a voyage round the world alone in a sloop, which he remodeled; or the voyages of Captain Cook in the South Seas.

2. In 1925, David Putnam, a boy of twelve years, went on a voyage with some scientists on the ship "Arcturus." He has told of his interesting experiences in a book called "David Goes Voyaging."

3. In 1923, a young man by the name of Alain Gerbault crossed the Atlantic alone in a small cutter, only 39 feet long and 8 feet 6 inches wide. He named his ship "The Firecrest," and has written a thrilling account of his voyage in a book called "The Fight of the Firecrest."

4. The travels of Marco Polo, telling of his adventure with his father and uncle in China, India, and Persia, make excellent reading. The Polos lived several centuries before Magellan.

5. "Story of Sir Francis Drake," by L. M. Elton. Dutton.
An interesting story of the exploits of this great sea-captain.

6. "Travels of Marco Polo," by T. W. Knox. Putnam.
One of the best accounts for young readers.

7. "Story of Captain Cook," by J. Lang. Dutton.
Strange adventures and discoveries in the South Sea Islands.

8. "Sailing Alone Around the World," by Joshua Slocum. Century.
A true story of exciting adventure.

9. "Magellan," by G. M. Towle. Lothrop.
A complete story of the life of Magellan.

THE CONQUEST OF THE POLES

For many thousand years men knew of the world only the small part in which they were born and raised. After Columbus had found the New World, there was much exploration in North and South America, but it was not until the nineteenth century that most parts of Africa came to be known; and there are still parts of Asia and of Africa that have not yet been mapped. The great difficulty and hardships from the intense cold kept both North and South Poles unknown until recent years.

THE DISCOVERY OF THE NORTH POLE

After you have finished reading this account of the discovery of the North Pole, you are going to read how the South Pole was found. If you are to have the fun of comparing the two stories —and they are very different—you must remember everything that is told in the first. It may help you if you keep in mind these four questions as you read. If you forget exactly what the questions are, read this paragraph again—and if necessary, oftener —until you remember them:

1. How far did Peary's use of his ship contribute to his success?
2. How far did his careful preparations in advance help him?
3. How was his success endangered by "leads"?
4. Could he have succeeded without using the "relay system"?

For hundreds of years men had been trying to find the North Pole. Ships and the lives of many men had been lost in the effort. After repeated discouraging failures, an American, Admiral Peary, finally succeeded.

He succeeded because he was slow to give up. "One fight more," he said in 1902. "One fight more," he said in 1905. "One fight more," he said in 1909. And this time he won.

He had sailed from New York in the summer of 1908, in the ship "Roosevelt"; and by August had arrived at Cape York, on the coast of Greenland, the home of the most northern tribe of Eskimos in the world. From Cape York the "Roosevelt" was driven north, "jamming and butting and dodging and hammering" her way through the ice until in September she reached Cape Sheridan, where she had to be laid up for the winter. We can understand what a terrible trip it must have been from Admiral Peary's own words:

"Imagine about three hundred and fifty miles of almost solid ice—ice of all shapes and sizes, mountainous ice, flat ice, ragged and tortured ice, ice that for every foot of height revealed above the surface of the water, hides seven feet below. . . .

"Then imagine a little black ship, solid, sturdy, compact, strong, and resistant as any vessel built by mortal hands can be, yet utterly insignificant in comparison with the white, cold adversary she must fight. And on this little ship are sixty-nine human beings, men, women, and children, whites and Eskimos, who have gone out into the crazy, ice-tortured channel between Baffin Bay and the Polar Sea— gone out to help prove the reality of a dream—in the pursuit of which men have frozen, and starved, and died. The music that ever sounded in our ears had for melody the howling of two hundred and forty-six wild dogs, for a bass accompaniment the deep, low grumbling of the ice surging around us with the impulse of the tides, and the shock and jar of our crashing assaults upon the floes."

During the worst parts of the journey Captain Bartlett, who had charge of the navigation of the ship, spent most of his time in the crow's nest.[1] Often Peary would be up there also, watching for the dangers that might at any moment destroy the ship. Sometimes he would hear the Captain shouting to the ship as if she were alive: "Rip 'em, Teddy! Bite 'em in two! Go it! That's fine, my beauty! Now—again! Once more!"

But after the ship was safe in winter quarters, the men had nothing to do but amuse themselves during the long winter night. They hunted walrus and musk oxen, and trained themselves in driving the dogs and managing the sledges on which food was to be carried to the Pole.

As soon as the sun came back in February, Admiral Peary and his men began to carry out their plan of reaching the Pole, which was more than five hundred miles from the ship. Peary's carefully worked-out plan was to drive the ship itself as far north as he could; then to do enough hunting during the autumn and winter to keep the party supplied with fresh meat so that they would not suffer from a terrible disease called scurvy.[2] They must have many more dogs than were needed, so that if more than half of

[1] crow's nest: a lookout high up on the mast of a ship; usually shaped like a barrel.
[2] scurvy: a disease caused by lack of fresh vegetable food, and marked by great weakness. Formerly common among sailors who used salty meats and no vegetables.

them were lost on the journey the expedition could still go on; and the best Eskimos that could be found, to help with their experience. They must transport supplies beforehand and have them at various points on the journey as far north as possible, so that it would not be necessary to carry everything at once. They must go and come back by the same route, so that they would have a trail made, and Eskimo houses already built for shelter. Finally, they must advance by relays; that is, have one party go ahead to make a sort of road as far as it was possible to do so, and another party to push forward where the first stopped and try to reach the Pole by forced marches. Besides these, other parties must bring up supplies as far as they could, and help the pioneer and the main party in case of danger or difficulty. Of the four relays with which Peary set out from the ship, he planned to have only one—that headed by himself—go as far as the Pole.

All the supplies for the party were packed on sledges drawn by dogs and guided by the man who drove the dog team. On each sledge were food for the men and dogs, and some extra clothing and tools. If one sledge had become separated from the others, the food on it would have kept the driver and the dog team from starvation for about fifty days. A special sledge for each party carried the alcohol stoves and the cooking utensils. But the other sledges were loaded as follows: On the bottom was a layer of red tins containing the pemmican that was fed to the dogs; above this two tins of biscuits and the blue tins containing the pemmican for the men; then tins of alcohol and condensed milk, a small skin rug for the man to sleep on in his snow-house at night; snowshoes and spare footgear, a pickax and a saw-knife for cutting ice blocks.

Men and dogs were kept on rations. For the men these were: 1 lb. pemmican, 1 lb. ship's biscuit, 4 oz. condensed milk, $\frac{1}{2}$ oz. compressed tea. This was all that they had to eat a day. For cooking there was an allowance of 6 oz. of liquid fuel per day.

This journey of five hundred miles was across a frozen sea. The greatest danger came from the fact that because of the winds and tides the ice was never still. The great ice floes or fields which covered nine-tenths of the surface were indeed safe enough, as they consisted of ice from twenty to one hundred feet thick. But they were being continually pushed about by the winds and tides in such a way that in some places they would be crushed together into great ridges, and in other places would be split apart. At any moment the solid ice might crack, and a great "lead" or street of open water show between the ice-fields. Sometimes these leads would be only a few inches wide, again, they would be too wide to jump, and at other times like great rivers of ice from half a mile to two miles wide. Sometimes the explorers would have to travel up and down such a lead trying to find a place where it was narrow enough to cross. Sometimes they could find or chop out a great cake of ice to use as a sort of ferryboat; but as each sledge weighed about five hundred pounds, this was not easy to do. Sometimes they had to camp by the side of the lead and wait for the winds and tides to close it again, or for the water to freeze until the ice was strong enough to bear the sledges as the men and dogs raced them across at full speed. This was very dangerous work, as the ice in the leads was often so thin that it would hardly bear the weight.

On the other hand, the "pressure ridges," as the ice floes were called when they were crushed together, made huge barriers where the men and dogs had to struggle to break through. Sometimes these ridges were only a few feet high, sometimes they were rods in height; sometimes they were narrow, sometimes a quarter of a mile wide. The blocks of ice in them might be as small as a golf ball, or as large as a small house.

The Peary expedition set out on this tremendous tramp across the frozen sea in a blizzard with a wind that made it almost impossible to see anything, and the thermometer at about thirty degrees below zero.

The second day out they saw before them the dark spots in the ice which showed open water. It proved to be a lead about a quarter of a mile wide. They camped for the night, and in the morning found the lead closing and filling up with a mass of young ice. Peary says that the crossing was like getting over a river on a mass of gigantic shingles, two or three deep, and all afloat and moving. However, they got across in safety, only to be stopped a few days later by a greater lead, by which they camped for six days, waiting in vain for it to close. At last, when they were nearly desperate, and when the Eskimos had begun to desert them, afraid to go farther, the temperature dropped to forty below zero, and the ice became strong enough to let them cross. That day they marched twelve miles, and had to cross no fewer than twelve of these leads.

Even before they reached the last stage of their journey they had several narrow escapes. One day one of the dog-teams broke through treacherous ice; but the man who was driving managed to keep the sledge with its precious load of supplies from sliding after, and then dragged the dogs back to safety. Some days later, just as Peary was dropping off to sleep, he heard the ice creaking and groaning close to his igloo or snow-hut. He thought nothing of it until he heard a yell outside. Looking out he saw that a broad lead of black water had come between his hut and the others. The break had happened within a few inches of the place where one of the dog-teams was fastened; and another team barely escaped being buried under a pressure ridge of ice. One of the camps was set floating on an ice-raft, and the other was in great danger of being carried off. However, Peary and his men succeeded in getting across to a larger floe, and then in helping the other men to escape from their icy island.

By April 2, Peary had sent on the return journey all the men except the four Eskimos and the negro whom he meant to take with him to the Pole. The weather was brilliant and sunny, and the temperature about twenty-five below zero—almost warm to men who had known it to be more than fifty below. As they had reduced the number of people and the amount of supplies to the lowest point, they could travel much more rapidly. The first day they made twenty-five or thirty miles. After some days of almost constant travel in clear, calm weather, with only a few hours' sleep, there came greater cold and a bitter wind that burned the men's faces until they cracked. Peary could scarcely sleep for the pain. But still they rushed along. The last part of the journey the ice was smoother and their difficulties were not so great. About ten o'clock in the morning of April 6, 1909, Peary was able to see that he was within a very few miles of the end of his journey, and that same day he wrote in his journal: "The Pole at last. The prize of three centuries."

—From "The North Pole," by Robert A. Peary.

FIRST AT THE NORTH POLE

As Peary writes in his story, "The North Pole," his thirty hours at the Pole were pretty well crowded with marchings and counter-marchings, and with the making of observation and records; but he said:

"I found time, however, to write Mrs. Peary on a United States postal card which I had found on the ship during the winter.

"It had been my custom at various important stages of the journey northward to write such a note in order that, if anything serious happened to me, these brief communications might ultimately reach her at the hands of survivors."

Here is what he wrote:

---

90 North Latitude
April 7th

My dear Jo,

    I have won out at last.

    Have been here a day.

    I start for home and you in an hour. Love to the "kiddies."

Bert

TESTING YOUR UNDERSTANDING

NOTE: Some of the following statements are *true* and some are *false*. Read each one carefully and decide whether it is true or false. On a clean sheet of paper set down the number of the statement and write *true* or *false* after it, as the case may be.

$$e.\,g.,\ 1 = false$$

Do not refer to the story until you have finished. Then check up and see how many you have are correct.

1. Admiral Peary sailed from New York in the summer of 1910.
2. His ship was named the "Roosevelt."
3. The "Roosevelt" was left at Cape York.
4. The surface of the ice was generally smooth.
5. During the worst parts of the voyage Captain Bartlett spent most of his time in the crow's nest.
6. Admiral Peary did not plan to take all his men to the Pole with him.
7. Each sledge carried only food enough to last the driver and dogs about thirty days.
8. The greatest danger on the ice came from winds and tides.
9. The weather was favorable on the day Peary set out over the ice toward the Pole.
10. On the last part of the journey, Peary made forced marches.

See if you can answer these questions:

1. What was Admiral Peary's plan for reaching the Pole? Make an outline of it.
2. What things were packed on each sledge? Make a list.
3. What kinds of food did the expedition have?
4. How did the winds and tides make the journey over the ice dangerous?
5. Make one or two good questions for the class to answer.

THINGS TO DO AND TALK ABOUT

1. Has this account of the discovery of the North Pole changed your ideas as to what it is like there? In what way?
2. What traits in Admiral Peary do you admire?
3. Did Admiral Peary really do the world a service in discovering the North Pole? Give specific reasons for your answer.
4. Bring to class information about the airplane flights of Captain Byrd and of Captain Amundsen to the North Pole. Compare their risks and achievements with Peary's.

BOOKS TO READ

1. "Last Secrets," by J. Buchan. Houghton.
   Heroic experiences of explorers.
2. "Conquest of the Poles," by Alfred Judd. Nelson.
   An interesting account of Arctic and Antarctic explorations.
3. "Farthest North," by F. Nansen. Harpers.
   A record of the voyage of the ship "Fram."
4. "Kak, the Copper Eskimo," by Vilhjalmur Stefansson. Macmillan.
   A story of an Eskimo boy; a true picture of Eskimo life.
5. "Northward, Ho!" by Vilhjalmur Stefansson. Macmillan.
   An interesting account of the Eskimos, with fine photographs.

THE DISCOVERY OF THE SOUTH POLE

Have you found that you can read as far as the commas without stopping? Can you sometimes read a whole short sentence without a pause? Have you tested yourself to find out the greatest number of words you can take in at a glance? Here is a short test to try:

Reread the first three sentences of the paragraph above. Then copy the following words, leaving space to write a sentence in, between the groups:

Have you found

Can you sometimes

Have you tested

Shut your books and try to write the whole of each of these three sentences without stopping until you reach the end.

As long ago as 1902, Captain Robert Scott, an Englishman, had succeeded in getting within six hundred miles of the South Pole, and in 1908, another Englishman, Captain [later, Sir Ernest] Shackleton, succeeded in reaching a point between one and two hundred miles from the Pole. Then it began to seem possible that the Pole itself might be discovered; and when in September, 1909, the news was cabled about the world that Admiral Peary had reached the North Pole, there seemed a better chance that the South Pole also could be found.

While Captain Scott in England was preparing to make another great effort, Captain Roald Amundsen, in Norway, who had been planning an exploring trip in the Arctic regions, decided to try his luck in the South. The two parties accidentally met in the Antarctic regions, February 4, 1911.

After that it was a race for the Pole. The two parties separated, and neither knew where the other was until after the Pole had been found. The adventures that happened to each expedition have been written in many books. We can read Captain Amundsen's account in his book called "The South Pole." Captain Scott did not write a book about his last voyage; but accounts of it by members of the expedition are found in Turley's "Voyages of Captain Scott" and Ponting's "The Great White South." From Ponting's book we know how the South Pole was twice "discovered" within about a month.

Captain Scott and his men were not so fortunate as Amundsen. They built a hut on a different part of the ice-barrier, which they called Hut Point. They also made short journeys to carry supplies as far as they could along the way and left them where they could be found when needed. It was particularly important to have them for the return journey from the Pole when the supplies on the sledges would have been used.

They did not make the start for the Pole until October 31, when Captain Amundsen and his men had been on the way more than three weeks. From the beginning they had a hard time. They tried to use motor-tractors to draw their sledges, but after many breakdowns they had to abandon the machines. The Siberian ponies that they had counted upon could not stand the strain and exposure, and had to be killed. After this, as they had no dogs, the men themselves had to draw the heavy sledges. They had terrific blizzards. For more than a hundred miles they were climbing a glacier which rose to a height of 10,000 feet. More and more men of the party were sent back, sorely against their will, to safety. Captain Scott was determined to reach the Pole, and he saw that his best chance was to have as few men as possible.

After two and a half months of almost superhuman effort, the little group of five who remained reached the top of the mountain pass. From this point they had a gradual descent of not much more than a hundred miles to the Pole. But because of the bad weather and the rough surfaces over which they had to pass, they were ten days in reaching it.

On January 15, Captain Scott wrote in his diary:

"It is wonderful to think that two long marches would land us at the Pole. . . . It ought to be a certain thing now, and the only appalling possibility the sight of the Norwegian flag forestalling ours."

The next day he wrote in his diary:

"The worst has happened, or nearly the worst. We marched well in the morning, and covered 7½ miles. Noon sight showed us in Lat. 89° 42′ S, and we started off in high spirits in the afternoon, feeling that tomorrow would see us at our destination. About the second hour of the march, Bowers's sharp eyes detected what he thought was a cairn; he was uneasy about it, but argued that it must be a *sastrugus* (hard ridge of snow). Half an hour later he detected a black speck ahead. Soon we knew that this could not be a natural snow feature. We marched on, found that it was a black flag tied to a sledge-bearer; near by the remains of a camp; sledge tracks and ski tracks going and coming, and the clear trace of dogs' paws—many dogs. This told us the whole story. The Norwegians have forestalled us and are first at the Pole. It is a terrible disappointment, and I am very sorry for my loyal companions. . . ."

Only a great man at such a moment would have thought of being more sorry for his companions than for himself. Disheartened as they were, the explorers pressed on, and, on January 18, arrived at the Pole, where the Norwegians had left records of themselves. Captain Scott wrote in his diary:

"Decided after summing up all observations that we were 3.5 miles away from the Pole—one mile beyond it and 3 to the right. More or less in this direction Bowers saw a cairn or tent.

"We have just arrived at this tent, 2 miles from our camp, therefore about 1½ miles from the Pole. In the tent we find record of five Norwegians having been here, as follows:

    Roald Amundsen
    Olav Olavson Bjaaland
    Hilmer Hanssen
    Sverre H. Hassel
    Oscar Wisting

16 Dec. 1911

"The tent is fine—a small compact affair supported by a single bamboo. A note from Amundsen, which I keep, asks me to forward a letter to King Haakon!

"Left a note to say I had visited the tent with companions. Bowers photographing and Wilson sketching. . . .

"We built a cairn, put up our slighted Union Jack, and photographed ourselves—mighty cold work all of it. . . .

"There is no doubt that our predecessors have made thoroughly sure of their mark and fully carried out their program. . . .

"We carried the Union Jack about three-quarters of a mile north with us, and left it on a piece of stick as near to the Pole as we could fix it."

In one of the photographs that they took of themselves at the Pole, four of them were laughing. Only brave men could have laughed after such a bitter blow.

Thinking of the journey back, Captain Scott wrote in his diary:

"Well, we have turned our backs now on the goal of our ambition and must face our 800 miles of solid dragging —and good-by to most of the day dreams. . . . Now for the run home and a desperate struggle. I wonder if we can do it."

Bad weather, bad traveling surfaces, and low temperatures were encountered from the outset of the return journey. For sixty days they struggled on through terrible gales, with the thermometer at from thirty to forty-seven degrees below zero. Thus they fought their way among dangerous crevasses, all of them suffering from frostbite and snow-blindness. Every day Captain Scott recorded in his diary the events of that day, and every day Doctor Wilson, the scientist, kept on the lookout for things of interest to carry back home, and added specimens to his collection.

Finally, conditions became so bad that two of the men died. The three who remained pitched their last camp, March 19. They were only eleven miles from their next depot, where they had food and fuel stored. The diary shows that they hoped to struggle on to it; but a blizzard set in which lasted for ten days. On March 29, Captain Scott made the last entry in his journal, in which he says: "We shall stick it out to the end, but we are getting weaker, of course, and the end cannot be far."

When they died is not known. Their bodies were found eight months after Captain Scott's last entry. The men had been so badly frozen by the terrible cold that even if they had reached safety they would have been crippled for the rest of their lives.

They died like the heroes they were, and later, at Hut Point, a cross was erected to their memory, inscribed with a line from Tennyson's "Ulysses," which sums up the way they had tried to live:

"To strive, to seek, to find, and not to yield."

—*Adapted from "The Great White South," by H. D. Ponting.*

TO SEE WHAT YOU CAN DO

1. Make up three questions to ask in class, which bring out three important points in the story.
2. Make a set of ten *true* and *false* statements, following the plan of the *true* and *false* test in the preceding story. Be sure to mix them up thoroughly. Give them to the class.
3. Give the list to your teacher to keep for a month and then take it as a test to see how much you remember.

THINGS TO THINK ABOUT AND DISCUSS

1. Compare the experiences of Captain Scott with those of Admiral Peary. In what way were their hardships and sufferings similar? In what way unlike?
2. In what way were their plans alike? unlike?
3. Why do you think Captain Scott failed while Admiral Peary succeeded?

THINGS TO DO

1. Make a list of all the characteristics a person should have to undertake what Peary and Scott did.
2. Compare the experiences of these intrepid explorers with the dangers and hardships and service of David Livingstone, missionary and explorer in darkest Africa.

BOOKS TO READ

1. "Last Secrets; the Final Mysteries of Exploration," by J. Buchan. Houghton.
   An interesting account of man's conquest of nature.
2. "Heroes of the Farthest North and Farthest South," by J. K. McLean. Crowell.
   A stirring story of great deeds.
3. "Voyages of Captain Scott," by C. Turley. Dodd.
   A fine account, with over twenty illustrations.

OUR COUNTRY

It is hard for those of us who have not traveled across the wide plains of the West to realize the vast size of the United States. It is likewise difficult for us to understand the dangers the pioneers met and conquered and the hardships and suffering they endured.

The first man who is known to have made that trip alone was Jedediah Smith. The story of his courage in setting off alone through an unknown land of Indians and desert in order to bring the East nearer to the West is a fine story for every boy and girl.

When you have read this story, you may be interested in Parkman's description of the way the Indians who once lived on the plains of the Middle West used to hunt the buffalo, which are now almost extinct.

The last story of the three tells how a man may be a pioneer even today. But he had to go to Alaska to have the kinds of adventures that our forefathers, less than a hundred years ago, used to have without going very far from their homes.

THE MAN WHO CROSSED THE RANGES

The men who crossed our country before railways were built learned the meaning of the words "three thousand miles." When you think how hard it is to walk ten miles in a good climate, with good roads and trails, with plenty of food, and with no fear of wild beasts and Indians, you begin to realize what it once meant to walk and ride, in a covered wagon or on horseback, three hundred times as far. This story tells about only one of the hundreds of heroes who crossed the ranges. Try to imagine yourself the man who crossed the ranges.

I

The story of the American onset to the West is one of the wonder tales of history. Over the natural waterway of the Great Lakes, down the road to Pittsburgh, along the trail that skirted the Potomac, and then down the Ohio, over the passes of the Cumberland into Tennessee, round the end of the Alleghanies into the Gulf States, up the Missouri, and so across the Rockies to the headwaters of the Columbia, or southwestward from St. Louis to the Spanish settlements of Santa Fé, the hardy pioneers poured in an ever-increasing stream. They carried with them little but ax, spade, and rifle, some scanty household effects, a small store of provisions, a liberal supply of ammunition, an unlimited faith, courage, and enterprise.

Undaunted by the menace of Mexican prisons, of Indian tortures, of savage animals, of thirst and starvation in the wilderness, the pioneers pushed westward and ever westward, until at last they were halted by the great range of the Sierra Nevada, snow-crested and believed to be impassable.

It was about the time of this halt in our westward progress that Captain Jedediah Smith came riding into the scene. Picture him as a gaunt-faced, lean-flanked, wiry man, with nerves of iron, sinews of rawhide, a skin like oak-tanned leather, and quick on his feet as a catamount.[1] He was bearded to the ears, of course, for razors formed no part of the scanty equipment of the frontiersman, and above the beard shone a pair of very keen, bright eyes, with the wrinkles about the corners that come of much staring across sun-swept spaces. He was sparing of his words, as are most men who dwell in the great solitudes. Like them he was devout, his stern and rugged features as well as his scriptural name showing the grim old Puritan stock from which he sprang. His hair was long and black, and would have covered his shoulders had it not been tied at the back of the neck by a leather thong. His dress was that of the Indian adapted to meet the requirements of the adventuring white man: a hunting-shirt and trousers of fringed buckskin, embroidered moccasins of elk-hide, and a cap made from the glossy skin of a beaver, with the tail hanging down behind.

On hot desert marches, and in camp, he took off the beaverskin cap and twisted about his head a bright bandanna, which, when taken with his gaunt, unshaven face, made him look like a pirate. Hanging on his chest was a

[1] catamount: cat of the mountain; usually, a lynx, cougar (mountain-lion).

capacious powder horn, and in his belt was a long, straight knife, very broad and heavy in the blade. He also carried a rifle with an altogether extraordinary length of barrel, which brought death to any living thing within a thousand yards on which its foresight rested. His mount was a plains-bred pony, as wiry and unkempt and enduring as himself.

II

The dates of Smith's birth and death are not known. As the nineteenth century was passing the quarter mark, Smith was the head of a firm of fur-traders, Smith, Jackson and Soublette, who had obtained from President John Quincy Adams permission to hunt and trade in the region lying beyond the Rocky Mountains.

In August, 1826, Smith and a small party of his hunters found themselves in the terrible Painted Desert, where the present states of Arizona, Utah, and Nevada meet. Water there was none, for the streams had run dry. The horses and pack mules were dying of thirst and exhaustion; the game had entirely disappeared; the supplies were all but finished, and five hundred miles of the most inhospitable country in the world lay between the pioneers and their camp on Great Salt Lake.

"What few supplies we have left will be used up before we get a quarter of the way back to camp," said Smith. "Our only chance—and I might as well tell you it's a mighty slim one, boys—is in pushing on to California."

"But California's a good four hundred miles away," expostulated his companions, "and the Sierras lie between, and no one has ever crossed them."

"Then I'll be the first man to do it," said Smith. "Besides, I've always had a hankering to learn what lies on the other side of those ranges. Now's my chance to find out."

History chronicles few such marches. Westward pressed the little troop of pioneers, across the sun-baked lava beds of southwestern Utah, over the arid deserts and the barren ranges of southern Nevada, and so to the foothills of that great Sierran range which rears itself ten thousand feet skyward, forming a barrier which had previously separated the fertile lands of the Pacific slope from the rest of the continent more effectually than an ocean. The lava beds gave way to sand wastes dotted with clumps of sagebrush and cactus; the cactus changed to stunted pines; the pines ran out in rocks, and the rocks became covered with snow; and still Smith and his hunters struggled on, emaciated, tattered, almost barefooted, lamed by the cactus spines on the desert, and the stones on the mountain slopes, until at last they stood upon the very summit of the range, and, like that other band of pioneers in an earlier age, looked down on the promised land after their wanderings in the wilderness. The little company of worn and weary men sighted the red-tiled roof of the mission just at sunset.

I doubt if there was a more astonished community between the oceans than was that of San Gabriel when this band of ragged strangers suddenly appeared from nowhere and asked for food and shelter.

"You come from the South—from Mexico?" queried the father superior, staring, half-awed, at these gaunt, fierce-faced, bearded men who spoke in a strange tongue.

"No, padre," answered Smith, calling to his aid the broken Spanish he had picked up in his trading expeditions to Santa Fé, "we come from the East, from the country beyond the great mountains, from the United States. We are Americans," he added a little proudly.

"They say they come from the East," the brown-robed monks whispered to each other. "It is impossible. No one has ever come from that direction. Have not the Indians told us many times that there is no food, no water in that direction, and that, moreover, there is no way to cross the mountains? It is, indeed, a strange and incredible tale that these men tell."

—Adapted from "Some Forgotten Heroes,"
by E. Alexander Powell.

TEST YOUR OBSERVATION

Here are some statements taken from the story which need to be completed to give full meaning. See how many of them you can complete from memory without looking at the text again. Write them out on a clean sheet of paper and then compare them with the statements in the story. This will show how keen an observer you are.

1. The story of the American onset to the West is one of the .... of history.

2. The hardy pioneers carried with them little but ...., ..., and ...., some scanty .... effects, a small store of ...., a liberal supply of ...., and unlimited ...., ..., and ....

3. The pioneers were undaunted by the menace of Mexican ...., of Indian ...., of savage ...., of thirst and starvation in ....

4. Jedediah Smith was a .... faced, ... flanked, wiry ...., with .... of iron, sinews of ...., a skin like ...., and quick on his feet as a ....

5. He was sparing of ...., as are most men who dwell in great ....

6. His hair was .... and ....

7. Water there was none, for the streams ....

8. Smith and his men were made lame by .... on the desert and by the stones on ....

Bring this to class with you:

1. An outline of the different routes the pioneers followed into the Great West. Look them up on a good map.

2. Who are other pioneers in an earlier age who looked down on the Promised Land after their wanderings in the wilderness?

THINGS TO THINK ABOUT

1. What would you name as the outstanding trait in the character of Jedediah Smith?
2. What are some of his other strong traits?
3. Do men who live in the city possess such traits?
4. Would you think Mr. Smith a good companion or not?
5. Compare Jedediah Smith with Daniel Boone or George Rogers Clark. In what points were they most alike?

THINGS TO DO

1. Find pictures of the Great Plains, the Painted Desert, pack-trains, mountain ranges, etc., and bring them to class.
2. Try to find in other books something about the monks and missions in the Far West, and how they came there.
3. Make a list of all the dangers and hardships the pioneers and trail-blazers had to meet and overcome.
4. Some one in the class may be interested to make a small model of a pioneer's covered wagon; a sand-table model of the Painted Desert; or a pioneer's camp modelled in sand and clay.

BOOKS TO READ

If you would like to know more of the times and experiences pictured in this story, read any one of these books:

1. "Kit Carson," by J. S. C. Abbott. Dodd.
   Hunting exploits and adventures in the Far West. Very interesting.
2. "Westward Movement," by C. L. Barstow. Century.
   Worth-while stories of wagon-trains, pony-express, pioneers, etc.
3. "Life and Adventures of Buffalo Bill," by William F. Walter Cody.
   The story of the Chief of Scouts as told by himself. A true picture of early Western life.

THE EXPLORER

We enjoy reading about the things we know best. The person who would get most pleasure out of "The Explorer" is one who has lived as an explorer. Those of us who know what it means to have picnics in the country will understand the poem better than those who have always lived in the city. And those who have pretended to go exploring—as many boys and girls do—will know better than those who have not played such games. But even when we have not the real experience to make us understand fully what we read, one book sometimes helps another. The story of Jedediah Smith will help you to like the poem.

As you read it the first time, make sure that you know the meaning of every word. Otherwise there will be gaps or holes in your understanding of it.

Read silently the first time. Then prepare for reading aloud in class. Pronounce the following words aloud:

cultivation (kŭl″tĭ-vā′shŭn)
conscience (kŏn′shĕns)
interminable (ĭn-tûr′mĭ-ná-bl)
everlasting (ĕv″ēr-lás′tĭng)
patience (pā′shĕns)
illimitable (ĭ-lĭm′ĭt-á-bl)
mutterings (mŭt′ēr-ings)
unimagined (ŭn-ĭ-măj′ĭnd)
self-delusion (sĕlf-dĕ-lū′zhŭn)

I

"There's no sense in going further—it's the edge of cultivation,"
So they said, and I believed it—broke my land and sowed my crop—
Built my barns and strung my fences in the little border station
Tucked away below the foothills where the trails run out and stop.

Till a voice, as bad as Conscience, rang interminable changes
On one everlasting Whisper day and night repeated—so:
"Something hidden. Go and find it. Go and look behind the Ranges—
Something lost behind the Ranges. Lost and waiting for you. Go!"

So I went, worn out of patience; never told my nearest neighbors—
Stole away with pack and ponies—left 'em drinking in the town;
And the faith that moveth mountains didn't seem to help my labors
As I faced the sheer main-ranges, whipping up and leading down.

March by march I puzzled through 'em, turning flanks and dodging shoulders,
Hurried on in hope of water, headed back for lack of grass;
Till I camped above the tree-line—drifted snow and naked boulders—
Felt free air astir to windward—knew I'd stumbled on the Pass.

'Thought to name it for the finder; but that night the Norther found me—
Froze and killed the plains-bred ponies; so I called the camp Despair

(It's the Railway Gap today, though). Then my whisper waked to hound me:—
"Something lost behind the Ranges. Over yonder. Go you there!"

II

Then I knew, the while I doubted—knew His Hand was certain o'er me.
Still—it might be self-delusion—scores of better men had died—
I could reach the township living, but . . . He knows what terrors tore me. . . .
But I didn't. . . . But I didn't. I went down the other side.

Till the snow ran out in flowers, and the flowers turned to aloes,
And the aloes sprung to thickets and a brimming stream ran by;
But the thickets dwined to thorn-scrub, and the water drained to shal'ows—
And I dropped again on desert, blasted earth, and blasting sky. . . .

I remember lighting fires; I remember sitting by them;
I remember seeing faces, hearing voices through the smoke;
I remember they were fancy—for I threw a stone to try 'em.
"Something lost behind the Ranges," was the only word they spoke.

I remember going crazy. I remember that I knew it
When I heard myself hallooing to the funny folk I saw.
Very full of dreams, that desert; but my two legs took
    me through it. . . .
And I used to watch 'em moving with the toes all black
    and raw.

But at last the country altered—White man's country,
    past disputing—
Rolling grass and open timber, with a hint of hills be-
    hind—
There I found me food and water, and I lay a week re-
    cruiting,
Got my strength and lost my nightmares. Then I entered
    on my find.

III

Thence I ran my first rough survey—chose my trees and
    blazed and ringed 'em—
Week by week I pried and sampled—week by week my
    findings grew.
Saul he went to look for donkeys, and by God[1] he found
    a kingdom!
But by God,[1] who sent His whisper, I had struck the worth
    of two.

Up along the hostile mountains, where the hair-poised
    snow-slide shivers—

[1] Through the help of God.

Down and through the big fat marshes that the virgin ore-bed stains,
Till I heard the mile-wide mutterings of unimagined rivers
And beyond the nameless timber saw illimitable plains!

Plotted sites of future cities, traced the easy grades between 'em;
Watched unharnessed rapids wasting fifty thousand head an hour;
Counted leagues of water-frontage through the ax-ripe woods that screen 'em—
Saw the plant to feed a people—up and waiting for the power!

Well I know who'll take the credit—all the clever chaps that followed—
Came, a dozen men together—never knew my desert fears;
Tracked me by the camps I'd quitted, used the water-holes I'd hollowed.
They'll go back and do the talking. They'll be called the pioneers!

They will find my sites of townships—not the cities that I set there.
They will rediscover rivers—not my rivers heard at night.
By my own old marks and bearings they will show me how to get there,
By the lonely cairns I builded they will guide my feet aright.

Have I named one single river? Have I claimed one single acre?
Have I kept one single nugget—(barring samples)? No, not I.
Because my price was paid me ten times over by my Maker.
But you wouldn't understand it. You go up and occupy.

Ores you'll find there; wood and cattle; water transit sure and steady.
(That should keep the railway rates down), coal and iron at your doors.
God took care to hide that country till He judged His people ready,
Then He chose me for His whisper, and I've found it, and it's yours!

Yes, your "Never-never country"—Yes, your "edge of cultivation."
And "no sense in going further"—till I crossed the Range to see.
God forgive me! No, I didn't. It's God's present to our nation.
Anybody might have found it—but His Whisper came to me.

—RUDYARD KIPLING.

THINGS TO THINK ABOUT

1. How did the "Explorer" differ from his neighbors as described in the first three stanzas?
2. What do you most admire about the "Explorer"?
3. Are there explorers other than those who seek new lands?
4. What makes the following quotation appropriate here?

"Now I see the secret of the making of the best persons. It is to grow in the open air and to eat and sleep with the earth."
—Walt Whitman.

THINGS TO DO

1. Memorize the "Whisper":

> "Something hidden—go and find it.
> Go and look behind the ranges.
> Something lost behind the ranges,
> Lost and waiting for you. Go!"

2. It is hard for us, in the days of good roads, automobiles, and trains, to understand the hardships described in this poem. Choose a phrase or sentence such as "sheer main-ranges, whipping up and leading down"; "above the tree-line—drifted snow and naked boulders." Prepare an explanation of it for your classmates, using your own experiences in the mountains or on the desert, pictures from magazines and books, slides, and so on.
3. There are many word-pictures here. Select the one that makes you see something most clearly.
4. Explain the full meaning in the poem of "illimitable plains," "hair-poised snow-slide"; "interminable changes"; "naked boulders."

RUDYARD KIPLING (1865-   )

Rudyard Kipling, a great British author, was born at Bombay, India, on December 30, 1865. Most of his first six years were spent in and around Bombay, which was then the most important city in the eastern world. When he was six years of age, his parents returned to England, but they were unable to remain there very long.

After spending several happy months together, his parents found it necessary to return again to India and leave Rudyard in England. He was placed in a school named Westward Ho, at Bideford, in Devonshire. Here he soon gained recognition on account of his reading of books of his own choice and on account of his original writing. His talents were such that he might have made a place for himself at the head of his class in all his studies but he was more interested in reading and writing. He became editor of the school paper and wrote some articles for the *Bideford Journal*. He wrote much verse and was venturesome enough to send some verses to a London paper, which, to his great delight, were accepted and published. Some of his verses were put together in a little volume and printed privately by his parents in India, with the title "Schoolboy Lyrics." It soon became clear that his future was to be in the field of literature.

He finished his course at school at the age of seventeen, and went out to India to be with his parents. There he worked on a paper for a number of years, writing verses and stories in addition to his newspaper duties.

These were happy years in the Kipling family. After five years, he was promoted to the editorial staff of *The Pioneer*, the greatest of all the Indian newspapers. From this time on his reputation and influence as a writer grew rapidly, until now he is known all over the world. His books are published in many languages and in every civilized country. He is now the most widely known of English authors.

You will enjoy Kipling's "Jungle Books."

PIONEERS! O PIONEERS!

When you have read "Pioneers! O Pioneers!" once silently, you will see that in some ways it is like "The Explorer." But if you answer the following questions, you will see that there are some important differences between them:

1. What difference is suggested by the two titles?
2. In which poem is the hero one man? in which a race of men?
3. In which poem is there much description? in which, exclamation? Why? Which do you prefer?
4. What is Kipling's feeling about his "Explorer"? Whitman's about his "Pioneers"?

    Come, my tan-faced children,
Follow well in order, get your weapons ready,
Have you your pistols? Have you your sharp-edged axes?
        Pioneers! O pioneers!

    For we cannot tarry here,
We must march, my darlings, we must bear the brunt of danger,
We the youthful sinewy races, all the rest on us depend,
        Pioneers! O pioneers!

    O you youths, Western youths,
So impatient, full of action, full of manly pride and friendship,
Plain I see you, Western youths, see you tramping with the foremost,
        Pioneers! O pioneers!

Have the elder races halted?
Do they droop and end their lesson, wearied over there
    beyond the seas?
We take up the task eternal, and the burden and the
    lesson,
        Pioneers! O pioneers!

All the past we leave behind,
We debouch upon a newer, mightier world, varied world,
Fresh and strong the world we seize, world of labor and
    the march,
        Pioneers! O pioneers!

We detachments steady throwing,
Down the edges, through the passes, up the mountains
    steep,
Conquering, holding, daring, venturing as we go the un-
    known ways,
        Pioneers! O pioneers!

We primeval forests felling,
We the rivers stemming, vexing we, and piercing deep the
    mines within,
We the surface broad surveying, we the virgin soil up-
    heaving,
        Pioneers! O pioneers!

Colorado men are we,
From the peaks gigantic, from the great sierras and the
    high plateaus,

From the mine and from the gully, from the hunting trail we come,
>Pioneers! O pioneers!

From Nebraska, from Arkansas,
Central inland race are we, from Missouri, with the continental blood intervein'd,
All the hands of comrades clasping, all the Southern, all the Northern,
>Pioneers! O pioneers!

>O resistless, restless race!
O beloved race in all! O my breast aches with tender love for all!
O I mourn and yet exult, I am rapt with love for all,
>Pioneers! O pioneers!
>>—WALT WHITMAN.

DIRECTIONS FOR STUDY

Nearly every line and sentence in the poem is full of meaning. Each stanza is a distinct picture of what the pioneers dared, endured, and conquered. The following directions will help you get from the poem its message:

1. For second reading study each stanza carefully. Try to think out what it means. Ask yourself questions about it. For example:

Stanza 1. Why "tan-faced children"? "Follow well in order"? Why mention pistols and axes?

Stanza 2. Why "we cannot tarry here"? Why "we must bear the brunt of danger"? Who depend upon us?

2. Ask yourself questions like these for each stanza. Write down one good question for your classmates to answer, which you think will help them to understand the meaning.

3. Use your dictionary for all new words and others not clear to you.

4. Learn by heart the stanza or stanzas you like best.

5. When you have finished, make a list of all the tasks that pioneers must do.

6. After completing a careful study of the poem as directed, read it again for pleasure, and see how much you have added to its meaning.

> Who loves the rain,
> And loves his home,
>   And looks on life with quiet eyes,
> Him will I follow through the storm,
> And at his hearth-fire keep me warm.
>
> —FRANCES SHAW.

WALT WHITMAN

You will be interested to know something of the author of "Pioneers! O pioneers!"

Walt Whitman (1819–1892) was an American poet, born at West Hills, Long Island.

His ancestors for generations had been men who earned their living with their hands. There was not one scholar among them.

Whitman himself left the Brooklyn schools at thirteen and learned his father's trade of carpentering. He also worked as a typesetter, taught school, wrote for magazines, and for a short time published a weekly newspaper. His leisure time he spent among the workers of the city studying their lives as one of them.

During the Civil War, Whitman volunteered as an army nurse, and became a close friend of Lincoln.

In his writings Whitman's purpose was to describe the development of America and to be a prophet of democracy, of freedom, and the brotherhood of man. His best known poem is that on the death of Lincoln, "O, Captain! My Captain!"

If you wish to become better acquainted with Walt Whitman, read Alfred Noyes's "Approach to Whitman."

THINGS TO THINK ABOUT

1. What lines in this poem remind you of experiences of Jedediah Smith?
2. Were there pioneers other than those who conquered the wilderness?
3. Are there pioneers today in education, industry, and science? Mention examples and show why you consider each a pioneer.
4. Can you name any pioneer in your community? Tell something about him.
5. Which of the two poems about the Pioneers do you like the better? Give your reasons.

THINGS TO DO

1. Be ready to read aloud the lines which best show the spirit and courage of the pioneers.
2. Make a list of the pioneers you have studied about in history.
3. Give illustrations from the history of our country, showing the truth of these lines from American pioneers:
   - *a.* "We must bear the brunt of danger."
   - *b.* "All the rest on us depend."
   - *c.* "All the past we leave behind."

BOOKS TO READ

If you wish to know about pioneers other than those who seek new lands, the following books will tell you about them:

1. "American Pioneers," by Mowry and Mowry. Silver, Burdett.
   Accounts of explorers, statesmen, educators.
2. "Boy's Life of Edison," by William H. Meadowcraft. Harper.
   An extremely interesting account of Mr. Edison's life and inventions, written by a member of his staff. Approved by Mr. Edison.
3. "Clara Barton" in "Group of Famous Women," by Edith Horton. Heath.
   Especially interesting and helpful.
4. "Heroines of Service," by Mary R. Parkman. Century.
   Short illustrated biographies of Clara Barton and others.
5. "Stories of Luther Burbank," by Effie Y. Slusser. Scribners.
   An interesting account of this great pioneer in plant cultivation.
6. "A Dutch Boy Fifty Years After," by Edward Bok. Scribners.
7. "The Boy Who Followed Ben Franklin," by Edward Bok. Scribners.

SONG TO THE MOUNTAINS
(PAWNEE) [1]

The songs and poetry of the Indian are not yet fully appreciated by the white man. They seem peculiar to us. But they possess a simple, natural beauty worthy of note. As you read the following poem observe the repetition in the opening of each stanza. Notice the advance upon the mountain until the peak is finally conquered.

Mountains loom upon the path we take;
Yonder peak now rises sharp and clear;
Behold! It stands with its head uplifted,
Thither we go, since our way lies there.

Mountains loom upon the path we take;
Yonder peak now rises sharp and clear;
Behold! We climb, drawing near its summit;
Steeper grows the way and slow our steps.

Mountains loom upon the path we take;
Yonder peak now rises sharp and clear;
Behold us now on its head uplifted;
Planting there our feet, we stand secure.

---

[1] Pawnee Indians are a tribe of North American Indians belonging to the Caddoan stock. The name, which is a native word meaning "horn," was given them because of the horn-like scalping-lock which they wore arranged in such a manner as to stand upright. Their home formerly was along the banks of the Platte River, in Nebraska. They raised grains and vegetables, and built permanent homes of logs and earth.

In 1874 they moved to a reservation in Indian Territory (now Oklahoma) where they now live.

Mountains loom upon the path we take;
Yonder peak that rose so sharp and clear;
Behold us now on its head uplifted;
Resting there at last we sing our song.

THINGS TO THINK ABOUT

1. This is called a lyric poem. Can you tell why?
2. How many of you have ever climbed a mountain?
3. In climbing a steep hill or mountain have you ever "experienced a feeling of exultation" when you reached the top?
4. Have you ever seen a steep hill or mountain "loom upon the path we take"; or the peak "that rose so sharp and clear"?
5. Why do you think the Indian was stirred to say: "We stand secure" when he had reached the top? Try also to explain his thought and feeling in the last line: "Resting there at last we sing our song."

THINGS TO DO

If you have records of Indian songs bring them to school and play them on the victrola.

BOOKS TO READ

If you are interested in knowing more about the Pawnee Indians you will enjoy reading:

"Pawnee Hero Stories and Folk Tales," by G. B. Grinnell. Scribners.

A wonderful story of Indian life, folklore, and customs
"Traditions of the Skidi Pawnee," by G. A. Dorsey.

In the Eskimaun lyric the speaker contemplates the mountain with its gathering clouds, and gives a picture of what he sees.

MOUNT KOONAK: A SONG OF ARSUT
(ESKIMAUN) [1]

I look toward the south, to great Mount Koonak,
To great Mount Koonak, there to the south;
I watch the clouds that gather round him;
I contemplate their shining brightness;
They spread abroad upon great Koonak;
They climb up his seaward flanks;
See how they shift and change;
Watch them here to the south;
How one makes beautiful the other;
How they mount his southern slopes,
Hiding him from the stormy sea,
Each lending beauty to the other.

—From "American Indian Lyrics,"
Selected by Nellie Barnes.

THINGS TO THINK ABOUT

1. Compare the two Indian lyrics. In what ways are they alike? In what ways different?

2. Can you describe the picture the speaker sees as he gazes at the mountain?

---

[1] The Eskimaun (from Algonken, Eskimautik, eaters of raw flesh) is a stock of North American Indians, whose habitat extends coastwise from eastern Greenland to western Alaska, and to the eastern extremity of Asia, a distance of over 5,000 miles.

The winter or permanent villages are usually along the coast. The interior is also visited for hunting deer and other animals, though the natives rarely go inland farther than fifty miles.

BOOKS TO READ

Vilhjalmur Stefansson has written an interesting story called "My Life with the Eskimos," published by Macmillan.

"Nanook of the North," by Julian W. Bilby, is the story of an Eskimo family. The author has lived more than fourteen years among Eskimos, and his picture of their manners and customs is the result of sympathetic and careful observation.

SILENT-READING TEST

The following story of a buffalo hunt will make a good silent-reading test. There are 1348 words in the story. Begin at a signal from the teacher or at a definite minute, if you are timing yourself. When you have finished, divide the number of words by the minutes it takes you to read the story. Include seconds to the nearest tenth of a minute. The quotient is your rate.

In the long sentences we cannot put in commas enough to show us always where to pause a second. We must ourselves learn to read at a glance the words that belong together and to separate them a little from the words not so closely connected with them. For example:

Half a century ago — there were still — herds of buffaloes — and tribes of Indians — living in Nebraska.

This is called phrasing or grouping. Do not go on from one group to another if you find that you do not understand.

Before you begin, make sure of the pronunciation and meaning of these words:

uneventful	reconnoitered
distorted	amphitheater
deceptive	stampede
lariat	deliberation
croup	toll

Remember what has been said about enunciation.

A PAWNEE BUFFALO HUNT

Half a century ago there were still herds of buffaloes and tribes of Indians living in Nebraska. The following story tells how a white man hunted the buffalo with the Pawnee Indians.

1. What was the plan of the hunt?
2. How and why was the hunt successful?

When we turned out of our blankets the next morning, a heavy mist hung over the prairie. This was unfortunate, for as long as the fog lasted it would be impossible for the scouts to see far enough to discover the buffaloes. The first few hours of the march were uneventful. Once or twice the huge bodies of a small band of buffaloes loomed up through the white mist, their size and shape greatly distorted by its deceptive effect. By midday the fog had risen from the ground, though still clinging in white cottony wreaths about the tops of the higher bluffs near us. We now could see for a long distance over the prairie. A little later the sun burst forth, and the sky became clear. Soon after noon we went into camp.

We had but just begun our dinner when a runner was seen coming at full gallop down the bluffs. It was one of the scouts. He dashed through the village, and did not check his pony's speed until he had reached the old chief's lodge. As he rode on and past us, he called out: "I saw many buffaloes," and we shouted back to him: "*Tu-ra-heh!* —It is good!"

At once the women began to take down the lodges and to pack the ponies. Orders had been issued to move the village to the creek by which the buffaloes were feeding, while the men should go at once and surround them. Leaving everything except guns and ammunition-belts in the wagon, we joined the crowd of men who were riding out of the village.

The scene that we now beheld was such as might have been witnessed here a hundred years ago. Here were eight hundred warriors, stark naked, and mounted on naked animals. A strip of rawhide, or a lariat, knotted about the lower jaw, was all they had to guide their horses. Among all these men there was not a gun nor a pistol, nor any indication that they had ever met with the white men. Their bows and arrows they held in their hands.

At a moderate gallop, we set off. Many of the Indians led a spare horse; often two men would be seen on the same animal, the one behind having the lariats of two led horses wound about his arm. Each naked Indian seemed a part of his steed, and rose and fell with it in the rhythmic swing of its stride. Out over each horse's croup floated the long black hair of his rider, spread out on the wings of the breeze. Gradually the slow gallop became fast. The flanks of the horses showed here and there patches of wet, which glistened in the slanting rays of the westering sun.

Eight, ten, a dozen miles had been left behind us, and we were approaching the top of a high bluff, when the signal was given to halt. In a moment, every man was off his horse. Two or three only rode up nearly to the top of the hill, dismounted, and then peered over; and a moment later, at another signal, all mounted and the swift gallop began again.

Over the ridge we passed, down the smooth slope, and across a wide, level plain, where the prairie dogs and the owls and the rattlesnakes had their home. Through the dog town we hurried on thundering hoofs, no doubt amazing the dogs, and perhaps even arousing some interest in the sluggish, stupid snakes.

Just before we reached the next high ridge, we were halted again. Two men reconnoitered and signalled that the buffaloes were in sight. The tired horses were now turned loose, and the fresh ones mounted.

As we rode slowly up the ridge, we saw spread out before us a wide valley, black with buffaloes. Two miles away, on the other side, rose steep, ragged bluffs, up which the clumsy buffaloes could make but slow progress, while the ponies could run there nearly as fast as on level ground.

At least a thousand buffaloes were lying down in this amphitheater. Here and there, away from the main herd on the lower hills, were old bulls, singly and by twos and threes, some of them quietly chewing the cud, others sullenly pawing up the dust, or grinding their battered horns into the yellow dirt of the hillsides. Not the slightest notice was taken of us as we rode down the slope at a pace that was almost a run, but still held in check by the leaders.

We had covered perhaps half the distance between the hilltop and the buffaloes when some of the outlying bulls seemed to observe us, and after looking for a moment or two, these started in rapid flight. This attracted the attention of the herd, and when we were yet half a mile from them they took the alarm. At once all were on their feet. For a moment they gazed bewildered at the dark line that was sweeping toward them, and then, down went every huge head and up flew every little tail, and the herd was off in a headlong stampede for the opposite hills. Then it was that the oldest man among the leaders, who was riding in the center of the line, turned back toward us and uttered a shrill *Lóo-ah!* It was the word we had waited for.

Like an arrow from a bow each horse darted forward. Now all restraint was removed and each man might do his best. What had been only a wild gallop became a mad race. Each rider hoped to be the first to reach the opposite ridge and to turn the buffaloes back into the valley, so that the surround might be completely successful. I had not gone much more than half way across the valley when I saw the leading Indians pass the head of the herd and begin to turn them back. This was the first object of the chase, for in a stampede the cows and young are always ahead, the bulls follow simply because they cannot run as fast as their wives and children. Bulls are never killed when cows and heifers are to be had.

Back came the herd, and I soon found myself in the midst of a throng of buffaloes, horses, and Indians. There was no yelling or shouting on the part of the men, but their stern, set faces, and the fierce gleam of their eyes told of the fires of excitement burning within them. Three or four times my rifle spoke out, and to some purpose, and one shot, placed too far back, drew on me a quick, savage charge from a young cow. My pony, while a good cattle horse, was new at buffalo running, and his deliberation in dodging caused me an anxious second or two, as I saw the cow's head sweep close to his flank.

Before I turned my horse's head toward the camp, the broad disk of the setting sun had rested on the tops of the western bluffs, and tipped their crests with fire. His horizontal beams lit up with a picturesque redness the dusky forms which moved about over the valley. Up the ravines and over the hills were stringing long lines of squaws, leading patient ponies, whose backs were piled high with dark meat and with soft, shaggy skins. Late into the night the work continued, and the loads kept coming into the camp. About the flickering fires in and before the lodges there was feasting and merriment. Marrowbones were tossed among the red embers, calf's-head was baked in the hot earth, fat ribs were roasted, and other parts boiled or eaten raw. With laughter and singing and story-telling and dance the night wore away.

Over the plain where the buffaloes had fallen, the gray wolf was prowling and with the coyote, the fox, and the badger, tearing at the bones of the slain. When day came, the golden eagle and the buzzard perched upon the naked red skeletons and took their toll.

—*Adapted from "The Oregon Trail," by Francis Parkman.*

THINGS TO TALK ABOUT

1. In what different ways did the Indians make use of buffaloes?

2. What really destroyed the great herds of buffaloes?

3. Are there any herds of buffaloes today?

4. There was also another kind of buffalo hunt. Fifty years ago or more, buffalo hides were in great demand for robes and coats. Hunting outfits were organized to go out on the plains to get hides. The meat was left to decay or for wolves to devour. Many of these outfits came into conflict with Indian hunting parties and robber bands. There were many bloody encounters. It may be some one in the class has read an account of this kind.

5. In Alaska there are now great herds of reindeer being cared for on the ranges, so that they may be used for meat and clothing. Why was not the buffalo kept in this way?

THINGS TO DO

1. Can you bring a good picture of a buffalo hunt to class?
2. Select from the story some part you think to be particularly vivid in description.

WORD STUDY

Have you ever thought how wonderful it is that we can use words? Animals have no words at all; babies learn one word at a time; little children have only a few hundred words to use. Probably you know more than a thousand. But a great writer uses many thousands of words to tell all that he sees and thinks and feels; and in the large dictionary there are nearly half a million words for us to use.

In studying words, it is important to know many; but it is more important to know the exact differences between words that mean almost the same thing. Look up in the dictionary and study the differences in meaning between the words grouped together in the following list:

> city, town, village, metropolis, capital, suburb, hamlet
> road, highway, street, avenue, boulevard, trail

See whether you can find interesting words in "A Pawnee Buffalo Hunt," which mean almost the same as some other words you know; and point out the differences.

BOOKS TO READ

1. "When Buffalo Ran," by George Bird Grinnell. Yale University Press.
   A vivid picture of Indian life in the Far West seventy-five years ago. The author is an Indian, and one of the greatest authorities on the subject.
2. "Wolf-Hunters: A Story of the Buffalo Plains." Scribners.
   A true story of the experiences of three soldiers during the winter of 1861–62 on the plains.

HOMESTEADING IN ALASKA

The pioneers are not all dead. Alaska is the land of pioneers today. At first men went to Alaska to find gold; now they go to make homes for themselves. This story of a man who took a claim of land in Alaska is as exciting as "Robinson Crusoe." The author had many strange and interesting adventures. There are several about bears which are exciting. You may wish to read the whole book. It is called "Alaska Man's Luck."

I

THE CLAIM

By Odin's Lake
March 30, 1916

I am sitting under a big spruce tree and in front of me a lusty campfire is burning, while beyond it lies Odin's Lake. It is covered with several feet of ice and snow, but it is very beautiful—a white glade amidst the woods.

I came to Haines several weeks ago and met all my old friends once again. They gave me a hearty welcome and asked what they could do for me. Jack asked me out to his ranch and I stayed there about ten days, helping him with this and that about the place. Then one day I decided to go down and see about my homestead.

I started out with a small blanket-roll and a little grub, a frying-pan, a stewpot, and a new rifle that I had bought in Juneau. It was a fine, cool day. There had been a frost in the night and the snow had frozen on top so that I could walk on it anywhere in the woods without breaking through. The trail led through the army post, across the peninsula to the Chilkat; then along the beach for five miles to Smokehouse Bay, where O'Brien has his homestead. I stayed with him for a while, had a cup of hot coffee, and then started out again through the pine woods across the peninsula to Flat Bay.

There is a ranch on this side of the peninsula, too, but there was no one there. I kept on along the beach a mile farther where the trail leads up to Odin's Lake. No one would know there was a trail there, the ground was covered so deeply with snow. There is a half-built log cabin near the beach, and I camped by it the first night. I slept under an overhanging spruce tree with a great fire built of driftwood to keep me warm. There was a mild south breeze and little waves lapped on the pebbly cove.

It was very wonderful to be alone in the peaceful woods. I lay long in the night and gazed into the fire and up into the sky where the stars were tumbling out, one by one and in clusters, blinking and twinkling down through infinity to me, filling me with cheer and hope. It seemed that they were laughing and singing to me, telling me that my troubles were over and that now I could take my reward— the earth, the woods, the fiord, the mountains, the beauty, and the peace. Then the wavelets lulled me to sleep and I woke up in the morning, joyous and happy to be there.

I cooked some hot cakes, ate, and went out to stake my claim. On a rocky point at the end of my cove, which I named Viking's Point, I chopped down my first spruce tree and made my first stake. From there I walked up through the woods in a southerly direction, blazing a tree now and then, and counting my steps. I would take my full allowance, three hundred and twenty acres. Seventeen hundred and sixty yards I stepped, and then made another stake and planted it, blazing trees all around to make the place conspicuous. It was not accurate measuring, but the law reads, to measure to one's best ability, and stepping off the distance was the only way I had of doing it.

Then I went eight hundred and eighty yards in a westerly direction along the side of the hill that lies behind Odin's Lake, and post number three was planted in a grove of big hemlocks with trees four feet in diameter, which will make good saw logs some day when I have a little sawmill rigged up on the creek that runs out of the lake. From post number three I walked straight down to the fiord again, and put up a stake at the right distance from post number one. My homestead was staked! I put up a notice in a box on a tree where the trail to the lake leaves the beach, and made a duplicate notice that I shall send to the land office when I get back to Haines.

This work took me all day, for there were many thickets to cut my way through, and several times I lost count and had to go back over my line to get it right. I moved my camp up to Odin's Lake in the evening and found a good place to camp under a branchy spruce tree. I have been resting for a few days, looking things over and trying to decide where is the best place to begin clearing, and where to build. Down by the cove there is a low beach that is covered with a thick growth of willows and alders. I think I will begin down there, making that my first field.

Odin's Lake lies in the center of my land, and around it is a valley with patches of alder, birch, and willow, and a sprinkling of spruce trees. It will be comparatively easy to clear, and if everything goes well, I ought to be able to make a good farm out of it. I shall try to get a little piece cleared this spring so that I can put in a small garden, and as soon as I can, I shall fell trees for the cabin. There is a fine grove of young spruce trees where I intend to build. All I have to do is to cut them down, notch them, and pile them up, and there is my house. I am full of plans for what I am going to do, and the only trouble is how to get the time! Yet Rome wasn't built in a day. Why worry about time?

I am going back to Haines tomorrow to get an outfit of grub, tools, and things, and I'll try to get a boat to transport them down here. The sun is going below the rim of the peaks. I had better stop writing and get my supper.

II

The Viking Ship

Viking's Cove
Haines, Alaska
April 20, 1916

When I came to Haines from Juneau, the school-teacher invited me to spend an evening with him and his wife.

We talked of Vikings and Norse mythology, and read poetry about Vikings. Then we agreed how much this country was like the Northland where the old Vikings had lived. It was this talk that caused me to name my point Viking's Point. When I rowed in here with my outfit the last time and the nice round cove seemed to welcome me, I named it Viking's Cove. Indeed, I felt like a Viking. Was I not from the land where the Vikings once lived, and was I not even now starting out, a young rover building my home in the wilderness of a new land as they did in the old days?

I bought a lot of things in Haines, a tent and more blankets, cooking utensils, and grub. I got a saw and a new ax, a grub hoe and a shovel, and the many other things I needed. Then I bought a fourteen-foot skiff from a soldier. It was not a very good boat, and one side was broken in, but I got it cheap and borrowed some tools from the post engineer to patch it up so that it would float. I got a gallon of coal tar from the painter, and when I have time some dry day, I'll haul the craft up on the beach and paint the bottom with tar. When I had everything bought and ready, I loaded my things into the skiff and began to row home.

It was a fine day and the fiord was as still as a millpond. In the afternoon I landed at my own beach. I carried my outfit up and made my camp under some big spruce trees near the spot where I intended to make my clearing.

The next day, after making my camp as comfortable as I could, I made a trail over to my future clearing and began cutting down trees and brush, and piling them in windrows on top of the snow. It was great fun, for my ax was sharp as a razor, and it fairly mowed down the alder brush. By nightfall on the first day, I had quite a hole cut in the woods, and I felt very proud and ambitious. I was hewing a farm out of the wilderness! I was putting my mark on the face of the earth! Where now stood great forests of brush and trees, I would have fields of clover and gardens full of fruit and flowers. I felt that I was doing good and really accomplishing something, not only for myself, but for the good of the whole country. I was making Alaska more habitable. That was worth working for.

I have been slashing two weeks now and have made a large clearing. Tomorrow I am going to Haines to buy a few things I need, and see whether I can get work when I have finished slashing and piling the brush on this five-acre piece I have started on. It takes money to build, and I must earn enough this summer to build a house and live all next winter.

Haines, Alaska
May 15, 1916

Time has passed swiftly and I have been very busy. I have finished slashing the five acres of my ranch, and as the brush was as yet too green to burn, I loaded my tent and household goods on my boat and came into town. I landed on the beach near Fort Seward and picked out a good place to pitch my tent, and then made my little home as comfortable as I could with a spruce-bough bed and a little table. I went over to Haines and bought a Yukon stove with a cast-iron top and put it in one corner of my tent. It looks like a little homely kitchen with my small pots and pans hanging about. I had brought my sourdough pot in with me, and I hung it in a good warm place. In the morning I have sour-dough hot cakes with an egg in them and lots of butter and syrup.

I have begun taking cold baths, plunging in the fiord in the morning. At five o'clock when the sun is only a little way above the mountain-top, and the little spears of grass that have just broken through the black earth are strung with drops of dew that gleam like diamonds in its rays, I roll out of my warm blankets, slip off my night-clothes and step out of my tent. Out there in the cool morning breeze my flesh shrinks from the touch of the wind, and only by clamping my teeth together can I keep them from chattering. My body says it would be much nicer to get into warm clothes, but my brain thinks how fine my body will feel after it is all over, and I walk determinedly down to the water's edge, wade in to my waist, and dive under.

Once under the water I usually get stricken with a joyous panic and scramble out as fast as I can, but sometimes I keep my head and swim around a little before I get out and climb up the beach. The wind no longer seems chill, and the sun seems to have become very warming. It envelops me in a billow of warmth as I rub myself dry, and my whole body tingles with the joy of life. I would like to run, run, run! Then I light my fire and my hot cakes begin to splutter in the skillet, and the coffee sends up a refreshing aroma. When my stack of three frying-pan-size cakes are baked and buttered and soaked in syrup, I sit down joyously to eat my breakfast.

Haines, Alaska
June 8, 1916

I have bought an old Indian war canoe, forty feet long and eight feet wide amidships. It looks more like a Viking ship than anything else I can think of; it is long, low, and has upturned ends. It belonged to some soldiers, but they had left it lying sideways on the beach where the waves reached and pounded on it every time there was an extremely high tide. I offered them five dollars for it and they were so happy that they gave me also wire for rigging, rigging-screws and blocks, ropes, two large sails, tools, and other things.

The canoe was rather battered and had two long cracks in the bottom, but I have her upon the beach above high tide, and I spend some time on her every morning before I go to work, and every evening when I can; and when I get her calked up and painted and her rigging on, she will be a real sailing ship. I will load her up with grub and things, sail her down and cast anchor in Viking's Cove. It will be great fun.

Haines, Alaska
June 15, 1916

My Viking ship is now ready to sail home. She lies at anchor out there in the bay, riding the waves gracefully, like a swan. I sailed down to the Chilkoot cannery one day and got two set-nets to fish with. I also got two pups that I intend to use as sleigh-dogs next winter. Now I am all ready to sail for Viking's Cove in the Viking ship. My nets and provisions are aboard, and tomorrow morning, if there is a north breeze, I set sail for home once more.

II

SALMON FISHING

Viking's Cove
July 5, 1916

In the evening I set out my nets. As it was not yet time to go to bed, I decided to go up to my clearing and see how my slashing would burn. We had had some dry weather and everything was dried out. I made a dozen small fires which soon spread till the flames roared and leaped away up into the air. They crackled and snapped and threw coals and cinders till I thought I had made a terrible mistake, and was about to set the whole country afire. Before long a tongue of flame stretched out toward the spruce woods, and the dry moss on the ground began to burn. I ran for the spring and brought a bucket of water, but that did no good at all.

Then I remembered that when I was in the army we

had put out a grass fire with wet gunny sacks; so I fetched another bucket of water and a sack, and went to work. I beat up and down along the edge of the woods, putting out fire after fire all night long, and succeeded in keeping the woods from catching fire. It seemed, though, that no sooner did I have one fire out, than another started somewhere else. Toward morning the long brush piles had all burned out, and there were no more fire sparks flying around, but there was one place where the fire had eaten down into the mossy bottom, and had worked underground for quite a distance into the woods.

I could see the smoke coming up through the moss and around the roots of several trees, and somehow I could not put it out. I had pick, shovel, and ax, and I dug and chopped and dug and shovelled the mossy ground out of the woods, but the fire kept on smoking and working its way deeper in. At last I was tired and gave it up, consoling myself by saying that if it was ordained that those woods were to burn, they would burn in spite of me.

I went down to the beach and was about to go to bed when I remembered that I had my nets out. I looked down that way and started. What was that? One of my nets, I could see, had drifted and half of it was up on the shore, but what were those shining things in it? I got into my skiff and rowed down there. I hardly dared believe that there were salmon in the net, but as I drew my boat nearer and the things looked more and more like fish, I had strength to go on. I worked along the net from the outside and took out sixteen salmon. They fought and wiggled with their tails as I took them out of the net, one by one, and it was no easy job. But, oh, how pretty they were! They seemed like a whole fortune to me as they lay there glistening in the bottom of the boat.

Then I put the net out again and rowed to the next cove to look at my other net. It, too, had drifted, and I took ten salmon out of it and put it back where it belonged. Then I rowed back and put all the fish in the Viking ship and went in to camp to get breakfast. There was a big smoke coming out of the woods, and as soon as I had eaten, I took a bucket of water up to the place and fought fire again for several hours. When I had the thing almost out, and there were only a few small wisps of smoke rising from the moss here and there, I went back to the beach, cooked a meal, and ate.

Evidently my nets were not put out right, for when I rowed out to them after I had eaten, I found that they had both drifted in again. I got twenty more salmon, however, making a total of forty-six. I had to take in the nets and put them out again. This took me fully three hours, and when I got back to the beach the fire in the woods was going again, fanned by a south wind that threatened to spread through the whole woods. There was no alternative. I ate some hardtack and a can of meat, then went up there and dug and dug and stamped out fires till toward evening I was exhausted. The fire wasn't out yet, but I gave up the struggle and went down to my tent and slept. When

I got up in the middle of the night to see how things were, my fire had gone out completely. Then I slept.

It was well along in the next day before I was rested enough to go out to my nets. They were both on the beach, but there were thirty-seven salmon in them, and I began to think that I was a fisherman. The cannery boat came, and I proudly pitched my catch on board, to the captain's great surprise; for no one else had caught any yet. That was yesterday, and today I took out one hundred and eleven salmon.

Viking's Cove
July 10, 1916

I have caught five hundred and fifty silvery-sided salmon. They come and come unceasingly. At first my nets kept drifting, but I put larger rocks on for anchors, and now they are secure enough. It is nice calm weather and the cork lines of my nets are stretched, beautifully arched in the sunshine out there in the coves. Whenever a salmon gets tangled in them, they bob and jerk back and forth. There must have been five that struck the net while I was looking at it this morning.

The weather was wonderful this morning, calm, clear, and cool. As I looked about me after I had taken my plunge, I was thrilled by the greatness, the vastness, the beauty of this wonderful land. The sun had risen over a distant row of mountain peaks in the northeast, and shone on the snow upon their crests and the glossy, wet sides of the great canyons everywhere, no matter where I turned. I could see each peak and canyon and cranny, oh, so clearly; and then the dark green, stately spruce woods, streaked with the light leaves of birch and willows, and splotched with the soft green velvet of alder patches, the black peaks towering to the sky, and the blue-green glaciers in the upper canyons contrasted splendidly with the big spots of unmelted white snow.

I have this to look at every day, and yet it doesn't grow old. I can go out at any time and be filled to the brim with the beauty of it. It is mine and it is priceless, and I am rich with it. I shall need no landscapes on the walls of my home; only large windows that will let in the light and air, and the outside that is so beautiful that any picture ever painted would be dwarfed by it.

A shadow has fallen over the earth, for it is nearly eleven o'clock and the sun has sunk below the mountains to the northward. It is not dark yet—it won't be till next month—but it is really night, for the owls are hooting in the woods, and all the other birds are asleep.

IV

Building the House

Viking's Cove
July 29, 1916

I have begun to build my house up by Odin's Lake. First, I picked out a good flat place near a rocky bluff, then I cleared it of brush and imagined a cabin standing there.

Young spruces grew all around, ranging from six inches to a foot in diameter. I began to fell them, trimming them and piling the branches in great heaps. I need only a few trees more to have enough for the cabin. When I row along the beach I see lumber that has drifted in and is lying among the seaweed and other driftage. I take this lumber to my beach where I have it piled according to size, shape, and condition.

Every time I go up to the lake, I take a load of lumber, and soon there will be enough for floor and ceiling.

I have cleared a little space in my slashing, and as it is too late to put in a garden, I will spend my time grubbing stumps and burning brush, so that next summer I can start in early to put a crop in some of my ground.

I am really proud of my work when I stand in my clearing and look about at the burned brush piles and the many stumps that I have already torn from their grasp in the soil. This clearing is the greatest thing I have ever accomplished. When I look at it, it seems almost impossible that one man could do so much in so short a time; my heart fills with the joy of achievement, and when I think of how I can make this land into a smooth, velvet field of clover, and of the two hundred odd acres up there around the lake that can be made into farm land, I could cry with the joy of it. I wouldn't change my place for the finest job in the finest city on earth.

*—Adapted from "Alaska Man's Luck,"
by Hjalmar Rutzebek.*

THINGS TO DO AND TALK ABOUT

1. Outline on the board the principal parts of this account. Which interested you most?
2. How was Mr. Rutzebek like a Viking? How was he different?
3. How does a person get land for homesteading? for taking other claims?
4. Is it better to stay in the city where there is not work enough for all, or to try to find land in the country, on which you can grow food for yourself and for others? State this as a proposition and plan a debate on the subject.
5. Make a map of the peninsula and mark the different points along the journey. Would you have chosen the site selected by the author? Give reasons for your answer.
6. What substitute did the author have for our moving-pictures and art galleries?
7. What are some of the things one might find to do in Alaska during the long winters?

BOOKS TO READ

This story may give you a new interest in Alaska. It is our greatest, undeveloped territory. Much of it has never been seen by white men. The United States Government has lately been mapping its mountain ranges, rivers, and lakes by the use of airplanes. There is an article in *The World's Work* for February, 1927, describing this survey. It is entitled, "The Aviator Maps Our Last Frontier." The article has many good pictures.

Alaska is a vast land of enormous natural resources. Some day it will be conquered and many people will live there.

The following books will tell you much of interest and value:

1. "Young Alaskans," by E. Hough. Harpers.
It tells of the life of Indians and of encounters with animals.
2. "Adventures in Alaska," by S. H. Young. Revell.

SOME FAMOUS PATRIOTIC POEMS

This statue has been placed at Concord Bridge so that people will remember the brave men who fought there for the freedom of our country. The poem will help you to understand the statue and the statue will help you to understand the poem.

CONCORD HYMN

Sung at the completion of the Battle Monument, April 19, 1836

By the rude bridge that arched the flood,
   Their flag to April's breeze unfurled,
Here once the embattled farmers stood,
   And fired the shot heard round the world.

The foe long since in silence slept;
    Alike the conqueror silent sleeps;
And Time the ruined bridge has swept
    Down the dark stream which seaward creeps.

On this green bank, by this soft stream,
    We set today a votive stone;
That memory may their deed redeem
    When, like our sires, our sons are gone.

Spirit, that made those heroes dare
    To die, or leave their children free,
Bid Time and Nature gently spare
    The shaft we raise to them and thee.

                      —RALPH WALDO EMERSON.

THINGS TO THINK AND TALK ABOUT

1. Tell the story of the Battle of Concord Bridge.
2. Explain the following words as they are used in the poem: embattled; votive; redeem; shaft.
3. How was "the shot heard round the world"?
4. Ralph Waldo Emerson was one of our great men of letters. He was a man of splendid character, and was beloved by all who knew him. He lived in Concord. Try to find some interesting facts about his life and home and work them up into a brief biography for the class. You will find Sara K. Bolton's "Famous American Authors" a good book for this purpose. Tassin and Maurice have given an excellent account of Emerson in their "Child's Story of American Literature" (Macmillan, 1923). Ida Prentice Whitcomb also has written about him in her "Young People's Story of American Literature."

THE "FIGHTING TEMERAIRE" TUGGED TO HER LAST BERTH
From a painting by J. M. W. Turner

OLD IRONSIDES

One day, while he was a student in Harvard University, Oliver Wendell Holmes noticed in the newspapers a dispatch saying that the Navy Department had issued orders for the breaking up of the old frigate "Constitution," then lying in Charleston Harbor. Seizing a scrap of paper, he dashed off the impassioned lines of "Old Ironsides."

The stirring words of the poem, copied in the press throughout the country, found a response in the heart of the people. Indignation blazed up everywhere. The astonished Secretary of the Navy made haste to recall his order, and the gallant vessel was spared as a relic of the heroic naval victories in the struggle for the freedom of the seas.

Ay, tear her tattered ensign down!
   Long has it waved on high,
And many an eye has danced to see
   That banner in the sky;
Beneath it rung the battle-shout,
   And burst the cannon's roar;—
The meteor of the ocean air
   Shall sweep the clouds no more.

Her deck, once red with heroes' blood,
   Where knelt the vanquished foe,
When winds were hurrying o'er the flood,
   And waves were white below,
No more shall feel the victor's tread,
   Or know the conquered knee;
The harpies of the shore shall pluck
   The eagle of the sea!

O, better that her shattered hulk
   Should sink beneath the wave;
Her thunders shook the mighty deep,
   And there should be her grave;
Nail to the mast her holy flag,
   Set every threadbare sail,
And give her to the god of storms,
   The lightning and the gale!

                —OLIVER WENDELL HOLMES.

WORD STUDY

The differences in meaning between the words grouped in the following list make an interesting study:

>ensign, flag, banner
>wave, flutter, flap
>shout, cry, outcry, uproar
>burst, break
>ocean, seaflood, tide, deep
>hurrying, hastening
>victor, conqueror, hero
>shore, beach, strand
>shattered, battered, smashed, ruined
>sink, drop, fall

Could any other word be substituted for those in the list which are used in the poem?

INTERESTING NOTES ABOUT "OLD IRONSIDES"

1. Her first flags and signals were made by Betsy Ross in Philadelphia; the bolts that fastened her timbers were made by Paul Revere.

2. Seeing the British solid shot bounding off the solid oak sides of the "Constitution" during the engagement with the "Guerrière," the American sailors called her "Old Ironsides," and she is known by that name throughout the world.

3. "May the spirit of 'Old Ironsides' go sailing on!" There is no relic in our country more symbolic of the early heroism of the Nation than the U.S.S. "Constitution." This fine old ship, whose every timber embodies the ideals of the Republic, is a living reminder of our glorious past, and an inspiration of patriotic citizenship to our children and our children's children. "She bears the scars of forty-two battles, and a score of vanquished captains brought their flags and swords for surrender to her victorious captain.

"'Old Ironsides' has never known defeat. The ravaging hand of Time now rests heavily upon this gallant old defender of our young Nation. She sends forth to the land an eloquent call to all America."—*Curtis D. Wilbur, Secretary of the Navy.*

4. Look up the story of "Old Ironsides." You will find a good account of this famous old ship in Charles Norris's "Heroes of the Navy," pp. 153–165, and in Blaisdell and Ball's "Hero Stories from American History," pp. 169–184.

SAVE "OLD IRONSIDES"

Plans are under way now to save the historic U.S.S. "Constitution" ("Old Ironsides") and to recondition her so that she may once more sail the seas. The restoration of this great old ship was authorized by Act of Congress, March 3, 1925, which also authorized the Secretary of the Navy to receive contributions for that purpose.

In a letter sent out on January 10, 1927, Rear-Admiral Philip Andrews, U. S. N., says, in part:

"The beloved United States Frigate 'Constitution' ('Old Ironsides') lies here today in the Boston Navy Yard, a valorous hulk honored and revered by a nation, but fallen into sad decay.

"'Old Ironsides' is more than a relic. She is a symbol of the spirit that preserved us as a nation. As such it should be as dear to the hearts of every American as the Liberty Bell or the Declaration of Independence. The Americanism that 'Old Ironsides' and her flag stand for is the sort that stimulates the young to virile aspirations, and gives to the masses high ideals of loyalty and set principles."

FOR FURTHER READING

Oliver Wendell Holmes was one of our most versatile early Americans. He graduated from Harvard College in the class which later came to be known as "the famous class of '29." A year after graduation he began the study of medicine, and in

1836 opened an office in Boston as a practicing physician. Later he was appointed Professor of Anatomy and Physiology in Harvard University. Among his many splendid works was the founding of *The Atlantic Monthly*, one of our well-known magazines today. The following books will tell you about him:

1. "Famous American Authors," by Sara K. Bolton. Crowell.
2. "Four American Poets," by S. Cody. American Book Co.
3. "Child's Story of American Literature," by Tassin and Maurice. Macmillan Company.
4. "Young People's Story of American Literature," by Ida P. Whitcomb. Dodd, Mead.

AN OLD-TIME SEA-FIGHT

Here are two poems of old-time sea-fights. These poems will help you to understand what "Old Ironsides" went through, and to appreciate the valor of naval heroes.

The two poems that follow are on the same subject; but one is by an American and the other by an Englishman. What ideas can you find in the two poems that are almost the same? What do you find that is very different?

Read aloud lines that show courage of captains and crews.

Would you hear of an old-time sea-fight?
Would you learn who won by the light of the moon and
    stars?
List to the yarn, as my grandmother's father, the sailor,
    told it to me.

Our foe was no skulk in his ship, I tell you (said he),
His was the surly English pluck, and there is no tougher
    nor truer, and never was, and never will be;
Along the lowered eve he came horribly raking us.

We closed with him, the yards entangled, the cannon touched,
My captain lashed fast with his own hands.

We had received some eighteen-pound shots under the water,
On our lower-gun-deck two large pieces had burst at the first fire, killing all around and blowing up overhead.
Fighting at sundown, fighting at dark,
Ten o'clock at night, the full moon well up, our leaks on the gain, and five feet of water reported,
The master-at-arms loosing the prisoners confined in the afterhold to give them a chance for themselves.

The transit to and from the magazine is now stopped by the sentinels,
They see so many strange faces they do not know whom to trust.

Our frigate takes fire,
The other asks if we demand quarter?
If our colors are struck and the fighting done?

Now I laugh content, for I hear the voice of my little captain:
"We have not struck," he composedly cries, "we have just begun our part of the fighting."

Only three guns are in use,
One is directed by the captain himself against the enemy's mainmast,
Two well served with grape and canister silence his musketry and clear his decks.

The tops alone second the fire of this little battery, especially the main-top,
They hold out bravely during the whole of the action.

Not a moment's cease,
The leaks gain fast on the pumps, the fire eats toward the powder-magazine.
One of the pumps has been shot away, it is generally thought we are sinking.

Serene stands the little captain,
He is not hurried, his voice is neither high nor low,
His eyes give more light to us than our battle lanterns.

Toward twelve, there in the beams of the moon, they surrender to us.

—WALT WHITMAN.

FOR DISCUSSION

1. Discuss the character of the captain; of "my grandmother's father, the sailor." Read the lines that prove your point in either case.

2. Compare the captains and the men in this and in the following poem.

THE OLD NAVY

This poem was written by an Englishman, Frederick Marryat (1792–1848), a captain in the British navy. We still enjoy reading his "Mr. Midshipman Easy" and "Masterman Ready."

Notice the fifth and sixth lines in each stanza.

Where does the captain make funny mistakes in his grammar? To make them complete, he should have said "*us* don't take *she*— and what else? Some people really make these mistakes.

The captain stood on the carronade: "First lieutenant," says he,
"Send all my merry men aft here, for they must list to me;
I haven't the gift of the gab, my sons—because I'm bred to the sea;
That ship there is a Frenchman, who means to fight with *we*.
  And odds bobs, hammer and tongs, long as I've been to sea,
  I've fought 'gainst every odds—but I've gained the victory!

That ship there is a Frenchman, and if we don't take *she*,
'Tis a thousand bullets to one, that she will capture *we*,
I haven't the gift of gab, my boys; so each man to his gun;
If she's not mine in half an hour, I'll flog each mother's son.
  For odds bobs, hammer and tongs, long as I've been to sea,
  I've fought 'gainst every odds—and I've gained the victory!"

We fought for twenty minutes, when the Frenchman had
> enough;
"I little thought," said he, "that your men were of such
> stuff";
Our captain took the Frenchman's sword, a low bow made
> to *he;*
"I haven't the gift of the gab, monsieur, but polite I wish
> to be.
>> And odds bobs, hammer and tongs, long as I've been to
>>> sea,
>> I've fought 'gainst every odds—and I've gained the
>>> victory!"

Our captain sent for all of us: "My merry men," said he,
"I haven't the gift of the gab, my lads, but yet I thankful
> be;
You've done your duty handsomely, each man stood to his
> gun;
If you hadn't, you villains, as sure as day, I'd have flogged
> each mother's son.
>> For odds bobs, hammer and tongs, as long as I'm at sea,
>> I'll fight 'gainst every odds—and I'll gain the victory."

—FREDERICK MARRYAT.

1. Compare this captain with Captain Isaac Hull of the illustrious U. S. S. "Constitution," and with our gallant John Paul Jones, who began the great tradition of the American Navy in the stirring naval battles of the American Revolution.

2. Do you know the story of Captain Jones and the "Bonhomme Richard"?

THE STAR-SPANGLED BANNER

Under a glass case in the Historical Museum at Washington there is a great flag. It is thirty feet wide and thirty-two feet long, as large as a large room. It was originally forty feet long, but it has been worn away so that now it is not much longer than it is wide. Each stripe is two feet wide, and it is two feet from point to point of each star.

This is the original Star-Spangled Banner which Francis Scott Key saw waving from Fort McHenry, the morning after it was bombarded by the British, in 1813. When Key wrote the poem, he was a prisoner on board one of the British ships. It is not strange that under the circumstances he was able to write the poem which has since become one of our national hymns.

Oh, say, can you see, by the dawn's early light,
  What so proudly we hailed at the twilight's last gleaming—
Whose broad stripes and bright stars, through the perilous fight,
  O'er the ramparts we watched were so gallantly streaming?
And the rockets' red glare, the bombs bursting in air,
Gave proof through the night that our flag was still there;
Oh, say, does that star-spangled banner yet wave
O'er the land of the free and the home of the brave?

On that shore dimly seen through the mists of the deep,
  Where the foe's haughty host in dread silence reposes,
What is that which the breeze, o'er the towering steep,
  As it fitfully blows, now conceals, now discloses?

Now it catches the gleam of the morning's first beam,
In full glory reflected now shines on the stream;
'Tis the star-spangled banner; oh, long may it wave
O'er the land of the free, and the home of the brave.

And where is that band who so vauntingly swore
    That the havoc of war and the battle's confusion
A home and a country should leave us no more?
    Their blood has washed out their foul footsteps' pollution.

No refuge could save the hireling and slave
From the terror of flight, or the gloom of the grave;
And the star-spangled banner in triumph doth wave
O'er the land of the free, and the home of the brave!

Oh, thus be it ever, when freemen shall stand
    Between their loved homes and the war's desolation!
Blest with victory and peace, may the heav'n-rescued land
    Praise the power that hath made and preserved us a nation.
Then conquer we must, when our cause it is just,
And this be our motto—"In God is our trust";
And the star-spangled banner in triumph shall wave
O'er the land of the free, and the home of the brave!

—FRANCIS SCOTT KEY.

> Speaking to a National Flag Conference, called by The American Legion, President Warren G. Harding said:
>
> "I should like to insist upon Americans being able to sing 'The Star-Spangled Banner.'
>
> "I have noted audiences singing—I should say trying to sing—the American national air, but, outside of about two per cent, they were only mumbling or pretending to sing. I should like to have the spirit of America show itself in song."

FOR STUDY

1. Make sure you understand the meaning of the following unusual expressions: perilous flight; o'er the ramparts; mists of the deep; dread silence reposes; towering steep; vauntingly swore; foul footsteps' pollution; war's desolation.

These expressions can best be understood in the lines where they occur. Why?

2. There are other words and phrases you will need to look up in your dictionary. Make a list of them.

THINGS TO TALK ABOUT

1. What other patriotic songs of our country do you know?
2. What other war songs do you know?
3. What national hymns of other countries do you know?
4. What good purposes does such a song have?

THINGS TO DO

1. Make up four questions to test your classmates. You may make up a "completion test" of one stanza and write it on the blackboard to be filled out by members you call upon.

2. Write a stirring account of the incident which led to this poem, using some of the graphic expressions of the poem. You might imagine you were writing it to a French boy or girl.

RESPECT THE FLAG

When you see the Stars and Stripes displayed, son, stand up and take off your hat. Somebody may titter. It is in the blood of some to deride all expression of noble sentiment.

But don't you mind! When Old Glory comes along, salute, and let them think what they please! When the band plays the "Star-Spangled Banner" in a restaurant or hotel dining-room, get up, even if you rise alone; stand there, and don't be ashamed of it either.

Don't be ashamed when your throat chokes and the tears come when you see the flag flying from the masts of our ships on the great seas, or floating from every flagstaff of the Republic. You will never have a worthier emotion. For of all the signs and symbols there is none more full of meaning than the flag of your country.

Other flags mean a glorious past; this flag means a glorious future. It is not so much the flag of our fathers as it is the flag of our children, and of countless children yet unborn. It is the flag of tomorrow, the signal of the "good time coming." It is not the flag of your king; it is the flag of yourself and your neighbors.

Your flag stands for humanity, for an equal opportunity to all the sons of men. Of course, we have not yet arrived at that goal; injustice still dwells among us; senseless and cruel customs of the past still cling to us, but the flag leads the way to righting the wrongs of men.

Our flag is the world's symbol of liberty. That piece of red, white, and blue bunting means five thousand years of struggle upward. It is the full-grown flower of generations fighting for liberty. It is the century plant of human hope in full bloom.

—ALVIN M. OWSLEY,
FORMER COMMANDER OF AMERICAN LEGION

PLEDGE TO THE FLAG

I pledge allegiance to the Flag of the United States of America and to the Republic for which it stands, one Nation indivisible, with liberty and justice for all.

NOTE: The approved form for pledging allegiance to the Flag of the United States of America is as follows:

Standing with face to the Flag, with the right hand over the heart, all repeat the pledge together. At the words, "to the Flag," the right hand is extended, palm upward, toward the Flag, and after the words, "justice for all" dropped to the side.

THE AMERICAN'S CREED

I believe in the United States of America as a government of the people, by the people, for the people; whose just powers are derived from the consent of the governed; a democracy in a republic; a sovereign nation of many sovereign states; a perfect union, one and inseparable; established upon those principles of freedom, equality, justice, and humanity for which American patriots sacrificed their lives and fortunes.

I therefore believe it is my duty to my country to love it; to support its constitution; to obey its laws; to respect its flag; and to defend it against all enemies.

—WILLIAM TYLER PAGE.

THE FLAG GOES BY

Hats off! Along the street there comes
   A blare of bugles, a ruffle of drums,
A flash of color beneath the sky;
   Hats off! The flag is passing by!

Blue and crimson and white it shines,
   Over the steel-tipped, ordered lines.
Hats off! The colors before us fly;
   But more than the flag is passing by.

Sea-fights and land-fights, grim and great,
    Fought to make and to save the State;
Weary marches and sinking ships;
    Cheers of victory on dying lips;

Days of plenty and years of peace;
    March of a strong land's swift increase;
Equal justice, right and law,
    Stately honor and reverend awe;

Sign of a nation, great and strong
    To ward her people from foreign wrong;
Pride and glory and honor,—all
    Live in the colors to stand or fall.

Hats off! Along the street there comes
    A blare of bugles, a ruffle of drums;
And loyal hearts are beating high:
    Hats off! The flag is passing by!

—HENRY HOLCOMB BENNETT.

WORD STUDY

This poem gives opportunity for an interesting word study. Find out the differences in meaning between the words grouped together in the following list:

bugle, horn, trumpet	weary, tired, worn out
blare, blast, fanfare	marches, tramps, walks
pride, honor, glory	justice, right, law
flash, flare, sparkle, gleam, glitter	honor, awe
crimson, red, scarlet	stately, reverend
grim, cruel, stern, harsh, severe	ward, watch, keep, protect

HEROES IN EVERYDAY WORK

There are many kinds of everyday work which require the finest kind of courage, self-control, physical fitness, and intelligence, which most of us never think about. We seldom think of the men who do this work as heroes, although their work calls for unflinching bravery.

The pilots who safely guide the great ships of the sea; the engineers who control the giant locomotives in all sorts of weather—in fog, flood, and sleet—with their tremendous loads of freight and human passengers; the structural-steel workers who erect the framework of our towering skyscrapers; the bridge-builders who throw marvellous roadways across our rivers and mountain chasms; the tunnel-makers who burrow roadways through mountains and under streams; the forest-rangers who fight devastating fires and protect our great forests; the beach patrol life-savers who keep lookout for disabled ships and rush to their rescue; the men who work in the steel-mills at the blast furnaces with white-hot molten metal; the log-men who bring the logs down the rivers to the lumber-mills; the fishermen who go to the Newfoundland Banks.

If you talk to the man who does this part of the world's work, you will often be surprised to find that he does not feel brave at all. He thinks of the dangers he faces as all a part of his work. His reply is: "It's all in the day's work."

Real courage means doing the job you have to do as well as it can be done, whether it is dangerous or not.

BOOKS TO READ ON HEROES AT WORK

If you become interested in this group of stories, you may want to read others like them. Here is a good reading list. It is not expected that you will read every book in the list. Select what you prefer or what you can get at the library.

1. "Book of Forest-Rangers," by Irving Crump. Dodd.
   This book tells of the importance of forestry work and the dangers and adventures that attend it.
2. "Beach Patrol," by William Drysdale. Wilde.
   A story of the life-saving service.
3. "Work-a-day Heroes," by C. C. Fraser. Crowell.
   It tells of the hazards of many occupations.
4. "Deeds of Doing and Daring," by W. A. Johnson. Wilde.
   Something like Fraser's "Work-a-day Heroes."
5. "Captains Courageous," by Rudyard Kipling. Doubleday.
   Life on a fishing schooner on the Newfoundland Banks.
6. "Careers of Danger and Daring," by Cleveland Moffett. Century.
   Vivid accounts of the courage and achievements of steeple-climbers, deep-sea divers, firemen, bridge-builders, and so on.
7. "Romance of Modern Engineering," by Archibald Williams. Lippincott.
   It tells of great dams, aqueducts, bridges, railways, tunnels, docks, canals, etc.

NOTE: There are many other interesting books on different kinds of bravery. Among the best is the H. W. Lanier "Book of Bravery," published by Scribners.

THE STEEPLE-CLIMBER

There are steeple-climbers all over the United States—all over the world. Wherever buildings with spires are going up, men risk their lives erecting them and painting or repairing them. We know that the steeple-climber of the story is in New York City because of the names used in the story. Broadway is one of the great business thoroughfares of the world, and Wall Street is famous for the bankers and business men who have offices there. Old Trinity and St. Paul's are two very old churches in New York.

In reading this story silently, see whether you can find out, before you finish it, answers to the following questions:

1. Why does a man become a steeple-climber?
2. How does he learn to do his work in safety?
3. Should you like to be a steeple-climber?

During the summer months of 1900 people on lower Broadway were constantly coming upon other people with chins in the air, staring up, and exclaiming: "Dear me, isn't it wonderful!" or "There's that fellow again; I'm sure he'll break his neck!"

The occasion of this general surprise and apprehension was a tall man dressed entirely in white, who appeared, day after day, swinging on a little seat far up the side of this or that church steeple, or at the top, hugging the gold cross or weather-vane, or, higher still, working his way, with a queer, kicking, hitching movement, up various hundred-foot flagpoles that rise from the heaven-challenging office buildings down near Wall Street.

"Steeple Bob" is what he was called in large black letters at the head of newspaper columns; but I came to know him, at his modest quarters on Lexington Avenue, as plain Mr. Merrill, a serious-mannered and unpretentious young man.

Merrill laughed about the climb up Old Trinity's spire, the first climb when he carried up the hauling-rope and worked his way clear to the cross, with nothing to help him but the hands and feet he was born with, and did it coolly, while men on the street below turned away, sickened with fear for him.

"I'm telling you the truth," said Steeple Bob, "when I say it was an easy climb; any fairly active man could do it if he'd forget the height. I'm not talking about all steeples—some are hard and dangerous; but the one on Trinity, in spite of its three hundred odd feet, has knobs of stone for ornament all the way up, and all you have to do is to step from one to another."

"How much of a step?"

"Oh, when I stood on one the next one came to my breast, and then I could just touch the one above that."

He called this easy climbing!

"The only ticklish bit was just at the top, where two great stones, weighing about a ton apiece, swell out like an apple on a stick, and I had to crawl around and over that apple, which was four feet or so across. If it hadn't been for grooves and scroll-work in the stone, I couldn't have done it, and even as it was I had two or three minutes of hard wriggling after I kicked off with my feet and began pulling myself up."

"You mean you hung by your hands from this big ball of stone?"

"I hung mostly by my fingers; the scrolls weren't deep enough for my hands to go in."

"And you drew yourself slowly up and around and over that ball?"

"Certainly; that was the only way."

"And it was at the very top?"

"Yes, just under the cross. It wasn't much, though; you could do it yourself.

"You would be surprised," he went on, "to feel the movement of a steeple. It trembles all the time, and answers every jar on the street below. I guess Old Trinity's steeple sways eighteen inches every time an elevated train passes. And St. Paul's is even worse. She rocks like a beautifully balanced cradle; it would make some people seasick. Perhaps you don't know it, but the better a steeple is built the more she sways. You want to look out for the ones that stand rigid; there's something wrong with them—most likely they're out of plumb."

"Isn't there danger," I asked, "that a steeple may get to swaying too much, say in a gale, and go clear over?"

"Gale or not," said Merrill, "a well-made steeple must rock in the wind as a tree rocks. That is the way it takes the storm, by yielding to it. If it didn't yield, it would probably break."

Then he explained that modern steeples are built with a steel backbone (if I may so call it) running down from the top for many feet inside the stone-work. At Trinity, for instance, this backbone (known as a dowel) is four inches thick and forty-five feet long, a great steel mast stretching down through the cross, down inside the heavy stones and ornaments, and ending in massive beams and braces where the steeple's greater width gives full security.

"What sort of work did you do on these steeples?" I asked.

"All kinds: stone-mason's work, painter's work, blacksmith's work, carpenter's work—a good steeple-climber has to know something about almost every trade. It's painting flagpoles, and scraping off shale from a steeple's sides, and repairing loose stones and ornaments, and putting up lightning rods, and gilding crosses, and cleaning smokestacks so high that it makes you dizzy to look up, let alone looking down, and a dozen other things. Sometimes we have to take a whole steeple down, beginning at the top, stone by stone—unless it's a wooden steeple, and then we burn her down, five or six feet at a time, with creosote painted around where you want the fire to stop; the creosote puts it out. Once I blew off the whole top of a steeple with dynamite; and I'll tell you about that some time."

"Do steeple-climbers always work in pairs?" I asked Mr. Merrill.

"Usually. It would be hard for one man to do a steeple alone. There are lots of places where you must have some one to fasten a rope, or hold the end of a plank or pass you something. Besides, it wouldn't be good for a man's mind to be spending days and days upon steeples all alone.

"I'll give you a case where a man alone could never have done the thing, I don't care how clever a steeple-climber he might be. It was on St. Paul's, New York, after we had finished the job and taken everything down. Then somebody noticed that the weather-vane on top of the ball wasn't turning properly. I knew in a minute what the matter was; it was easy enough to fix it, but the thing was to reach the weather-vane. I don't mean that the climb up the steeple was anything; we had done that before; but if I tried to climb around that big ball again (it was the same sort of a wriggling business as that over the bulging stones at Trinity) I should certainly scrape off a lot of the fine gilding we had just put on. And yet I couldn't get at the weather-vane without getting over the ball. I studied quite a while on this little problem, and solved it with my partner's help. We both climbed the steeple as far as the ball; we went up the lightning rod; then we roped ourselves on the steeple-shaft by life lines, and then my partner stood on my shoulders and did the job. You see it was easy enough that way."

—Adapted from "*Careers of Danger and Daring*," by Cleveland Moffett.

THINGS TO TALK ABOUT

1. What did you admire most about the steeple-climber in the story?
2. What are the greatest dangers to the steeple-climber?
3. What measures does he take for safety?
4. Make an outline of the different tasks steeple-climbers do?
5. Was there anything in the story that particularly surprised you—something you hadn't realized before? Had you known that steeples sway? Why must steeples sway?
6. Read to the class and discuss the part that seemed most interesting to you.
7. Perhaps you can bring to class tomorrow a list of some of the occupations that require daily courage in your community.

WORK

Let me but do my work from day to day,
In field or forest, at the desk or loom,
In roaring market-place or tranquil room;
Let me but find it in my heart to say,
When vagrant wishes beckon me astray,
"This is my work; my blessing, not my doom;
Of all who live, I am the one by whom
This work can best be done in the right way."

Then shall I see it not too great, nor small
To suit my spirit and to prove my powers;
Then shall I cheerful greet the laboring hours,
And cheerful turn, when the long shadows fall
At eventide, to play and love and rest,
Because I know for me my work is best.

—HENRY VAN DYKE.

THE BRIDGE-BUILDER

When you look at a great railway bridge, do you wonder how it could have been built? It is only within the last hundred years or so that men have learned to build great iron bridges across wide rivers.

What do you suppose is the oldest kind of bridge? What kind of bridge might you find in a forest where no man has ever been? in a rocky mountain valley? Suppose you found a tree lying across a stream, and farther along, you found that you could step from one great boulder to another all the way across the stream—do you see how the first bridges came to be built?

Why is a suspension bridge better than one built on arches? What are some of the greatest difficulties in building a suspension bridge?

The writer of the story printed below went into dangerous places to see how a great bridge is built; but the workmen risk their lives there every day. When you read the story, you will feel almost as if you had been on the unfinished bridge yourself.

I

First we clambered, pyramid fashion, up the pile of granite, big as a church, that will hold the cable-ends; they call it the anchorage. From the top of this we could look along the iron street that stretched away in a slight up-grade toward the tower. We were on a level with the roadway of the bridge, and far below us spread the house-tops of Brooklyn. Between our stone precipice and the iron street-end yawned a gulf that we drew back from, with water in its deepest bottom. Here the cables would be buried some day, sealed, and cemented, piled over with masonry, to hold for centuries.

Somehow, seen from here, the iron street looked delicate, not massive; its sides were trelliswork, its top frames gently slanting, and one could fancy the whole thing beaufully grown over with vines, a graceful arbor-way suspended in mid-air. And down the length of this came the strangest sounds—one would say a company of woodpeckers of some giant sort making riot in an echoing forest. *Br-r-r-ip-ip-ip-ip—br-r-r-r-up-up-up—br-r-r-ap-ap-ap-ap-ap*. What was it? Now from this side, *up-up-up-br-r-r-up-up*, and ending abruptly. Then straightway from near the top on the other side, *ap-ap-ap-br-r-r-r-ap-ap-ap*. Then fainter from halfway down the street, and then from all points at once, a chorus of hammer-birds making the bridge resound in call and in answer, hammer-birds with strokes as swift as the roll of a drum. What is it?

And look! Those points of fire that glow forth here and there and vanish as the eye perceives them, tiny red lights, tiny yellow lights, that flash from far down the iron street and are gone, that flash from all along the iron street and are gone! What are they? What strange work is doing here?

It was the riveters driving the endless red-hot bolts that hold the bridge together, driving them with hammers that are worked with triggers, and aimed like a fireman's hose, hammers with rubber pipes dragging behind that feed in compressed air from an engine. Long past are the days when bolts were driven by brawny arms and the slow swing of a sledge. Now the workman, leaning his stomach against an iron club, touches a spring, and, presto! the hard-kicking, pent-up air inside drives the darting club-head back and forth, back and forth, quick as a snake strikes, *br-r-r-r-r-ip-ip-ip*, against whatever the steering arms may press it. Driving rivets nowadays is something like handling a rapid-fire gun. And how your body aches from the bruise of that recoil!

"We must get nearer to those fellows," said the artist; and presently, after some mild hazards, we were safely over on the span, quite as near as was desirable to a gang of riveters dangling twenty feet above us on a swing. For presently, with a sputter of white sparks, a piece of red-hot iron struck the girder we were straddling, and then went bounding down—down——down—

Crouching under cover of a wide steel beam, we watched another gang of riveters on the structure opposite, where we had a better view, watched the forge-man pass along the glowing rivets, and the buffer-man slip them through ready holes, and the hammer-man flatten the flaming ends into smooth, burnished heads. And presently a riveter, in black cap and faded blue jersey, climbed down from the swing overhead, and explained things to us. We watched his descent in wonder and alarm, for it involved some lively gymnastics, which he entered upon, however, with complete indifference. First he swung across from the scaffolding to a girder, the highest rail of the bridge, and along this he walked as coolly as a boy on a wide fence-top, only this happened to be a fence one hundred and fifty feet high. Then he bent over and caught one of the slanting side supports, and down this worked his way as a mountain-climber would work down a precipice. Presently he stepped off at our level, never having taken the pipe from his mouth.

When we asked how he dared go about so carelessly over a reeling abyss, he said they all did it; they got used to it, or else got killed.

II

Then he went on to tell us how the riveters often get into tight places, say on the tower, where there is so little room for the forge-man to heat his bolts that he has to throw them up to the hammer-man, twenty or thirty feet.

"What!" exclaimed the artist. "Throw red-hot bolts twenty or thirty feet up the tower!"

"That's what they do; and we've got boys who are pretty slick at it. They'll grab a bolt out of the fire with long-handled nippers, and give her a swing and a twist, and away she goes sizzling through the air, straight at the man above; and say, they don't miss him once in a hundred times; and, what's more, they never touch a truss or a girder. If they did there'd be a piece of red-hot iron sailing down on the lads below, and that wouldn't be good for their health."

"How does the hammer-man catch these red-hot bolts?" I asked.

"In a bucket. Catches 'em every time. That's a thing you want to see, too."

There were so many things we wanted to see in this strange region! We set forth down the iron street, keeping in mind a parting caution of the riveter not to look at our feet, but at the way before us, and never to look down.

Presently we came to the busiest scene on the structure, down where the covered part ended and the iron roadway reached on, bare of framework, to the tower. Here the "traveler"[1] was working with a double gang of men, raising a skeleton of sides and cross-beams that were pushing on, pushing on day by day, and would finally stretch across the river. Once on the "traveler's" deck, we breathed more easily, for we were safe from fearsome crevasses, safe on a great wide raft of iron and timber, set on double railroad tracks, a lumbering steam-giant that goes resounding along, when the need is, with its weight of four locomotives, its three-story derricks swinging out great booms at the corners, its thumping engines (two of them) for the hoisting, its coal-bins, its water-tanks, its coils of rope, its pile of lumber, and its mascot kitten curled up there by the ash-box in a workman's coat. They say the bridge has to wait when that kitten wants her dinner, and woe to the man who would treat the little thing unkindly!

[1] A traveling steam or electric crane. Look it up in the dictionary.

This "traveler," with its gangs, is a sort of gigantic sewing-machine that stitches the bridge together; it lifts all the parts into place and binds them fast, as it were, with basting-threads of temporary iron, to hold until the riveters arrive for the permanent sewing. Five or six tons is the weight of ordinary pieces handled by the "traveler," but some pieces weigh twenty tons, and, on a pinch, forty tons could be managed, the weight of six elephants like Jumbo. Of course, when I say that the "traveler" "stitches" these pieces together, I really mean that the "traveler" gangs do this, for the big brute booms can only lift things and swing things; the bolt-driving and end-fitting must be done by little men.

When we arrived, the "traveler" was bringing to one spot the massive parts of a cross-section in our arbor-way. It was a stretched-out iron W, flattened down between girders across top and bottom. This, we learned, was a "strut," and it weighed sixteen tons, and it would presently be lifted bodily overhead to span the roadway. We waited a full hour to see this thing done—to watch another stitch taken in the bridge; and it seems to me, as I think of it, that I can recall no hour when I saw so many perils faced with such indifference.

First, the booms would drop down their clanking jaws and grip the chain-bound girders from little delivery cars, then swing them around to the lifting-place at the farther end of the "traveler." Now we understood what our friend down the way meant by "skipping along lively when the falls come at you." He meant this boom-tackle and its load as they sweep over the structure in blind, merciless force. And, indeed, they did skip along, the bridge-men, as the "traveler" turned its arms this way and that, and several times I saw a man slip as he hurried, and barely save himself. A single misstep might mean the crush of a ten-ton mass, or a plunge into space, or both. It seemed a pretty shivery choice.

Soon we were joined by another bridge-man, who told us how they ride the big steel columns from the ground clear to the cap of the tower. Two men usually ride on a column, their duty being to keep her from bumping against the structure as she lifts, and then bolt her fast when she reaches the top. Of course, as a tower grows in height, these rides become more and more terrifying, so that some of the men who are equal to anything else draw back from riding up a column.

III

These fears were justified in the last stage on the New York tower when a man named Jack McGreggor had an experience that might well have blanched his hair. They had reached the 325-foot level, and were placing the last lengths of column but one, and McGreggor was riding up one of these lengths alone. It was a huge mass, twenty-five feet long, square in section, and large enough to admit a winding ladder inside. It weighed eighteen tons. As the overhead boom lifted the pendent length (with McGreggor astride) and swung it clear of the column it was to rest on, the foreman, watching there like a hawk, wiggled his thumb to the signal-man on a platform below, who pulled four strokes on the bell, which meant "boom up" to the engine-man. So up came the boom, and in came the column, hanging now in true perpendicular, with McGreggor ready to slide down from his straddling seat for the bolting.

Now the foreman flapped his hand palm down, and the signal-man was just about to jerk two bells, which means "lower your load," when rip—smash—tear! Far down below a terrible thing had happened: the frame of the engine had snapped right over the bearing, and out pulled the cable-drum that was holding the strain of that eighteen-ton column, and down came the falls. It was just like an elevator breaking loose at the top of its shaft. The column started to fall; there was nothing to stop it; and then—and then a miracle was worked; it must have been a miracle; it is so extraordinary. That falling column struck squarely, end to end, on the solid column beneath it, rocked a little, righted itself, and stayed there! Which was more than Jack McGreggor did, for he came sliding down so fast— he came with a wild, white face—that he all but knocked the foreman over; and the foreman was white himself. And what that eighteen-ton column would have done to the bridge, and the boys on it, had it crashed down those three hundred and twenty-five feet, is still a subject of awed discussion.

All this time a dozen men have been swarming over the

strut, hammering bolts, tightening nuts, hitching fast the "falls," making sure that all parts are rigid and everything ready for the lifting. At the front of the "traveler" two foremen, "pushers" they are called, yell without ceasing: "Hey, Gus! Hey, Jimmie! Put that winch in! Slack away them falls! What the mischief are you doing? Hey! Hey!" And they shake their hands and dance on their toes, for all the world like a pair of mad auctioneers.

The men work faster under this vigorous coaching. Four or five are stretched flat on their stomachs along the top girder, as many more cling to steep, slanting braces, and some hang fast to the uprights, with legs twisted around them like Japanese pole-climbers. No matter what his position, every man plies a tool of some sort—wrench, chisel, or sledge—and presently all is ready.

Now the engines start with a pounding and sputtering that make the bridge quiver. The big spools haul fast on the ropes, the falls stiffen, the booms creak, and with shouts from every one, the strut heaves and lifts and hangs suspended. The "pushers" yell at the engines to stop. The men swarm over the load, studying every joint, then wave that all is well, and come sliding, twisting down just as the engines start again, all but two men, who sit at the ends and ride along with the hoist. Meantime the others are racing up the side frames, from slant to slant to the top of the truss, where they wait eagerly, yelling the while at the points on either side where presently the strut-ends must be adjusted and then bolted fast.

It seems like some mad schoolboy game of romps. Now we'll all swing over this precipice! Whoop-la! Now we'll all run across this gulf! Wow! wow! wow! Every man in that scrambling crew is facing two deaths, or three deaths, and doing hard work besides. Look! There comes the strut up to its place, and nearly crushes Jimmie Dunn with its sharp edge, as a strut *did* crush another lad not so long ago. And see that man hang out in a noose of a rope, hang out over nothing, and drive in bolts. And see this fellow kick off on the free pulley-block and come sliding down. Hoooo! And there are the others jumping at the falls after him, and coming down with a rush, laughing. Risking their lives? One would say they never thought of it.

"Why, that's nothing!" said one of them; "we used to slide down the falls from the top of the tower. But you've got to know the trick or the ropes 'll burn through your trousers. It's a great slide, though."

"Aren't you ever afraid of falling?" I asked a serious-faced young man who was running one of the engines.

"I'll tell you how it is," said he; "we're not afraid when a lot of us do a thing together, but each one might be afraid to do it alone. In our hearts I guess we're all afraid."

—Adapted from "Careers of Danger and Daring," by Cleveland Moffett.

DIRECTIONS FOR STUDY

1. Read the story through again, noting words and phrases that you do not understand. Look up as many of these as you can and ask about the others in class.

2. Then read it again and find these points. Satisfy yourself as to what they mean.

(1) Where and how were the cables buried?
(2) What made the sounds like a flock of giant woodpeckers?
(3) How did the riveters get their red-hot rivets?
(4) What was "the traveler," and what did it do?
(5) Why do men ride up on the giant pieces of steel?
(6) What signals do the bridge men use?
(7) What answer did the bridge-worker make to the question: "Aren't you ever afraid of falling?"

3. Write down a list of all the words and phrases about bridge-building which are new to you. Bring them to class.

THINGS TO TALK ABOUT

1. Have you ever watched the work on a great bridge?
2. Have you ever observed riveters at work?
3. What expression is used in the story to describe the noise the riveters make? See if you can make the sound.
4. Have you ever seen a steam-crane at work? Where? Or a steam-shovel? Where? Tell how it seemed to work.
5. Mention things in the story that impressed you.
6. What was the "near accident" which the story relates?
7. How do the men get up and down to their work?

THINGS TO DO

1. Bring to class pictures of bridges, steam-cranes.
2. Look up in some encyclopædia about different kinds of bridges and report to class what you find.

Some people live dull and unhappy lives because they never find out the meaning of work. They think it is only something that must be done to get money for food and clothes and other things that they need. They don't know that it is one of the principal ways by which men and women can keep on growing finer and better all their lives. Nor do they know that the joy of work well done is one of the greatest joys in the world. It is worthwhile whether or not it is rewarded, because it makes the worker feel that he is doing his share to make the world a better place to live in. People who understand what work can do for them are likely to sing at their work. Perhaps this is what Whitman had in mind when he wrote his poem.

You will find these lines pleasant to read aloud. They almost sing themselves.

I HEAR AMERICA SINGING

I hear America singing, the varied carols I hear,
Those of mechanics, each one singing his as it should be blithe and strong.
The carpenter singing his as he measures his plank or beam,
The mason singing his as he makes ready for work, or leaves off work,
The boatman singing what belongs to him in his boat, the deckhand singing on the steamboat deck,
The shoemaker singing as he sits on his bench, the hatter singing as he stands,
The wood-cutter's song, the ploughboy's on his way in the morning, or at noon intermission or at sundown,
The delicious singing of the mother, or of the young wife at work, or of the girl sewing or washing,
Each singing what belongs to him or her and to none else,
The day what belongs to the day—at night the party of young fellows, robust, friendly,
Singing with open mouths their strong melodious songs.

—WALT WHITMAN.

SUGGESTIONS

1. Read the poem through as a whole.
2. List in order the different kinds of work mentioned.
3. Try to picture in your mind each worker mentioned.
4. Learn the poem by heart. See how quickly you can memorize it.

FOR DISCUSSION

1. What have you seen each of these workmen do that Whitman does not mention? What other workers might have been named in the poem? What could have been said about each?

2. Here are the names of some different kinds of poetry that can be sung: carols, hymns, anthems, psalms, lyrics, catches, lullabies, ballads. Tell how some are different from others.

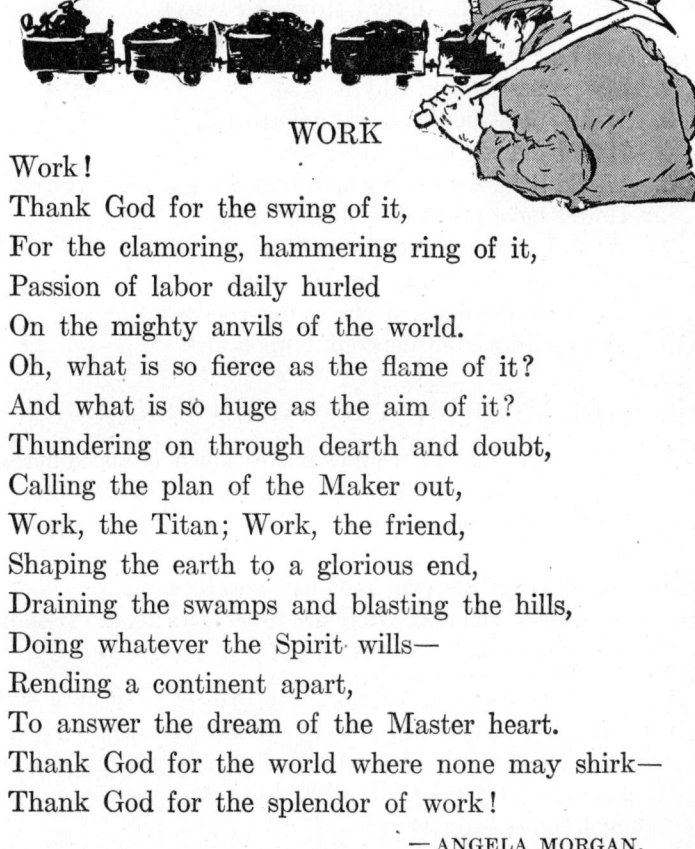

WORK

Work!
Thank God for the swing of it,
For the clamoring, hammering ring of it,
Passion of labor daily hurled
On the mighty anvils of the world.
Oh, what is so fierce as the flame of it?
And what is so huge as the aim of it?
Thundering on through dearth and doubt,
Calling the plan of the Maker out,
Work, the Titan; Work, the friend,
Shaping the earth to a glorious end,
Draining the swamps and blasting the hills,
Doing whatever the Spirit wills—
Rending a continent apart,
To answer the dream of the Master heart.
Thank God for the world where none may shirk—
Thank God for the splendor of work!

— ANGELA MORGAN.

TWO-MINUTE TALKS

Now that you have been giving some attention to the best way of learning, it may be of interest to use the following topics for two-minute talks and short written paragraphs. Which of the topics have most to do with *Good Reading?*

TOPICS FOR ORAL AND WRITTEN WORK
(On Learning How to Study)

1. My best study: why I like it.
2. My poorest study: why it is so.
3. Weak spots shown on my report-card.
4. How I did my best in one study.
5. Would it be a good thing to post the grades in our class?
6. How I have profited by home study.
7. What I study at home; how I do it.
8. The fault of working just for marks.
9. The characteristics of one of our good students.
10. The foolishness of depending upon luck.

THE WORK OF THE EYE IN READING

What the eye does in reading makes much of the difference between poor readers and good readers. A poor reader takes in only a word or part of a word at a glance, and often repeats his look at a word. A good reader takes in more than one word at a glance and keeps his eyes moving forward along the lines of print in a series of glances. Here are three facts about eye-movements you should know:

1. The eye should move along the lines of print in a series of quick glances. These are called "eye-sweeps."
2. At the end of each "eye-full" there is a very brief pause; but it should be very brief. It is at these very brief pauses that the thought comes into the mind.

3. The number of pauses varies with the kind of reading, the purpose for which it is read, and the reader's familiarity with the words and thought presented.

One's rate of reading is likely to become a fixed habit, as difficult to change as any other habit. It is therefore important:

1. To practice longer eye-sweeps—which means to take in as many words as possible at one glance.
2. To make as few pauses as possible at one glance.
3. To keep the eye moving forward along the line in regular sweeps like this:

4. To keep one's mind fixed upon what is being read so that the eyes will not need to move back and forth along the line in irregular fashion.

Try to practice these points. Print some short "sentence flashcards" with a rubber-stamp alphabet, and see who can take in the most at one glance. Test yourself on sentences in this book.

However well and rapidly you may read now, you will go on practicing to make your eye-sweeps longer and longer, without losing any of the sense, if you wish to get the most out of books.

There's a song that the world is singing,
  A resonant, splendid song
    Of its work, work, work,
    With never a shirk,
    Of its battles won,
    Of its labors done—
  And of Right that masters Wrong!

—ISABEL BOWMAN FINLEY.

TWO WAYS OF MAKING THE WORLD BETTER

Any one who really wishes to make the world better knows that he need not go from home to do so. Wherever fortune sends you, there is work to do, and you have the chance to leave the world better or worse than you found it in that place.

The first of the next two stories tells how a young Dutchman was sent to a lonely island where the people were hardly civilized. It tells what he did for them.

The second story tells of the great work of caring for helpless animals, which has been going on now in our own country for a long time. The account of the Humane Association was written for this book by Dr. William O. Stillman.

If you were to try to make a list of good work that is being done in different parts of the world, you would be surprised to see how quickly you could get a long list.

Can you think of anything that needs to be done especially in your neighborhood? How could it be done?

Many persons would like to help their country or their town if they knew how to begin. What one man does, another may. When we read what some one has accomplished, we may think of things that we ourselves could do.

WHAT ONE MAN DID FOR THE PLACE HE LIVED IN

NOTE: This is a true story of the author's grandparents, who built their home on a desert island off the coast of Holland. Edward William Bok tells how they transformed the barren island into a place of beauty and usefulness by planting trees.

As you read, decide whether or not the following quotation applies:

"Nature ever yields reward
To him who seeks and loves her best."
—BRYAN WALLER PROCTER.

CARING FOR TREES AND BIRDS

Along an island in the North Sea, five miles from the Dutch coast, stretches a dangerous ledge of rocks that has proved the graveyard of many a vessel sailing that turbulent sea. On this island once lived a group of men who, as each vessel was wrecked, looted the vessel and murdered those of the crew who reached shore. The government of the Netherlands decided to exterminate the island pirates, and for the job King William selected a young lawyer at The Hague.

"I want you to clean up that island," was the royal order. It was a formidable job for a young man of twenty odd years. By royal proclamation he was made mayor of the island, and within a year, a court of law being established, the young attorney was appointed judge.

The young man now decided to settle on the island, and began to look for a home. It was a grim place, barren of tree or living green of any kind; it was as if a man had been exiled to Siberia. Still, argued the young mayor, an ugly place is ugly only because it is not beautiful. And beautiful he determined this island should be.

One day the young mayor-judge called together his council. "We must have trees," he said, "we can make this island a spot of beauty if we will!" But the practical seafaring men demurred; the little money they had was needed for matters far more urgent than trees.

"Very well," was the mayor's decision—and little they guessed what the words were destined to mean—"I will do it myself." And that year he planted one hundred trees, the first the island had ever seen.

"Too cold," said the islanders; "the severe north winds and storms will kill them all."

"Then I will plant more," said the unperturbed mayor. And for the fifty years that he lived on the island he did so. He planted trees each year; and, moreover, he had deeded to the island government land which he turned into public squares and parks, and where each spring he set out shrubs and plants.

Moistened by the salt mist, the trees did not wither but grew prodigiously. In all that expanse of turbulent sea—and only those who have seen the North Sea in a storm know how turbulent it can be—there had not been a foot of ground on which the birds, storm-driven across the water-waste, could rest in their flight. Hundreds of dead birds often covered the surface of the sea. Then one day the trees had grown tall enough to look over the sea, and, spent and driven, the first birds came and rested in their leafy shelter. And others came and found protection, and gave their gratitude vent in song. Within a few years so many birds had discovered the trees in this new island home that they attracted the attention not only of the native islanders, but also of the people on the shore five miles distant, and the island became famous as the home of the rarest and most beautiful birds. So grateful were the birds for their resting-place that they chose one end of the island as a special spot for the laying of their eggs and the raising of their young, and they fairly peopled it. It was not long before ornithologists from various parts of the world came to "Eggland," as the farthermost point of the island came to be known, to see the marvelous sight, not of thousands but of hundreds of thousands of bird eggs.

A pair of storm-driven nightingales had now found the island and mated there; their wonderful notes thrilled even the souls of the natives; and as dusk fell upon the seabound strip of land the women and children would come to "the square" and listen to the evening notes of the birds of golden song. The two nightingales soon grew into a colony, and within a few years so rich was the island in its nightingales that over to the Dutch coast and throughout the land and into other countries spread the fame of "The Island of Nightingales."

Meantime, the young mayor-judge, grown to manhood, had kept on planting trees each year, setting out his shrubbery and plants, until their verdure now beautifully shaded the quaint, narrow lanes, and transformed into wooded roads what once had been only barren wastes. Artists began to hear of the place and brought their canvases, and on the walls of hundreds of homes throughout the world today hang bits of the beautiful lanes and wooded spots of "The Island of Nightingales." The American artist, William M. Chase, took his pupils there almost annually. "In all the world today," he declared to his students, as they exclaimed at the natural cool restfulness of the island, "there is no more beautiful place."

The trees are now majestic in their height of forty or more feet, for it is nearly a hundred years since the young attorney went to the island and planted the first tree; today the churchyard where he lies is a bower of cool green, with the trees that he planted dropping their moisture on the lichen-covered stone on his grave.

This much did one man do. But he did more.

Making a True Home

After he had been on the barren island two years he went to the mainland one day, and brought back with him a bride. It was a bleak place for a bridal home, but the young wife had the qualities of the husband. "While you raise your trees," she said, "I will raise our children." And within a score of years the young bride sent thirteen happy-faced, well-brought-up children scampering over that island, and there was reared a home such as is given to few. Said a man who subsequently married a daughter of that home:

"It was such a home that once you had been in it you felt you must be of it, and that if you couldn't marry one of the daughters you would have been glad to have married the cook."

One day, when the children had grown to man's and woman's estate, the mother called them all together and said to them: "I want to tell you the story of your father and of this island," and she told them the simple story that is written here.

"And now," she said, "as you go out into the world I want each of you to take with you the spirit of your father's work, and each, in your own way and place, to do as he has done; make you the world a bit more beautiful and better because you have been in it. That is your mother's message to you."

The first son to leave the island home went with a band of hardy men to South Africa, where they settled and became known as "the Boers." Tirelessly they worked at the colony until towns and cities sprang up and a new nation came into being: The Transvaal Republic. The son became secretary of state of the new country, and today the United States of South Africa bears tribute, in part, to the mother's message to "make the world a bit more beautiful and better."

The second son left home for the Dutch mainland, where he took charge of a small parish; and when he had finished his work he was mourned by king and peasant as one of the leading clergymen of his time and people.

A third son, scorning his own safety, plunged into the boiling surf on one of those nights of terror so common to that coast, rescued a half-dead sailor, carried him to his father's house, and brought him back to a life of usefulness that gave the world a record of imperishable value. For the half-drowned sailor was Heinrich Schliemann, the famous explorer of the dead cities of Troy.

The first daughter now left the island nest; to her inspiration her husband owed, at his life's close, a shelf of works in philosophy which today are among the standard books of their class.

The second daughter worked beside her husband until she brought him to be regarded as one of the ablest preachers of his land, speaking for more than forty years the message of man's betterment.

To another son it was given to sit wisely in the councils of his land; another followed the footsteps of his father. Another daughter, refusing marriage for duty, ministered unto and made a home for one whose eyes could not see.

So they went out into the world, the girls and boys of that island home, each carrying the story of their father's simple but beautiful work, and the remembrance of their mother's message. Not one from that home but did well his or her work in the world; some greater, some smaller, but each left behind the traces of a life well spent.

And, as all good work is immortal, so today all over the world goes on the influence of this one man and one woman, whose life on that little Dutch island changed its barren rocks to a bower of verdure, a home for the birds and the song of the nightingale. The grandchildren have gone to the four corners of the globe, and are now the generation of workers—some in the far East Indies; others in Africa; still others in our own land of America. Each has tried, according to his talents, to carry out the message of that day, to tell the story of the grandfather's work; just as it is told by the author of this book, who, in the efforts of his later years, has tried to carry out, so far as opportunity has come to him, the message of his grandmother:

"Make you the world a bit more beautiful and better because you have been in it."
—EDWARD W. BOK.

COMPARING IDEAS

To see how your ideas compare with those of your classmates, prepare a definite statement on each of the following points, and bring them up in class for discussion:

1. What did the young mayor really do to make his island safe and beautiful?
2. How did his attitude toward his work aid it and make success certain?
3. Select a few striking words to compare the condition of the island at the time of the mayor's arrival with the condition at the time of his death.
4. What traits of character do you notice in the family? Select two or three of the finest characteristics and prove each by reading a passage of the story.
5. What was the mother's ambition for her children? How did she try to impress this ideal on them?
6. Write out a statement making perfectly clear the two beautiful ways by which the man actually made the world better.

THINGS TO THINK AND TALK ABOUT

1. What things can young people actually do to make the place they live in more beautiful and attractive?
2. Suggest some worthy project for the class to undertake if they would like to do something as a group.
3. Give reasons why our trees should be cared for.
4. If birds could talk, what laws do you think they would ask the people to make?
5. It may be some one in the class is doing something worthy of note to attract and care for birds. Tell of it in class.

TOPICS FOR TWO-MINUTE TALKS

1. Things That Make an Ideal Home.
2. How a Happy Well-Kept Home Benefits a Community.
3. How to Care for Trees.
4. How to Attract Birds.
5. Ways of Making the Place We Live in More Attractive.

BOOKS TO READ

Here are two books which tell about other ways of making the world a better place to live in:

1. "A Labrador Doctor," by Wilfred Thomason Grenfell. Houghton.
  The story of the life and work of a medical missionary on the bleak coasts of Labrador and Newfoundland—and told by himself.
2. "Johnny Appleseed," by Elizabeth Harrison.
  Johnny Appleseed, whose real name was John Chapman, was born in New England in 1775. The story tells how, for forty-six years, he walked barefoot and unarmed through the western wilderness of the United States, planting apple-seeds that would some day grow into trees whose fruit would feed his fellow man.

TREES

"A people without children would face a helpless future; a country without trees is almost as helpless; forests which are so used that they cannot renew themselves will soon vanish and with them all their benefits. When you help to preserve our forests, or plant new ones, you are acting the part of good citizens."
—THEODORE ROOSEVELT.

LOVELIEST OF TREES

Loveliest of trees, the cherry now
Is hung with bloom along the bough
And stands about the woodland ride
Wearing white for Eastertide.

Now, of my threescore years and ten,
Twenty will not come again,
And take from seventy springs a score,
It only leaves me fifty more.

And since to look at things in bloom
Fifty springs are little room,
About the woodlands I will go
To see the cherry hung with snow.
—A. E. HOUSMAN.

FOR CLASS DISCUSSION

1. What does each stanza tell about? Read the words that connect the third stanza with the second. Then read those that connect the third stanza with the first. Do you see how beautifully the whole poem expresses one idea about the cherry in spring? What is the idea? Do you have that feeling in spring?

If you learn the poem now, you may like to say it when you are "three score and ten."

2. What is your favorite tree? Why?
3. Do you know other poems about trees? If you have a favorite one bring it in to class.
4. At what season of the year do you enjoy trees the most?

OTHER POEMS ABOUT TREES

1. "Trees," Bliss Carman.
2. "Shade," Theodosia Garrison.
3. "Salute to the Trees," Henry van Dyke.
4. "Birches," Robert Frost.

THE AMERICAN HUMANE ASSOCIATION
What It Is and What It Does

The first society for the prevention of cruelty was organized by Henry Bergh, in New York City, in 1866. It was named the American Society for the Prevention of Cruelty to Animals. At that time no state or territory in the United States had any laws preventing cruelty to animals. In 1874 he rescued a little girl from cruel treatment, and this led to the founding of a Society for the Prevention of Cruelty to Children.

Another result of his work is the ambulance corps for removing disabled animals from the street. He also originated an ingenious invention which substitutes artificial birds for live pigeons as marks for the sportsman's gun. In 1877, the various societies were brought together into a national association, known as The

American Association for the Prevention of Cruelty to Animals and Children. Now every state in the Union has laws against cruelty.

This account was written by Dr. William O. Stillman, who has been president of the organization for many years. He tells: (1) How the association came to be founded. (2) What it does now. (3) What it hopes to do. If, as you read, you take notes on each of these points you can have a discussion afterwards, and perhaps suggest other work that the association might do.

The American Humane Association exists for the prevention of cruelty to children and animals, and for the promotion of kindness. Every city of importance has a society organized for this purpose. There are more than six hundred of these societies, each working independently in its own territory, but all combined as a national force in the American Humane Association.

The first American society to protect animals was founded in New York in 1866, by Henry Bergh. The first society in the world to protect children was formed in New York, in 1874, through the efforts of Henry Bergh and two others. In a few years the movement spread to other important cities. Both classes of societies were established to guarantee to children and animals the protection of the law, and to have new laws made when needed. In those early days horses were beaten almost to death on the public streets, overloaded, and made to work when sick or lame. Animals of all kinds were tortured and neglected, starved, and abused. Children were treated like slaves, whipped, clubbed, crippled, and starved.

In 1877 the different local societies held a meeting at Cleveland, and formed the American Humane Association. In 1905 I was appointed president of the national body, and the headquarters of the association was moved to Albany, New York.

The American Humane Association is constantly forming new societies in different parts of the country, and building up those in need of help. Its correspondence is heavy, amounting to hundreds of letters every day. It publishes tons of literature. Its monthly magazine, *The National Humane Review*, published at a dollar a year, is the world's leading magazine devoted to the prevention of cruelty. Every year it promotes competitions for humane posters, and also for humane essay writing. Hundreds of thousands of boys, girls, and adults compete. It works for new laws to help the spread of kindness and the prevention of cruelty. It sends lecturers, organizers, and investigators to all parts of the country. When it was found that millions of cattle and sheep were turned out to starve in the terrible winters of the West, it sent its own officers to see how conditions were, and what could be done. When the magnificent herds of elk in the neighborhood of Yellowstone Park were dying of starvation, the American Humane Association gave money to buy the hay which saved these beautiful animals. When mules were being abused and worked almost to death in the oil-fields, the Association's officers were sent to protect them. During the World War vast quantities of supplies were given to relieve the suffering of the hundreds of thousands of animals, and sixty thousand dollars was spent in purchasing ambulances so that sick and wounded horses might be taken to hospitals.

The world is getting better, but there is still much cruelty. Probably there will always be cruelty, always something for the American Humane Association to do. There are men who promote brutal sports, such as dogfighting, cockfighting, and other sports cruel to animals. There are men trying to introduce bullfighting, the debasing entertainment of Spain, Mexico, and other countries. There are cruelties in the city, on the farm, and away in the wilds. There are the cruelties of the slaughterhouse, and of the transportation of animals to the slaughterhouse from the country. There is the destruction of birds for sport and personal adornment, the catching of millions of helpless wild creatures in steel-jawed traps to provide furs for human decoration.

It is to fight all forms of cruelty that the American Humane Association exists, and that is just what it does.

—WILLIAM O. STILLMAN.

GENERAL QUESTIONS AND TOPICS FOR DISCUSSION

1. In what ways can you show kindness to animals?
2. Give instances where you have seen animals respond to kind treatment.
3. Have you ever "made friends" with a bird? If so, tell your classmates about it.
4. Ernest Thompson Seton says "we and the beasts are kin." What does he mean?

5. What is done in your community to prevent cruelty both to children and to animals?

6. Find all you can about the "Jack London Club," in Boston.

7. Look up George F. Hoar and find what he did for the protection of birds.

8. Learn about the protection of animals in parks.

9. What is the obligation of the Boy Scouts toward animals?

10. The celebrated Frenchman, Louis Pasteur, known for his scientific discoveries and for his humanitarian interests, said: "We do not ask a sufferer, 'What is your country or your religion?' We say, 'It is enough that you are suffering. You belong to me, and I will care for you.'"

VOLUNTEER READING

Perhaps some member of the class will be pleased to volunteer to read and report on "The Call of the Wild," by Jack London; "Stickeen," by John Muir; "Adrift on an Ice Pan," by W. T. Grenfell. These are three wonderful books, full of human interest. They tell of wonderful dogs and men.

SUGGESTIONS FOR ORAL COMPOSITIONS

1. One of My Animal Friends.
2. How Horses Help in Time of War.
3. The Society for the Prevention of Cruelty to Animals.
4. What We Can Do to Prevent Cruelty to Animals.
5. Present-Day Methods of Training Wild Animals.

LIBRARY READING

1. "Michael, the Brother of Jerry," by Jack London.
A dog story that shows the cruelty involved in the training of animals for public performances. As a result of this book a

club was formed in Boston called the Jack London Club, which tries to prevent such training.
2. "Gulliver, the Great," by Walter Alden Dyer.
A story of how a man who disliked dogs was changed into a man who loved them.
3. "Black Beauty," by Anna Sewell.
A story written to teach kindness, sympathy, and common sense in the treatment of horses.
4. "Wild Animal Ways," by Ernest Thompson Seton.
5. "The Grizzly King," by James Oliver Curwood.
In this story, Mr. Curwood tells us the experience that changed him from a hunter of big game to a friend of animals.
6. "Smoky," by Will James.
This book was awarded the John Newberry medal in 1927, as being the most distinguished children's book published during the year 1926.

FOUR LITTLE FOXES

Have you ever thought of the dangers and fears that wild animals must experience in their struggle for food and shelter, and from the pursuit of man?

How does the author make us feel his sympathy for the "babes in the woods" in his poem "Four Little Foxes"?

Speak gently, Spring, and make no sudden sound;
For in my windy valley, yesterday I found
New-born foxes squirming on the ground—
      Speak gently.

Walk softly, March, forbear the bitter blow;
Her feet within a trap, her blood upon the snow,

The four little foxes saw their mother go—
          Walk softly.

Go lightly, Spring, oh, give them no alarm;
When I covered them with boughs to shelter them from harm,
The thin blue foxes suckled at my arm—
          Go lightly.

Step softly, March, with your rampant hurricane;
Nuzzling one another, and whimpering with pain,
The new little foxes are shivering in the rain—
          Step softly.
                    —LEW SARRETT.

THE RUNAWAY

    There is an old-fashioned idea that poetry is something apart from our daily lives and full of fine phrases that people admire without really understanding them. There is poetry of this kind; but most of it is very bad. Some of the finest poetry in the world is about things that might happen to any of us any day, and told in simple language that makes us, not merely understand, but wake up and feel the beauty of what it says. Consider how this is true of "The Runaway":

Once when the snow of the year was beginning to fall,
We stopped by a mountain pasture to say "Whose colt?"
A little Morgan had one forefoot on the wall,
The other curled at his breast. He dipped his head
And snorted to us. And then he had to bolt.

We heard the miniature thunder where he fled
And we saw him or thought we saw him dim and gray,
Like a shadow against the curtain of falling flakes.
"I think the little fellow's afraid of the snow.
He isn't winter-broken. It isn't play
With the little fellow at all. He's running away.
I doubt if even his mother could tell him, 'Sakes,
It's only weather.' He'd think she didn't know!
Where is his mother? He can't be out alone."
And now he comes again with a clatter of stone
And mounts the wall again with whited eyes
And all his tail that isn't hair up straight.
He shudders his coat as if to throw off flies.
"Whoever it is that leaves him out so late,
When other creatures have gone to stall and bin,
Ought to be told to come and take him in."

—ROBERT FROST.

FOR DISCUSSION

Does the poem make you see the colt? Read the lines that help you to see him. Does it make you feel that if you had seen him, you would want him to be taken in? Then it is a good poem.

Do you find many words in the poem that are not used in everyday life? Is the poem about something that might have happened to any one in the country?

Do you think of anything else of the kind about which a good poem might be written?

What do you think of these subjects about which Frost has also written poems?

1. Birches.
2. The Woodpile.
3. Mending Wall.
4. After Apple-picking.

NATURE'S FRIEND

Say what you like,
   All things love me!
I pick no flowers—
   That wins the Bee.

The summer's Moths
   Think my hand one
To touch their wings
   With Wind and Sun.

The garden Mouse
   Comes near to play;
Indeed, he turns
   His eyes away.

The Wren knows well
   I rob no nest;
When I look in,
   She still will rest.

The hedge stops Cows,
   Or they would come
After my voice
   Right to my home.

>   The Horse can tell
>   Straight from my lip
>   My hand would not
>   Hold any whip.
>
> Say what you like,
>   All things love me!
> Horse, Cow, and Mouse,
>   Bird, Moth, and Bee.
>
> —WILLIAM H. DAVIES.

CLASS ACTIVITIES

1. List the ways Davies showed his love for nature.
2. Explain the second stanza.
3. Do you know some one who is Nature's friend?

VOLUNTEER

Write a stanza or short poem showing love for trees or flowers.

William Davies wrote many poems about nature. Here are the names of some you may wish to read:

1. Truly Great.
2. Early Morn.
3. Robin Redbreast.
4. Joy and Pleasure.

NEW LIGHT ON OLD HEROES

Much as you have read about Lincoln, perhaps you have never heard how he made his famous Gettysburg speech. This account was written especially by Mr. Oliver N. Goldsmith, a soldier in the Civil War, who stood in front of the platform at Gettysburg when the speech was made.

When you heard Longfellow's poem about Hiawatha, you probably did not think that there was once a real Indian named Hiawatha, and that he was a great man. The story you are going to read tells how he tried to do what men today have not yet accomplished—tried to bring peace to all the world.

We are so accustomed to think of Washington as a general and as the President of the United States, that we forget that he always thought of himself as a farmer, and that he believed it to be as much his duty to manage well his land at Mount Vernon as it had been to lead the American armies to success, and to govern the country well while he was President.

There have been many stories written about Benjamin Franklin; but the story you will read here is taken from his diary, and some of it is quoted in his own words.

When you read of the poverty, hardships, and disappointments of the men in these stories, who were once boys like you, there will come to you a finer appreciation of their true greatness.

SOMETHING TO DO

Have you been experimenting with your flash-cards? How many words can you now read as a group? You might have a competition.

BOOKS THAT WILL INTEREST YOU

Among the many books written about Washington, Franklin, and Lincoln, you will find the following most helpful at this time. These books really ought to be in your school library. It may be you can find some way to secure them if they are not already there. The public library may also have them.

One of the best ways to improve reading is to read extensively, and to supplement one's reading by reference to other books on the same subject. To read widely is to increase word-mastery and accumulate a rich store of facts and ideas. Such experience improves both rate of reading and understanding of what is read.

Books on Washington

1. "Washington, the Young Leader," by G. W. Gerwig. Scribners.
2. "On the Trail of Washington," by F. T. Hill. Appleton.
3. "Washington, the Man of Action," by F. T. Hill. Appleton.
4. "Washington, a Virginia Cavalier," by W. H. Mace. Rand.
5. "George Washington," by H. E. Scudder. Houghton.

Books on Lincoln

1. "The True Story of Abraham Lincoln," by E. S. Brooks. Lothrop.
2. "Abraham Lincoln," by W. F. Gordy. Scribners.
3. "Lincoln, the Man of the People," by W. H. Mace. Rand, McNally.
4. "The Boy's Life of Abraham Lincoln," by H. Nicolay. Century.
5. "The Boy Scout's Life of Lincoln," by I. M. Tarbell. Macmillan Co.

Books on Franklin

1. "Autobiography," by Benjamin Franklin. Houghton, Mifflin.
2. "True Story of Benjamin Franklin," by E. S. Brooks. Lothrop.

It will prove helpful if you will read some of these books while studying "New Light on Old Heroes," and be ready to report from them on interesting topics. You might keep your notes in a loose-leaf notebook as follows:

A LOOSE-LEAF NOTEBOOK FOR HEROES

Make a loose-leaf notebook in which to put things that you wish to remember about the great men. A good form would be:

Name:	Service for which he is noted:	Traits of character:	Other remarks:

Use as few words as possible in the notes. As the list grows check up on the character traits. See which are mentioned most often. You will find some of the same characteristics mentioned for every person. What does this prove?

A Soldier's Recollections

Very few men are now alive who saw Lincoln. Fewer still there are who heard him make his famous speech at Gettysburg, which is one of the most beautiful pieces of writing in the world. You are going to read first an account of Lincoln by a soldier who heard him at Gettysburg, then the speech itself.

The soldier has described the scene at Gettysburg very vividly. As you read the description of the procession, stop and try to imagine Lincoln in his high top-hat and the "notables" riding solemnly down the road with the crowd of people following. Picture the semicircle formed by the soldiers standing at attention while the address was being given.

LINCOLN AT GETTYSBURG

When President Lincoln delivered his celebrated address at Gettysburg, November 19, 1863, I was nineteen years of age and was a private in F, Fifth Company, New York Heavy Artillery. Our regiment, stationed at Baltimore in the fortifications there, was selected as the President's regimental escort on this occasion, and, moving by rail to Gettysburg three days in advance of the date set, went into camp there to await the day.

We had a regimental band and when President Lincoln arrived on the evening of the 18th, we serenaded him at the home of the Honorable David Wills, where he was stopping. He showed himself to the crowd, but when they called for a speech he seemed reluctant to make one, and, indeed, what he said was in reality only an explanation of why he did not wish to make a speech at that time.

On the following day, November 19th, the exercises at the Cemetery were held. There had been a large temporary platform erected at the place now known as "The Semi-Circle," decorated with bunting and the Stars and Stripes, and large enough to seat all the distinguished personages who were present. An imposing procession moved from the town up the pike by way of what is now Hancock

Avenue, at the head of which pageant was our regimental band, and then our regiment of soldiers, and then President Lincoln on horseback. Just before entering the cemetery, our regiment formed in two lines, open order, at the side of the road, and presented arms as the President and a long column of distinguished men, mounted on horses, passed by. These were members of the President's cabinet, foreign ambassadors, in their national dress, generals of the army and officers of the navy who could be spared from the front, senators and representatives, governors of the Northern States, each wearing a high silk hat and accompanied by his uniformed mounted staff. We soldiers stood at present arms while all this pageant passed. The President took off his silk hat and carried it in his hand as he rode by. After this great cavalcade had passed, our regiment marched up and formed a semicircle in two columns in front of the platform on which the notables were then seated. The civilian part of the audience stood or sat upon the ground, as there were no seats for them. It would seem that the comfort of the audience had not been considered.

We soldiers stood at parade throughout the exercises, which lasted probably about three hours. I will not attempt to recall the program of the day. The principal orator was Edward Everett, who made a long, eloquent address. The President was then introduced and made the short speech that has become famous as one of the most beautiful pieces of writing in English. When he stopped, there was a silence. Whether it was because people were surprised that he did not go on longer, or that they were moved by what he did say, I do not know. I heard little or no comment among the soldiers. Perhaps we were too young to realize the greatness of what we had just heard. On my own mind, however, the words made a deep impression. I felt that the President's address alone had accomplished the purpose of the occasion, that it dedicated and hallowed the ground where the martyred dead were sleeping.

It was clear to me that Lincoln's mind was dwelling upon the immeasurable importance of the test that our government was then undergoing. With this thought in mind, he remembered the price that had been paid in lives of soldiers who had fought and died for the cause of union and liberty; and he realized that no words could consecrate the ground where they lay—that they themselves had consecrated it by the sacrifice of their lives. This feeling it was that gave such impressiveness to his speech when he urged upon us the need to take the high resolve that the dead should not have died in vain, and that government of the people, by the people, and for the people, should not perish from the earth.

—*Adapted from Oliver N. Goldsmith.*

How was the soldier's account of Lincoln like your own idea of him? How was it different?

What qualities made Lincoln a great man?

THE GETTYSBURG ADDRESS

Delivered on the battlefield of Gettysburg, November 19, 1863, when the national cemetery was dedicated for the soldiers who fell during the battle, July 1–3, 1863.

Fourscore and seven years ago our fathers brought forth on this continent a new nation, conceived in liberty, and dedicated to the proposition that all men are created equal.

Now we are engaged in a great civil war, testing whether that nation, or any nation so conceived and so dedicated, can long endure. We are met on a great battlefield of that war. We are met to dedicate a portion of that field as a final resting-place for those who gave their lives that that nation might live. It is altogether fitting and proper that we should do this.

But in a larger sense we cannot dedicate, we cannot consecrate, we cannot hallow this ground. The brave men, living and dead, who struggled here, have consecrated it far above our poor power to add or detract. The world will little note nor long remember what we say here, but it can never forget what they did here. It is for us, the living, rather to be dedicated here to the unfinished work which they who fought here have thus far so nobly advanced. It is rather for us to be here dedicated to the great task remaining before us—that from these honored dead we take increased devotion to that cause for which they gave the last full measure of devotion; that we here highly resolve that these dead shall not have died in vain; that this nation, under God, shall have a new birth of freedom, and that government of the people, by the people, for the people, shall not perish from the earth. —ABRAHAM LINCOLN.

FOR DISCUSSION

In the best writing not a word can be spared. Every word contributes something of value. Read again slowly Lincoln's Speech. Could it have been shorter and still have said the same thing? Would it have been as good if it had been longer?

In the best writing the reader is made to feel what the writer wishes him to feel, more by what is left unsaid, to be imagined, than by what is actually put into the words. What does Lincoln leave unsaid about the soldiers? What does he say that makes you realize all that they did? It is difficult to imagine a man who knew this speech by heart going out into life and becoming a mean, selfish, dishonest citizen.

THINGS TO DO

1. Study pictures of Lincoln and see if you can imagine him speaking these words to the great audience on the battlefield.

2. Memorize the address. It will help you to realize that the only life that counts is the life of service.

3. "The Perfect Tribute," by Mary Raymond Shipman Andrews, expresses beautifully the spirit of Lincoln in the writing of the address. Read it.

LINCOLN'S LIFE AS WRITTEN BY HIMSELF

The compiler of the "Dictionary of Congress" states that while preparing that work for publication in 1858, he sent to Mr. Lincoln the usual request for a sketch of his life, and received the following reply:

Born February 12, 1809, in Hardin Co., Kentucky.

Education defective. Profession a Lawyer. Have been a Captain of Volunteers in Black Hawk War. Postmaster at a very small office. Four times a member of the Illinois Legislature, and was a member of the Lower House of Congress.

Yours, etc.
A. Lincoln.

SOMETHING TO THINK ABOUT

When you read Lincoln's own account of his life, does it not make you realize his keen sense of humor? He was always extremely modest, and realized how little any of us can do compared with the great amount there is to be done. He left it to us to find out the details about him. Would it not be a wonderful thing if our lives could be so helpful that people would eagerly seek to know every little thing about us without our having to tell them?

He knew to bide his time,
    And can his fame abide,
Still patient in his simple faith sublime,
    Till the wise years decide.
Great captains, with their guns and drums,
    Disturb our judgment for the hour,
But at last silence comes;
    These are all gone, and, standing like a tower,
Our children shall behold his fame.
    The kindly-earnest, brave, foreseeing man,
Sagacious, patient, dreading praise, not blame,
    New birth of our new soil, the first American.

—JAMES RUSSELL LOWELL.

FOR STUDY

1. What is the significance of these words, "But at last silence comes"?

2. What have you read about Lincoln that justifies the words Lowell uses about him?

3. Memorize all of the verse if you have time. Be sure to memorize the last three lines.

THE TRUE STORY OF HIAWATHA[1]

Do you remember how little Hiawatha was brought up by his grandmother? how he learned to shoot and to fish? how he made his first canoe? and how he became a great man among this people? If you have not read Longfellow's poem about him, this is a good time to read it. For there was a real Hiawatha. He lived many hundreds of years ago, but he had the great ideal which white men are trying to accept nowadays, that nations should try to live at peace with one another. The real Hiawatha had a hard fight for peace. He had to leave his own people and live among strangers; but he would not give up. A brave man who knows he is right and who never gives up can accomplish wonders in any age.

Among the Indian tribes in this country were the Iroquois,[2] who lived in what is now called New York. The Iroquois were divided into five clans or groups, sometimes called the Five Nations. In one of these clans, long before Columbus discovered America, there lived a chief called Hiawatha. At a time when England was being ruined by civil war, and when civilized men in Europe were like the Indians of this country, always ready to fight one another, this great Indian chief dreamed of universal peace, and tried to bring it about among his own people.

His plan was that all the Iroquois should come into a great league or federation.[3] Each tribe was to manage the affairs of the village in which it lived, but no tribe should go to war without the consent of all the others.

---

[1] Hiawatha (hī″ a-wô′thà): chief of the Mohawk Indians.

[2] Iroquois (Ĭr′ŏ kwoi′): one of the most important groups of North American Indians. Look them up in a history or encyclopædia.

[3] federation: a union of several states or tribes.

Each tribe was to elect certain of its members to attend a council, and this council alone should decide matters that concerned all the Indians, especially questions of peace and war. Any tribe that wished to join the federation should be allowed to do so, and the government set up in the beginning was to last forever. If Hiawatha's plan had been carried out, there would not have been any wars among the Indians after that time.

When he had thought out his plan, he called his own tribe, the Onondagas,[1] to a council. They came in their canoes over the lakes and along the creeks and rivers to the council fire, to hear what Hiawatha had to say. Among them came Atotarho,[2] who was the greatest chief among them, and a mighty warrior who did not wish war to end. Not only was he a great man himself, but he had a strong band of followers who always did as he told them, even to the point of killing in secret those who opposed him. During the council Atotarho went about, grim and silent; and all the people saw that he would not agree to Hiawatha's plan. They knew also that he never hesitated to kill or to have killed any one against whom he had a grudge. So they were afraid to vote for the plan for perpetual peace, and Hiawatha failed.

But he was not a man to give up for one failure. After a time, he sent out runners again, asking the Indians to come to another council. But when they came, there were

---

[1] Onondagas (Ŏn'on-dä'găs): one of the nations of the Iroquois.
[2] Atotarho—Ä'tō-tär'ho.

not nearly so many as at the first meeting. And among them went the followers of Atotarho, who discouraged and frightened them so that they would not vote for the plan.

Still Hiawatha did not give up. He sent out his runners once more to call a third meeting. But this time no one came.

Then Hiawatha was sorrowful. He sat down on the ground alone and covered his head with his mantle of skins, to hide his grief. For a long time he sat there, sad and alone, wondering what he should do next to make people believe in his great plan. He knew that it was for the good of all.

At last he made up his mind that if his own people would not listen to him, he must go alone among other tribes. He must try to make them join a league for peace. Then he arose and went out of the village. Outside the village, not far away, there was a spring of water. Beside this spring Hiawatha saw sitting alone Atotarho, the man who had ruined his hope. The two chiefs looked at each other, but neither spoke. And so Hiawatha went alone into exile.

He journeyed through forests; he climbed mountains; he crossed a lake; and finally in a canoe he floated down the Mohawk[1] River.

About Hiawatha's wanderings there are many strange stories. One of these stories tells how he crossed a lake

---

[1] Mohawk (mō'hôk): Indians originally occupying the Mohawk valley in New York. Once the leading nation of the Iroquois Confederacy. During the war of the Revolution, they fled to Canada. They are now most prosperous farmers.

on the shores of which there were many small white shells. These he gathered and made into strings and hung on his breast as a token that he went as a messenger of peace. Beads used in this way the Indians called wampum. And it is by wampum beads hundreds of years old that the story of Hiawatha is remembered among the Indians of today. They have strings of wampum which are arranged in patterns. Each string reminds the Indians of one part of the story.

At last, after long wandering, Hiawatha arrived early one morning in a village of the tribe of the Caniengas. He seated himself on a log near a spring from which he knew the village people would come to draw water. One of the Indian women came out of the long house in which many families lived together, and came to the spring with a vessel of elm bark. Hiawatha sat, silent and motionless, and she was afraid to speak to him. She went back to the house and said to the chief of the Caniengas, whose name was Dekanawidah, "A man, or a figure like a man, is seated by the spring, having his breast covered with strings of white shells."

"It is a guest," said the chief. "Go and bring him in."

Thus Hiawatha and the chief of the Caniengas met, and Hiawatha told about his plan. Dekanawidah at once saw that it was for the good of the people. He called a council, and before long the whole tribe of the Caniengas had agreed to begin a league for peace.

Then Dekanawidah sent messengers to another tribe, the Oneidas,[1] who lived near and were related to the Caniengas. The Oneidas were friendly to the plan, but it took them a year to make up their minds. At the end of that time, however, they joined the Caniengas in making a league for peace.

Then the two tribes thought that they were strong enough to propose the plan for peace to Atotarho again. They thought he might change his mind when he saw other tribes agreeing to the plan. So they sent ambassadors to Atotarho, laying the plan before him again; but as before, the great war-chief of the Onondagas would have nothing to do with it.

Then Hiawatha and his friend Dekanawidah, and the

---

[1] Oneidas (ō-nī′dȧs): one of the Iroquois nations. They lived by Oneida Lake, New York.

chief of the Oneidas sent messengers to the Cayugas,[1] who were related to the people of Atotarho, and persuaded these to join the league for peace.

When Atotarho saw that still other tribes were joining the new league, he at last allowed his people to join also.

Last of all, the Senecas[2] were brought in; and then the dream of Hiawatha was partly realized. He had all the five nations of the Iroquois united in a league against war among themselves.

The first meeting of the league was near Onondaga Lake. All the chiefs came together and a vast concourse of their followers. They made laws by which the nations in the league should be governed. And from that time until the Revolutionary War of 1776, the tribes of the Iroquois kept these laws. They lived in peace with one another and gave friendship and protection to many a poor Indian from other tribes who had been ruined by war.

But in the Revolution the Iroquois took sides with the British. Our government was obliged to break up the Iroquois league and the work of Hiawatha was forgotten.

From the time when Hiawatha won the friendship of Dekanawidah, he was received among the Caniengas and made a chief by them; but of his history after the foundation of the league we know nothing. He is still revered by the Indians as one of their greatest chiefs.

[1] Cayugas (kā-you'gȧs): an Iroquois nation. Their home was in western New York. Now they live in Canada.
[2] Senecas (sĕn'e-kȧs): warlike tribe of Indians originally living in western New York. One of the Iroquois nations.

SUGGESTIONS AND QUESTIONS FOR DISCUSSION

1. Outline all you can remember of the story under the following heads:

        Facts about Hiawatha
        Condition of the times
        The league
        The last days of Hiawatha

Then read the story to check facts you have overlooked.

2. A weak man gives up after several failures. What did Hiawatha do?
3. Compare traits of character of Hiawatha with other heroes.
4. Do you believe there is good in all races of people? Longfellow believed that every one who earnestly tries to find the good will find it no matter to what race he belongs.
5. What was Hiawatha's way of securing peace? What do you think of it as a plan? What other plan can you think of that would keep the world at peace?
6. Why should the story of Hiawatha be included in the group of old heroes?

NOTE: Dr. Charles Eastman, whose Sioux name is Ohiyesa, has written for children a splendid collection of books on Indians and their lives. Read his "Indian Boyhood" and you will want to read others of the collection.

NOTE: You may desire to read more about Indian life. The following books will please you:

1. "Indian History for Young Folks," F. S. Drake. Harpers.
2. "Indian Child Life," Charles Eastman. Little.
3. "Hero of the Longhouse," Mary E. Laing. World Book Co.
4. "Blackfeet Indian Stories," G. B. Grinnell. Scribners.
5. "Legends Every Child Should Know," H. W. Mabie. Grossett.
6. "The Song of Hiawatha," H. W. Longfellow. Houghton, Mifflin.

THE AUTOBIOGRAPHY OF BENJAMIN FRANKLIN

It is interesting to read the autobiography of a great man. He better than any one else can tell us how he lived and how he did the work that made him great. "The Autobiography of Benjamin Franklin" is more interesting even than most books of this kind: for one reason, because Franklin began as a poor boy and worked his way up until he became one of the wisest and greatest men in the land; for another, because it tells much about life in our country in the days of the early settlers. He is still regarded as one of the best American prose writers. Some day you will wish to read the whole book in which he tells about his life.

Franklin's Boyhood

Franklin was born in Boston in 1706; and he says in his book that he cannot remember the time when he could not read. When he went to school he did so well in his classes that his father hoped to send him to college so that he could become a minister. But there were more than a dozen children in the family, and when Franklin was only ten years old, he had to leave school and help his father in his business of making soap and candles.

He did not like making soap and candles; he wanted to go to sea. So when he was twelve years old, his father tried to find for him a trade that he could like. He took him to see joiners,[1] bricklayers, turners,[2] braziers,[3] and other workmen at their work. From that time on, Franklin always liked to watch a man handling tools well, and he

---
[1] joiners: skilled workmen, who finish the inside woodwork for houses.
[2] turners: workmen who shape things with lathes.
[3] braziers (brā′zhẽrs): those who work in brass.

himself became very clever in doing little jobs about the house and in handling different kinds of tools. This skill was useful to him later on.

But he always had a book in his hands. Among his favorites at this time were Bunyan's "Pilgrim's Progress" and Plutarch's "Lives." At last Franklin's father, seeing his interest in books, apprenticed[1] him to his brother, who was a printer. He had to sign papers that he would work for his brother for nine years—until he was twenty-one. He would have his board and lodging and clothes, and wages the last year. This was the way that boys used to learn trades.

Franklin liked printing much better than candle-making. He came to know the apprentices of booksellers, and sometimes they would lend him books to read. Sometimes he would sit up all night to finish a book that he must return early in the morning, and he always returned it clean.

After he had read many books, he began to wish to write. He set to work to teach himself, and he learned to write better than most men of the time who had all the advantages of education.

In 1720 or 1721, Franklin's brother began to print a newspaper which he called the *New England Courant*. It was the second newspaper published in America. At first Franklin's business was to carry the paper to subscribers; that is, he was a newsboy.

---

[1] apprentice: one who is bound by contract to serve another in order to learn a trade.

But he happened to hear people talk about writing for the newspaper, and he decided to try what he could do. He knew his brother would think him too young to have anything printed. So he copied in a different handwriting a little piece of his own, and put it at night under the door of the printing-house. In the morning he was greatly pleased to see his brother showing the piece to friends, and to hear all of them wondering who had written it. They were greatly surprised to find that it had been written by a boy.

Franklin's First Trip Out into the World

Some time after this, Franklin had a quarrel with his brother. He admitted in his autobiography that perhaps he had been "too saucy and provoking." But the end of it was that he ran away without finishing his apprenticeship. He tried at first to get work as a printer in New York; but upon being recommended to a printer in Philadelphia, he went there. He had already come three hundred miles from home, alone, friendless, and almost penniless; and he had to go a hundred miles more for work.

The first part of the journey was by water. But in a sudden storm the boat was almost wrecked and its passengers suffered great hardship from cold and hunger before they finally reached the shore safe. There Franklin fell ill of a fever, but none the less he set out the next day to walk fifty miles on his way to Philadelphia. All day long it poured with rain; but he managed to walk almost forty of the fifty miles. When he arrived the next day at

Burlington, where he expected to take the boat for Philadelphia, he found that he had missed it, and that there would not be another for several days.

Hard luck as this seemed, it was not so bad. An old woman from whom he had bought gingerbread offered to give him a bed and food; and in the evening, as he was walking by the river, he saw a boat with people in it rowing to Philadelphia. They took him aboard and, as there was no wind, he helped them row until after midnight. Then, thinking that they must have passed the city in the dark, they landed in a little creek, made a fire with fence rails, as it was a cold October night, and spent the night there. The next morning they found that they had passed the city, rowed back, and landed about eight or nine o'clock on a Sunday morning. It is interesting to read in Franklin's own words what happened to him next:

"I was in my working dress, my best clothes being to come round by sea. I was dirty from my journey; my pockets were stuffed out with shirts and stockings, and I knew no soul nor where to look for lodging. I was fatigued with traveling, rowing, and want of rest; I was very hungry, and my whole stock of cash consisted of a Dutch dollar and about a shilling in copper. The latter I gave the people of the boat for my passage, who at first refused it on account of my rowing; but I insisted on their taking it. A man is sometimes more generous when he has but a little money than when he has plenty, perhaps through fear of being thought to have but little.

"Then I walked up the street, gazing about till near the market-house I met a boy with bread. As I had made many a meal on bread, I inquired where he got it, and went immediately to the baker's he directed me to, in Second Street, and asked for biscuit intending such as we had in Boston; but they, it seems, were not made in Philadelphia. Then I asked for a three-penny loaf, and was told they had none such. So I bade him give me three-penny worth of any sort. He gave me, accordingly, three great puffy rolls. I was surprised at the quantity, but took it, and having no room in my pockets, walked off with a roll under each arm, and eating the other. Then I went up Market Street as far as Fourth Street, passing by the door of Mr. Read, my future wife's father. She, standing in the door, saw me and thought I made, as certainly I did, a most awkward, ridiculous appearance."

Then Franklin wandered down to the river to get a drink of water; and, being satisfied with his one roll, gave the other two to a woman and child who had come in the boat with him and were there waiting to be taken farther.

Franklin as a Printer

Soon he got work as a printer. He was even sent to England to buy types and other things that he needed for his business. Letters of introduction to people in England did not come, and he was obliged to work there as a printer. He remained there for a year and a half, and might have stayed on but for a Quaker friend who offered him a good position in America if he would return.

After various adventures, he set up a printing-office in Philadelphia with a friend. It was thought that they would fail, as there were already two printers in the city. But one old gentleman who used to pass the printing-office thought differently. He said: "The industry of that Franklin is superior to anything I ever saw of the kind. I see him still at work when I go home from club, and he is at work again before his neighbors are out of bed."

By working in this way, Franklin not only made his printing business succeed, but was able to establish a newspaper of his own. The friend who had gone into business with him was a good-for-nothing, and when after some years he withdrew, Franklin bought out his share and carried on the work alone. He obtained the printing of the speeches made in the state legislature; he got orders for the printing of paper money. He set up a stationer's shop. To show that he was not proud, he sometimes wheeled home in a wheelbarrow the paper that he had bought for his printing.

In 1730 he married the girl who had seen him arrive in Philadelphia munching his roll. Mrs. Franklin not only helped her husband by doing all her housework, but she assisted him in his business by folding and stitching pamphlets, and by tending shop and doing other useful work.

At that time there was not a single good bookstore in America south of Boston. People who liked to read had to send to New England for all their books. As there were no railways, no express, no parcel post, this was a slow and expensive business. When Franklin was in England, he remembered how as a boy he used to borrow books from booksellers, and he arranged to pay an English bookseller a fixed sum for the privilege of reading books, provided that they were returned uninjured. At home, he had this in mind when he established a circulating subscription library

in Philadelphia. From the first the plan was a success, and Franklin himself was one of the people who read most in the library. He had studied in school a little Latin, and long after he was married he taught himself French, Italian, and Spanish.

Franklin's Rules for Improving His Character

About this time he got the idea of trying to improve his own character. He drew up a list of rules and decided that he would make himself follow them. They were these:

1. Temperance: Eat not to dullness; drink not to elevation.
2. Silence: Speak not but what may benefit others or yourself; avoid trifling conversation.
3. Order: Let all your things have their places; let each part of your business have its time.
4. Resolution: Resolve to perform what you ought; perform without fail what you resolve.
5. Frugality: Make no expense but to do good to others or yourself; *i. e.*, waste nothing.
6. Industry: Lose no time; be always employed in something useful; cut off all unnecessary actions.
7. Sincerity: Use no hurtful deceit; think innocently and justly; and if you speak, speak accordingly.
8. Justice: Wrong none by doing injuries, or omitting the benefits that are your duty.
9. Moderation: Avoid extremes; forbear resenting injuries so much as you think they deserve.
10. Cleanliness: Tolerate no uncleanliness in body, clothes, or habitation.
11. Tranquillity: Be not disturbed at trifles, or at accidents common or unavoidable.
12. Chastity.
13. Humility: Imitate Jesus and Socrates.

To help himself keep these rules, he made a kind of calendar, in which he gave himself black marks whenever he broke them. From these marks we can tell that his greatest fault was disorder; and that it was a fault that he tried hard to overcome.

Another plan of his for regulating his life every day may have had something to do with his success in business. This was the way he spent his day at that time:

The Morning. Question: What good shall I do this day?	5–7	Rise, wash, and dress. Pray. Plan the business of the day and make resolutions for the day, including the study of the virtues, and breakfast.
	8–12	Work.
Noon.	12–1	Read, or overlook accounts, and dine.
	2–6	Work.
Evening. Question: What good have I done today?	6–10	Put things in their places. Supper. Music or amusement, or conversation. Examination of the day.
Night.	10–5	Sleep.

The effort to plan our lives from day to day goes far toward success in whatever we undertake.

Franklin's Public Services

About 1732, Franklin began to hold public office, first as clerk in the legislature, and then as postmaster in Philadelphia. As soon as he had the opportunity, he began to find ways of serving his fellow citizens.

One thing he did was to show them how much better it was, instead of taking turns as watchmen to protect property, to pay the city to hire men whose regular business it was to protect lives and property. This was the beginning of our police system.

At that time, when a fire broke out in a city, all the neighbors ran to put it out. They formed lines from the nearest wells and passed buckets from hand to hand along the lines between men at the wells and men nearest the fire. Franklin wrote an article pointing out the great loss through fires, and suggesting that people form a company for putting out fires and saving goods at fires. It was agreed that the company should provide a certain number of leather fire-buckets and of strong bags and baskets for carrying out goods, and that they should meet once a month to try to find ways to improve their system of putting out fires. The small fines paid by members who were absent from the monthly meetings were used for buying fire engines, ladders, fire-hooks for pulling down dangerous walls, and other appliances. In those days all such things were much smaller and less expensive than they are now. And that was the beginning of our fire companies.

After teaching people how to keep their houses safer from fire, Franklin showed them how their homes could be heated with less expense. He invented a small stove which could be used with the doors either open or shut, and which burned much less fuel than the large open fireplaces then in use. Not many years ago many of these Franklin stoves could be seen about the country. This kind of stove was such a success that Franklin was offered a patent on it by which he could have made a fortune; but he refused it, saying that, "as we enjoy great advantages from the inventions of others, we should be glad of an opportunity to serve others by any inventions of ours; and this we should do freely and generously."

In 1747 the province of Pennsylvania was in some danger from the wars of the Spanish, French, and English, in their possessions surrounding it. Franklin wrote a paper showing what would happen if the citizens did not take measures for their own protection. This he printed. It created such an effect that there was a mass meeting of citizens at the end of which twelve hundred men had signed for a militia training, and this number was soon increased to ten thousand. The men furnished their own arms and chose their own officers. The Philadelphia men chose Franklin as their colonel; but he refused the honor, saying that he was not suited to the position, and continued to serve in the militia as a private.

Although he would not accept a dignity for which he felt himself unfitted, with regard to a political office, in which he felt that he had the ability to serve his country, he expressed a different view. He said that he would "never *ask*, never *refuse*, nor ever *resign* an office." He meant that although he would never seek office for his personal advantage, he would not refuse a public duty, nor would he allow personal considerations to draw him from the performance of a duty he had once undertaken.

Besides giving much time to the services of his country, Franklin was very busy with the study of science. He established in Philadelphia a society which is still carrying on the ideals that he set for it. One of his most important experiments was his famous use of a kite to prove that lightning is electricity. By sending up a kite in a thunderstorm, he was able to conduct lightning down the cord to a metal key at the end, where it showed itself as electric sparks. The practical result of this experiment was the invention of the lightning rod for the protection of buildings. By the use of it, lightning that might otherwise strike the building is led into the earth, where it can do no damage.

Franklin was never allowed long to be out of public service of some kind. He was made justice of the peace, then alderman, and finally chosen to the legislative assembly of Pennsylvania, where he sat for ten years. At the time when the English general Braddock arrived in this country to fight the French and Indians, Franklin was postmaster-general, and he was sent to Braddock to help establish the quickest and most certain communications between the English army and the governors of the nearest provinces. Not only did he work out a splendid system of providing transport wagons and supplies, but, like Washington, he tried in vain to persuade Braddock that he knew nothing about fighting Indians, and would have saved him from the disaster that followed if Braddock had listened. After the Revolution, when we had set up a government independent of England, Franklin went as our representative to France, and in his old age won as much respect in Europe as he had won among his countrymen at home.

But far more important than the holding of offices was the work that Franklin did as a private citizen for bettering the conditions of life. He was troubled that there was so little education in Pennsylvania. He wrote a pamphlet explaining what he thought could be done, and sent out a subscription list. The result was the founding of an academy which later developed into the great institution now called the University of Pennsylvania.

One of Franklin's friends, Dr. Thomas Bond, wished to found a hospital for the sick poor. He asked Franklin to help him with a subscription fund because he had found out that when people heard that Franklin approved of a plan, it was certain to be good. Franklin helped Bond, and the result was a free hospital.

Franklin lived near the Jersey Market, and often saw people obliged to wade in the mud to make their purchases. So he suggested that it would pay to have the whole market paved. From observing the good result of this paving, people came to the idea of having all the streets paved. To Franklin is due also the beginning of street-cleaning in Philadelphia. He arranged with a man to sweep the market pavements twice a week and to carry off the rubbish, and with the market people to pay the man so much a month for doing it. Before Franklin went to England he drew up a bill for the legislature, providing for the paving of the whole city. With this bill there was also a provision for street lamps. Although Franklin said that the honor of thinking of these did not belong to him but to a Mr.

John Clifton, he greatly improved the usefulness of the lamps, and made them much cheaper to replace when broken. He also brought back from England the idea of scavengers' carts to carry off the rubbish before people were up in the morning. He had in mind the advantages of daylight saving when he wrote:

"In walking through the Strand and Fleet Street one morning at seven o'clock, I observed there was not one shop open, though it had been daylight and the sun up above three hours; the inhabitants of London choosing voluntarily to live much by candlelight and sleep by sunshine, and yet often complain, a little absurdly, of the duty on candles and the high price of tallow."

It is a pity that Franklin did not live to finish his "Autobiography." It stops in the middle of a sentence concerning the year 1757, and Franklin did not die until 1790. He began his book in 1771, but dropped it and did not take it up again until after the Revolution, in 1784, when he was a very old man. We should like to know more about him because he was not only a successful business man, but he owed his success as much to his honesty as to his cleverness, and he used his success not for his own advantage but, throughout his long life, in the service of his country and of the people of his time.

STUDY HELPS

1. Make a short outline of the main facts in Franklin's life.
2. Make another outline, on a different plan from the first, showing the different ways in which he served his country.
3. Make a third outline, on a still different plan, naming all the things that show he was a great man.
4. What were Franklin's rules for improving his character? Which of them do you think are most useful to any one?
5. What was Franklin's plan for his day? If you were asked to make a plan for your day, how would it read?
6. How was the America of Franklin's day different from the America of today? How did Franklin help to bring about modern improvements?

A GOOD EXERCISE

Here are listed various kinds of modern public needs and activities. Perhaps you can think of others. Copy the list in your best handwriting. Put a cross before every one that Franklin influenced in his time.

Churches	Paved streets	City offices
Public schools	Sewers	State offices
Colleges	Street lighting	National offices
Libraries	Transportation	International offices
Clubs	Police protection	Investigations
Hospitals	Fire protection	Discoveries
Thrift	Taxation	Inventions

WASHINGTON AT HOME

When the Revolutionary War came, Washington was sorry to leave his beautiful country home on the Potomac; and when the war was over, and he had gone back home to live, he was unwilling to leave it, even to be President. He could not refuse the office because his country needed him as it had needed him to lead the army. But he was never so happy as at Mount Vernon.

If you go to Mount Vernon, even as it stands today, you can easily see why Washington cared so much for his home. From the river rises the hill covered with grass and shrubs and trees, many of which Washington planted himself; and at the top is the big white house, not at all splendid or pretentious—just a big comfortable home. It is a house to work in, to play in, to read and to talk and to have music in; a house to rest in and to be happy in. Some day perhaps you can go to Mount Vernon. After you have seen the library where Washington read his books, the bedroom where he slept, the old-fashioned kitchen, the beautiful garden, and the many things that belonged to him and his family, you will not only know him better but you will love him as a man who was good as well as great.

Mount Vernon, on the Potomac River, about fifteen miles below the city of Washington, is one of the most delightful homes that could be imagined. It was built by Washington's elder brother as a small but comfortable farmhouse; but when Washington inherited it, he twice enlarged it, and made it the stately house that it is today.

The house stands on a hill above the river, with a wide view of wooded hills and water. Washington must have loved this view, as it was his habit to pace up and down the ninety-foot long porch for an hour every day, winter or summer.

There is no doubt that his heart was in Mount Vernon and in the improvement of the great estate by which it was surrounded. In 1785 he told a visitor that it was his ambition to become the first farmer in America. He gradually increased his land until he had eight thousand acres about Mount Vernon, and of this not far from half was actually under cultivation.

He spent much time and money making the grounds and gardens as beautiful as possible. He laid out a fine approach from the river, added a shrubbery,[1] a botanical garden,[2] and a paddock[3] full of deer. He had almost a menagerie of animals sent to him from all parts of the world—Chinese pheasants and geese, French partridges, guinea pigs, and all sorts of curious or beautiful plants and trees.

When he was at home, Washington gave most of his time to the study of agriculture and to trying out various methods of farming on his estate. In 1792 he grew more than 5,000 bushels of wheat. Besides wheat, he had many other crops, especially flax, hay, clover, buckwheat, turnips, and potatoes. One year he sowed twenty-seven bushels of flaxseed, and planted more than three hundred bushels of potatoes.

At that time nearly everything used on a great plantation was made there, and what could not be made was or-

---

[1] a shrubbery: a place planted with shrubs.
[2] botanical garden: a piece of ground set apart for the cultivation and study of flowers, vegetables, etc.
[3] paddock: a small field for pasture.

dered once a year from England. Washington's directions to his overseers were to buy nothing they could make on the plantation.

A corps of workmen were kept on the estate. Some worked in the blacksmith-shop. Others were wood-burners and supplied charcoal. There was always a gang of carpenters busy, and also a brick-maker and masons. The gardener and his men set out thousands of grapevines, fruit-trees, and other plants. There was a water-mill, which ground especially fine flour. There were coopers to make the barrels in which it was packed, and Washington's own schooner carried it to market.

The estate had its own shoemaker, and a staff of weavers was trained. In 1768 they produced hundreds of yards of cotton, linen, linsey, and woollen cloth. Later they made all sorts of different cloths, such as dimity, broadcloth, silk and cotton mixture, and other kinds of striped, plaid, and figured materials.

There was a fishery on the estate, and much fish was salted down.

There was a splendid stable, as Washington rode every day about the farms and often went hunting. He had several famous horses. One was called Magnolia, another Nelson, another Blueskin. In 1793, besides the riding horses there were fifty-four draught-horses. At the same time there were three hundred and seventeen cattle—cows and oxen used for ploughing; and there was a dairy in which butter was made for the use of the family. There were also more than six hundred sheep, and many hogs running wild through the woodland.

A careful account of all these things had to be kept, just as any business accounts are kept.

Washington himself tells us how he passed his days at Mount Vernon. He was up at sunrise, and if he found his men not at work at that time, he used to send them word that he was sorry they were ill! Then he looked into whatever estate business seemed most pressing. At seven o'clock he had breakfast. For breakfast he usually had three corncakes, honey, and three cups of tea.

After breakfast, he rode round the farms, looking into everything that called for attention, and did not usually return until it was time to dress for dinner at three o'clock. A visitor at Mount Vernon said of him that he "often works with the men himself—strips off his coat and labors like a common man. The General has a great turn for mechanics. It's astonishing with what niceness he directs everything in the building way, condescending even to measure the thing himself, that all may be perfectly uniform."

In the afternoon he would stay at home and read or write, have tea half an hour before sunset, and go to bed regularly at nine o'clock.

Sometimes for amusement he would join with the other gentlemen of the countryside in fox-hunting. He kept a fine breed of hounds. You may like to know some of their names: Mopsey, Pilot, Tartar, Jupiter, Trueman, Juno,

Duchess, Ragman, Lady, Searcher, Rover, Sweetlips, Vulcan, Singer, Music, and Forester. He also liked duck-hunting and fishing. He liked concerts and plays and other amusements of the kind, such as the circus, waxworks, puppet-shows, and he paid to see all sorts of animals, such as a dancing bear, an elk, a lioness, and a tiger.

In bad weather he would play cards or billiards, and read, more or less, though he never became a lover of books except those about agriculture. Although he never felt that he could write as well as he wished, when he found time he became a writer of letters and had correspondents in many parts of the world.

He was very fond of children, although he had none of his own. But he loved his two stepchildren as if they had been his own. In the very first order for goods that he sent to England after he had married their mother, we find the following items: "10 shillings worth of toys," "6 little books for children beginning to read," and "1 fashionable-dressed baby (doll) to cost 10 shillings." Later he ordered another fashionable doll, which was to cost twice as much, and a box of gingerbread toys or little figures in sugar candy, and other things for the children, including a Bible and prayer book for each, "neatly bound in Turkey" leather, with the name in gilt letters on the inside of the cover.

In 1783, when Washington was going home for Christmas, after resigning from the army at the end of the War —going home for the first time in eight years—he stopped for some hours in Annapolis, buying Christmas presents. We have still the memorandum that he made in his notebook, showing that he bought a locket, 3 small pocketbooks, 3 sashes, a dress cap, a hat, a handkerchief, children's books, a whirligig, a fiddle, and some boxes of games. Can you imagine what a happy Christmas they had at Mount Vernon?

TEST YOUR MIND'S EYE

1. When you think of Mount Vernon, what particular things can you imagine you see?
2. When you think of the work done there, what can you see? Pantomime the work that seems most interesting to you for the rest of the class to guess.
3. When you think of Washington at this home what do you see him doing? Describe just how he looks.
4. Can you see one of the workers receiving a message from Washington saying: "I am sorry that you are ill"? How does he look?

A VIRGINIA PLANTATION

Read rapidly and silently. Try to imagine a picture of each important scene described. Write down a list of words that seem to you particularly descriptive.

Let us visit in imagination a Virginia plantation, such as was to be found when Washington was a child, and see what sort of life was led upon it.

To reach the plantation one will ride for some distance through the woods. The country is not yet cleared of the forest, and each planter, as he adds one tobacco field to another, has to make inroads upon the great trees.

We have been told there were then scarcely any towns or villages in Virginia, so one might fancy there was some mistake; for here is a great collection of houses. Surely this is a village; but look closer. There are no stores or shops or churches or schoolhouses. Rising above the rest is one principal building. It is the planter's own house, which probably is surrounded by beautiful trees and gardens. At a little distance are the cabins of the negroes, and the gaping wooden tobacco-houses, in which the tobacco is drying, hung upon poles and well sunned and aired, for the houses are built to allow plenty of ventilation and sunlight. The cabins of the negroes are low wooden buildings, the chinks filled in with clay. Many of them have kitchen gardens about them, for the slaves are allowed plots of ground on which to raise corn and melons and small vegetables for their own use. The planter's house is sometimes of wood, sometimes of brick, and sometimes of stone. The one feature, however, which always strikes a stranger is the great outside chimney—usually there is one at each end of the house—a huge pile of brick or stone, rising above the ridgepole. Very often, too, there are wide verandas and porches. In this climate, where there are no freezing-cold winters, it is not necessary to build chimneys in the middle of the house, where the warmth of the bricks may serve to temper the air of all the rooms. Moreover, in the warm summers it is well to keep the heat of the cooking away from the house, so the meals are prepared in kitchens built separate from the main house. Inside the great house, one finds oneself in large, airy rooms and halls; wide fireplaces hold blazing fires in the cool days, and in the summer there is air on all sides. Sometimes the rooms are lathed and plastered, but often they are sheathed in the cedar and other woods which grow abundantly in the country.

The planter has no market near by to which he can go for his food; accordingly he has his own smokehouse, in which he cures his ham and smokes his beef; he has outhouses and barns scattered about, where he stores his provisions; and down where the brook runs is the spring-house, built over the running stream. Here the milk and butter and eggs are kept standing in buckets in the cool, fresh water. The table is an abundant but coarse one. The woods supply game, and the planter has herds of cattle. But he raises few vegetables and little wheat. Now and then one of the negro women has a genius for cooking and can make dainty dishes. The living, however, is rather profuse than nice.

It fits the rude, outdoor life of the men. The master of the house spends much time in the saddle. He prides himself on his horses, and keeps his stables well filled. It is his chief business to look over his estate. He has, to be sure, an overseer, or steward, who takes his orders and sees that the gangs of negroes do their work; but the master, if he would succeed, himself must visit the several parts of his plantation and make sure that all goes smoothly.

With horses in the stable and dogs in the kennel, the Virginian is a great hunter. He lives in a country where he can chase not only the fox but the bear and the wildcat. With other planters he rides after the hounds. The man who can ride the hardest, shoot the surest, lift the heaviest weight, run, leap, and wrestle beyond his fellows is the most admired.

With so free and independent a life, the Virginian is a generous man who is hospitable both to his neighbors and to strangers. If he hears of any one traveling through the country and putting up at one of the uncomfortable little inns, he sends for him to come to his house, without waiting for a letter of introduction. He entertains his neighbors, and there are frequent gatherings of old and young for dancing and merrymaking.

The Virginian does not often go far from his plantation. His chief journey is to the capital at Williamsburg, where he goes when the colonial House of Burgesses is in session. Then he gets out his great yellow coach, and his family drive over rough roads, meeting other planters and their families driving through the woods in the same direction. At the capital, during the session, are held balls and other entertainments. The men discuss the affairs of the colony.

But what does the Virginia lady do at home? It is not hard to see, when one thinks of the great house, the many servants, the hospitality shown to strangers, and the absence of towns. She is a home-keeping body. She has to provide for her household, and, as she cannot go shopping to town, she must keep abundant stores of everything she needs. Often she must teach her children, for very likely there is no school near to which she can send them. She must oversee and train her servants, and set one to spinning, another to mending, and another to sewing; but she does not find it easy to have nice work done; her black slaves are seldom skilled, and she has to send to England for her finer garments. There is no doctor near at hand, and she must try her hand at prescribing for the sick on the plantation, and must nurse white and black.

In truth, if it were not for the Virginia lady, the men would be rude and barbarous; but they treat her with unfailing respect, and she gives the gentleness and grace which they would quickly forget. Early in 1800 some one went to visit an old Virginia lady, and she has left this description of what she saw:

"On one side sits the chambermaid with her knitting; on the other, a little colored pet learning to sew; an old woman is there with her table and shears, cutting out the negroes' winter clothes; while the old lady directs them all, incessantly knitting herself. She points out to me several pairs of nice colored stockings and gloves she has just finished, and presents me with a pair half-done, which she begs I will finish and wear for her sake."

The old lady thus described was the widow of George Washington, and so little had life in Virginia then changed from what it had been when Washington was born, in 1732, that the description might easily stand for a portrait of George Washington's mother.

—Adapted from "George Washington,"
by Horace E. Scudder.

COMPARISONS AND QUESTIONS

1. In what ways is the description of life on the Virginia plantation like that at Mount Vernon?
2. Can you give a reason for this?
3. We often hear Southern ladies spoken of as "gracious." Which parts of this story show why?
4. We also often hear of "Southern hospitality." What does that mean?

SUGGESTIONS

1. Draw a map showing location of important things mentioned in the story, or construct a Virginia plantation on your sand-table, and invite the children of the primary grades to see where Washington lived when he was a boy.
2. Dramatize the visit to an old Virginia lady, showing the different people at work and the industry and graciousness of the "old lady." What did she do that was especially gracious?

THE AMERICAN BOY

Theodore Roosevelt was a great lover of boys and girls. Knowing them as he did—he had six children—he wrote the following to show what an American boy should be.

It will help you to understand his thought if you make sure of the meaning of these words before you read the selection:

    stalwart   straightforward
    depraved   objectionable
    hearty   indignation
    incapable   incalculable
    prig   decency

Notice how Mr. Roosevelt uses these words. Read the selection through rapidly to see what the main thought seems to be, and then go over it again for a careful study of each paragraph. Then work out the directions at the end of the selection.

Perhaps you know some boy who is like this.

Of course, what we have a right to expect of the American boy is that he shall turn out to be a good American man. Now, the chances are strong that he won't be much of a man unless he is a good deal of a boy. He must not be a coward or a weakling, a bully, a shirk, or a prig. He must work hard and play hard. He must be clean-minded and clean-lived, and able to hold his own under all circumstances and against all comers. It is only on these conditions that he will grow into the kind of American man of whom America can be really proud.

The boy can best become a good man by being a good boy—not a goody-goody boy, but just a plain good boy. "Good," in the largest sense, should include whatever is fine, straightforward, clean, brave, and manly. The best boys I know—the best men I know—are good at their studies or their business, fearless and stalwart, feared by all that is wicked and depraved, incapable of submitting to wrongdoing, and equally incapable of being aught but tender to the weak and helpless. A healthy-minded boy should feel hearty contempt for the coward, and even more hearty indignation for the boy who bullies girls or small boys, or tortures animals.

The effect that a thoroughly manly, thoroughly straight and upright boy can have upon the companions of his own age, and upon those who are younger, is incalculable. If he is not thoroughly manly, then they will not respect him, and his good qualities will count for but little; if he is mean, cruel, or wicked, then his physical strength and force of mind merely make him so much the more objectionable a member of society. He cannot do good work if he is not strong and does not try with his whole heart and soul to count in any contest; and his strength will be a curse to himself and to every one else if he does not have thorough command over himself and over his own evil passions, and if he does not use his strength on the side of decency, justice, and fair-dealing.

In short, in life, as in a football game, the principle to follow is:

Hit the line hard; don't foul and don't shirk, but hit the line hard!
—THEODORE ROOSEVELT.

DIRECTIONS FOR STUDY

Note: Do you know what the word *trait* means? A trait is a particular quality in the nature of a person. For example, *kindness* is a trait or quality of character. Traits are best understood by ways of acting, which we sometimes call conduct or behavior. Traits of character make a person what he really is.

Paragraph 1. What desirable traits are suggested in this paragraph? Keep this in mind: Mr. Roosevelt sometimes suggests desirable traits by naming their opposite. For example, in paragraph 1, "He must not be a coward or a weakling" calls for *courage* and *strength* of character.

Paragraph 2. Explain in other words the expression "goody-goody." What traits of character does he say the best boys and men possess? Select two or three strong, meaningful expressions from this paragraph.

Paragraph 3. What effect does Mr. Roosevelt point out that a manly boy has on his companions?

What traits necessary for the highest success are mentioned?

FOR CLASS DISCUSSION

1. Outline on the blackboard the ideals which Roosevelt emphasizes in this selection.

2. Do you know any boy who fits Theodore Roosevelt's word-picture of his ideal American boy? Do you admire him? Why?

3. List the desirable traits suggested in this selection, then in another column write their opposites. Example:

strength   weakness

4. Here is a list of ideals from the sayings of Roosevelt. Do you know other persons in history and in real life of whom they are also true?

"I believe in honesty, sincerity, and the square deal."
"Making up one's mind what to do and doing it."

"I believe in fearing God and taking one's own part."
"I believe in hitting the line hard when you are right."
"I believe in speaking softly and carrying a big stick."
"I believe in hard work and honest sport."
"I believe in a sane mind in a sane body."
"I believe we have room for but one soul loyalty, and that is loyalty to the American People."

5. Compare these ideals with:

(1) The Boy Scout Laws.   (2) The Athenian Boys' Oath.

BOOKS TO READ

Here are three interesting books. In them you find many traits of character. You notice different ideals. See how those of the Indian boys compare with those of the New England boys.

1. "The Story of a Bad Boy," by Thomas Bailey Aldrich. Houghton, Mifflin.
Mr. Aldrich based this story on his boyhood life. It tells of the fun and mischief of a New England boy. It is humorous and delightful. The "bad boy" was not so bad after all.
2. "Indian Boyhood," by Charles Eastman. Little, Brown. The author is a full-blooded Sioux. He describes his own boyhood, playmates, games, hunting, forest adventures.
3. "Yourself and Your Body," by Wilfred Grenfell. Scribners. An interesting book by a wonderful man. Vivid illustrations.

WORD STUDY: SYNONYMS

How many words are there in the English language? How could you find out?

Words that have almost the same meaning are called *synonyms*. In the study of synonyms it is important to try to find why no synonym can take the place of the word used. In other words, in the study of synonyms, it is the differences, not the resemblances, that must be emphasized. In all good writing, there is, as a rule, only one right word for a particular place. Every synonym that can be substituted changes the meaning, and usually spoils it.

For practice study of synonyms, find the exact differences in meaning between the members of the following groups of words:

>coward, skulker, slacker
>fearless, rash, bold, brave, daring, hardy
>stalwart, strong, stout, fat
>story, legend, anecdote, fib
>dumb, mute, still, speechless, quiet, silent

Make a list of ten interesting words from some story and write beside each, one or two synonyms. Then, using your dictionary, find how the words in each group of your list differ. Discuss the lists in class.

FOUR POEMS TO LEARN

The Noble Nature

It is not growing like a tree
In bulk, doth make Man better be;
Or standing long an oak, three hundred year,
To fall a log at last, dry, bald, and sere;
A lily of the day
Is fairer far in May,
Although it fall and die that night—
It was the plant and flower of Light.
In small proportions we just beauties see;
And in short measures life may perfect be.

—BEN JONSON.

1. Which lines in this poem express the thought?
2. Do you think the comparison between the oak and the lily is a good one for the author's purpose? Why?

Do You Fear The Wind?

Do you fear the force of the wind,
The slash of the rain?
Go face them and fight them,
Be savage again.
Go hungry and cold like the wolf,
Go wade like the crane:
The palms of your hands will thicken,
The skin of your cheek will tan,
You'll grow ragged and weary and swarthy,
—But you'll walk like a man.

—HAMLIN GARLAND.

1. Do you like this poem? Why?
2. Do you read this poem more quickly or more slowly than you read the one by Ben Jonson?
3. What does it mean to "walk like a man"?
4. What traits of character are suggested here?
5. See how quickly you can learn this poem.

A Nation's Strength

Not gold, but only men can make
    A people great and strong—
Men, who for truth and honor's sake,
    Stand fast and suffer long.

—RALPH WALDO EMERSON.

Opportunity

This I beheld, or dreamed it in a dream:
There spread a cloud of dust along a plain,
And underneath the cloud, or in it, raged
A furious battle, and men yelled, and swords
Shocked upon swords and shields. A prince's banner
Wavered, then staggered backward, hemmed by foes.

A craven hung along the battle's edge,
And thought, "Had I a sword of keener steel—
That blue blade that the king's son bears—but this
Blunt thing—" he snapped and flung it from his hand
And lowering, crept away and left the field.

Then came the king's son, wounded, sore bestead,
And weaponless, and saw the broken sword
Hilt-buried in the dry and trodden sand,
And ran and snatched it, and with battle shout
Lifted afresh, he hewed his enemy down
And saved a great cause that heroic day.

—EDWARD ROWLAND SILL.

GOING FOR THE DOCTOR

Were you ever awakened in the middle of a dark, rainy night and asked to go alone on some errand? Here is a story that tells of the actual experience of a brave country boy who had to ride to town one dark, stormy night for the doctor. The place was on the lonely prairies in Iowa before the telephone and automobile had come into use.

Read silently as rapidly as you can, keeping in mind *who, what, when,* and *where*. Then follow the directions at the end of the story.

There are some unusual expressions that will attract your attention. See if you can get their meaning:

garret eaves	poignant note
fleet but treacherous Morgan	impassive face
wonderful staying power	imperative jingle
swales full of water	nigh horse

1. One night as I lay buried in deep sleep close to the garret eaves, I heard my mother call me—and something in her voice pierced me, roused me. A poignant note of alarm was in it.

"Hamlin," she called, "get up—at once. You must go for the doctor. Your father is very sick. *Hurry!*"

I sprang from my bed, dizzy with sleep, yet understanding her appeal. "I hear you, I'm coming," I called down to her as I started to dress.

"Call Hattie. I need her, too."

The rain was pattering on the roof, and as I dressed I had a disturbing vision of the long cold ride which lay before me. I hoped the case was not so bad as mother thought. With limbs still numb and weak I stumbled down the stairs to the sitting-room, where a faint light shone.

Mother met me with a white, strained face. "Your father is suffering terribly. Go for the doctor at once."

2. I could hear the sufferer groan even as I moved about the kitchen, putting on my coat and lighting the lantern. It was about one o'clock of the morning, and the wind was cold as I picked my way through the mud to the barn. The thought of the long miles to town made me shiver, but as the son of a soldier I could not falter in my duty.

In their warm stalls the horses were resting in dreamful doze. Dan and Dick, the big plough team, stood near the door. Jule and Dolly came next. Wild Frank, a fleet but treacherous Morgan, stood fifth, and for a moment I considered taking him. He was strong and of wonderful staying powers, but so savage and unreliable that I dared not risk an accident. I passed on to bay Kittie, whose bright eyes seemed to inquire: "What·is the matter?"

Flinging the blanket over her and smoothing it carefully, I tossed the light saddle to her back and cinched it tight, so tight that she grunted. "I can't take any chances of a spill," I explained to her, and she accepted the bit willingly. She was always ready for action and fully dependable.

Blowing out my lantern, I hung it on a peg, led Kit from her stall out into the night, and swung to the saddle. She made off with a spattering rush through the yard, out into the road. It was dark as pitch, but I was fully awake now. The dash of the rain in my face had cleared my brain, but I trusted to the keener senses of the mare to find the road, which showed only in the strips of water which filled the wagon tracks.

We made way slowly for a few minutes until my eyes expanded to take in the faint lines of light along the lane. The road at last became a river of ink running between faint gray banks of sward, and my heart rose in confidence. I took on dignity. I was a courier riding through the night to save a city, a messenger on whose courage and skill thousands of lives depended.

"Get out o' this!" I shouted to Kit, and she leaped away like a wolf, at a tearing gallop.

She knew her rider. We had herded the cattle many days on the prairie, and in races with the wild colts I had tested her speed. Snorting with vigor at every leap she seemed to say: "My heart is brave, my limbs are strong. Call on me."

Out of the darkness John Martin's Carlo barked. A half-mile had passed. Old Marsh's foxhound clamored next. Two miles were gone. From here the road ran diagonally across the prairie, a velvet-black band on the dim sod. The ground was firmer but there were swales full of water. Through these Kittie dashed with unhesitating confidence, the water flying from her drumming hoofs. Once she went to her knees and almost unseated me, but I regained my saddle and shouted, "Go on, Kit!"

The fourth mile was in the mud, but the fifth brought us to the village turnpike, and the mare was as glad of it as I. Her breath was labored now. She snorted no more in exultation and confident strength. She began to wonder—to doubt, and I, who knew her ways as well as I knew those of a human being, realized that she was beginning to flag. The mud had begun to tell on her.

It hurt me to urge her on, but the memory of my mother's agonized face, and the sound of my father's groan of pain steeled my heart. I set lash to her side and so kept her to her highest speed.

At last a gleam of light! Some one in the village was awake. I passed another lighted window. Then the green and red lamps of the drug-store cheered me with their promise of aid, for the doctor lived next door. There too a dim ray shone.

Slipping from my weary horse, I tied her to the rail and hurried up the walk toward the doctor's bell. I remembered just where the knob rested. Twice I pulled sharply, strongly, putting into it some part of the anxiety and impatience I felt. I could hear its imperative jingle as it died away in the silent house.

At last the door opened and the doctor, a big blond handsome man in a long nightgown, confronted me with impassive face. "What is it, my boy?" he asked kindly.

As I told him he looked down at my water-soaked form and wild-eyed countenance with gentle patience. Then he peered out over my head into the dismal night. He was a man of resolution but he hesitated for a moment. "Your father is suffering sharply, is he?"

"Yes, sir. I could hear him groan.—Please hurry."

He mused a moment. "He is a soldier. He would not complain of a little thing—I will come."

Turning in relief, I ran down the walk and climbed upon my shivering mare. She wheeled sharply, eager to be off on her homeward way. Her spirit was not broken, but she was content to take a slower pace. She seemed to know that our errand was accomplished, and that the warm shelter of the stall was to be her reward.

Holding her down to a slow trot I turned often to see if I could detect the lights of the doctor's buggy, which was a familiar sight on our road. I had heard that he kept one of his teams harnessed, ready for calls like this, and I confidently expected him to overtake me. "It's a terrible night to go out, but he said he would come," I repeated as I rode.

3. At last the lights of a carriage, crazily rocking, came into view, and pulling Kit to a walk, I twisted in my saddle, ready to shout with admiration of the speed of his team. "He's driving the 'Clay-Banks!'" I called in great excitement.

The Clay-Banks were famous throughout the county as the doctor's swiftest and wildest team, a span of bronchos whose savage spirits no journey could entirely subdue, a team he did not spare, a team that scorned petting and pity—bony, sinewy, big-headed. They never walked, and little cared for mud or snow.

They came rushing now with splashing feet and foaming, half-open jaws, the big doctor, calm, iron-handed, masterful, sitting in the swaying top of his light buggy, his feet against the dashboard, keeping his furious span in hand as easily as if they were a pair of Shetland ponies. The nigh horse was running, the off horse pacing, and the splatter of their feet, the slash of the wheels, and the roaring of their heavy breathing, made my boyish heart leap. I could hardly repress a yell of delight.

As I drew aside to let him pass, the doctor called out with mellow cheer: "Take your time, boy, take your time!"

Before I could even think of an answer he was gone, and I was alone with Kit and the night.

4. My anxiety vanished with him. I had done all that could humanly be done, I had fetched the doctor. Whatever happened, I was guiltless. I knew also that in a few minutes a sweet relief would come to my tortured mother, and with full faith and loving confidence in the man of science, I jogged along homeward, wet to the bone, but triumphant. *—From "A Son of the Middle Border," by Hamlin Garland.*

THE POINTS OF A GOOD STORY

NOTE: To tell or write a good story one must keep in mind the following points:

1. The situation or problem upon which the story is based.
2. Interesting incidents or events which lead up to what is called "the turning point."
3. The turning point in the story.
4. The close or ending of the story.

Other points are also considered but these are the main ones. This story is an excellent illustration of all these points. To help you make a thorough study of it, the story is grouped into sections, each of which is numbered at its beginning paragraph. Now see what you can do with it.

Section 1: The Introduction.

1. Which paragraph presents the situation upon which the story is based?
2. What details are worked into the introduction to add interest and color?
3. Does the conversation add anything?

Section 2: Interesting Incidents and Events.

1. Select a number of incidents in this section which carry the story forward and make you want to read it.

Section 3: The Turning Point.

1. Where does it come? Read carefully to find it and give your reasons. What sentence really expresses it?

Section 4: The Ending.

1. What point is mentioned to bring the story neatly to a close?

FOR COMMENT AND DISCUSSION

1. How did the thought that he was the son of a soldier help Hamlin?
2. Explain the reference to the horse, Frank, as a "fleet but treacherous Morgan." Have we lost anything by not having horses in common use today?
3. Why did he trust to his horse to keep the road?
4. How did Hamlin use his imagination to help him on his night ride? Find the paragraph which proves it.
5. What memories of home kept coming into Hamlin's mind?
6. Why did the doctor say: "He is a soldier . . . I will come"?
7. What traits of character would you say the doctor had?
8. What points did you notice about the boy?
9. Select several fine descriptive expressions in the story and have them written on the board, *e. g.*, "as I lay buried in deep sleep"; "the horses were resting in dreamful doze."
10. What conversations add to the interest of the story?

NOTE: This story would make good oral reading. Perhaps some of the class will volunteer to read it for your enjoyment.

MORE SYNONYMS: A PRACTICE EXERCISE

In the following sentences taken from the story you have just read, choose the best synonyms you can find for each word in italics. Prove that no other words will do as well.

1. Mother met me with a white, *strained* face.
2. I can't take any chances of a *spill*.
3. She was always ready for action and fully *dependable*.
4. Then he *peered* out over my head into the *dismal* night.
5. I could hardly *repress* a yell of *delight*.
6. My anxiety *vanished* with him.
7. Whatever happened I was *guiltless*.

BOOKS TO READ

Hamlin Garland has two books you will enjoy. He is known as one of our most interesting story-writers. Ask your library for them.

1. "Boy Life on the Prairie," by Hamlin Garland. Harpers. Gripping stories of herding cattle, ploughing and sowing, harvesting, spearing fish, hunting prairie chickens, killing wolves, etc., on the prairies of Iowa when he was a boy.
2. "The Book of American Indians," by Hamlin Garland. Harpers. Illustrated by Frederic Remington.

There is another story by another author, of the same kind as "Boy Life on the Prairie," called "Prairie Rose." It is written by Bertha Bush, and tells of a pioneer girl who also lived on the prairies. She has all sorts of amusing and dangerous experiences. Perhaps some girl in the class would like to get this book and report on it in class, or read a story from it for you.

THE YELLOW MAIL

Jimmie Bradshaw was a freight engineer who wanted a chance to show what he could do with an engine on a fast run. This is how he got his chance.

The railway company had agreed to carry the mail from coast to coast in a certain time. A test run was to be made with a special train, to carry mail only, called the Yellow Mail because of the color of the cars. If this succeeded, the Government would let the railroad have the contract to carry the mail regularly.

In the Mountain Division of the road, on the morning that the trial run was to be made, the fireman for Engine 1012, which was to be used, had been drunk the night before, and could not be trusted. Then Jimmie Bradshaw asked if he might have the chance. The story tells what he made of the chance.

There are some people who can always be depended upon to do what they undertake to do.

The other principal characters in the story are:

Neighbor, the superintendent at Piedmont.
Doubleday, the master mechanic at Medicine Bend.
McTerza, the engineer who brought the mail from the east on engine No. 808.
Sollers, the engineer who carried it westward on engine No. 1012.

Special Directions

This is a good story for silent reading. The action is rapid and exciting. There are some words and phrases that have a particular meaning about engines and railroads. As you read the first time, quickly jot down the words you do not understand. Then read again to see if you can get the right meaning from the rest of the sentence or paragraph. Use your dictionary.

At class time, ask the boys who know more about railroads and engines to help clear up these meanings, a paragraph at a time. Here are some of them:

big drivers
drumming at her gauge
shivering pointer

blocked the spurs
high pressure
sickening slew

Stop at the end of I and make a note of what you think is going to happen to stop the mail and how it will concern Jimmie?

I

In the east the sun was breaking over the sandhills, and below it a haze of black thickened the horizon. It was McTerza with No. 808 and the Yellow Mail. Neighbor, the superintendent, looked at his watch. The train was, if anything, a minute to the good.

When McTerza blocked the big drivers at the west end of the depot, every eye was on the new train. Three standard railway mail-cars, painted in varnished buttercup yellow, strung out behind the sizzling engine, and they looked as pretty as cowslips. While Neighbor was wondering how to get a fireman without a moment's delay, Jimmie Bradshaw, just in from a night run down from the Bend, walked across the yard.

"What are you looking for, Neighbor?" he asked.

"A man to fire for Sollers—up. Do you want it?"

Neighbor threw it at him crossly and carelessly, not having any idea that Jimmie was looking for trouble. But Jimmie surprised him; Jimmie did want it.

There wasn't much time to look for any one else. The 1012 was being coupled to the mail for the hardest run on the line.

Jimmie lost no time climbing in. The 1012 was drumming then at her gauge with better than two hundred pounds of steam. Adam Shafer, conductor for the run, ran backward and forward, examining the air. At the final word from his brakeman he lifted two fingers at Sollers; Oliver opened a notch, and Jimmie Bradshaw stuck his head out of the gangway. Slowly, but with swiftly rising speed, the yellow train began to move out through the long lines of freight-cars that blocked the spurs. Those who watched that morning from the Piedmont platform thought a smoother equipment than this mail train never drew out of the mountain yards.

Jimmie Bradshaw jumped at the work in front of him. He had never lifted a pick in such a cab. He had never seen so much play for a shovel in his life, and he knew the trick of his business better than most men, the trick of holding the high pressure every minute, of feeling the drafts before they left the throttle. As Oliver let the engine out very, very fast, Jimmie sprinkled the grate-bars craftily and blinked at the shivering pointer, as much as to say: "It's you and me now for the Yellow Mail, and nobody else on earth."

There was a long reach of smooth track in front of the foothills. It was there the big start had to be made, and in two minutes the bark of the big machine had deepened to a chest tone, full as thunder. It was all fun for an hour, for two hours. Then the ambitious fireman realized what the new speed meant: the sickening slew, the lurch on lurch so fast that the engine never righted, the shortened breath along the tangent, the giddy roll to the elevation, and the sudden shock of the curve, the roar of the flight on the ear, and, above and over it all, the booming purr of the steel.

When they struck the foothills Sollers and Jimmie looked at their watches and looked at each other like men who had turned their backs on every mountain record. There was a stop for water, an oil round, an anxious touch on the wheels; then the Yellow Mail drew reeling into the hills. Oliver eased her just a bit for the heavier curves, but for all that the train writhed, and the men remembered, in spite of themselves, the mountain curves ahead. The worst of the run lay ahead, because the art in mountain running is not alone or so much in getting up hill; it is in getting down hill. But by the way the Yellow Mail got that day up hill and down, it seemed that the 1012 actually would pull the stamps off the letters. Before they knew it they were through the gateway, out into the desert country, up along the crested buttes, and then, suddenly, the wheels of the 1012 struck a tight curve, a rail sprang out like a knitting-needle, and the Yellow Mail shot staggering off the track.

II

There was a crunching of truck and frame, a crashing splinter of varnished cars, a scream from the wounded engine, a cloud of gray ash in the burning sun, and a ruin of human effort in the ditch. In the twinkle of an eye the mail train lay spilled on the alkali.

It was hardly more than a minute before, like ants out of a trampled hill, men began crawling from the yellow wreck. And first on his feet, with no more than scratches, and quickest back under the cab after his engineer, was Jimmie Bradshaw, the fireman.

Sollers, barely conscious, lay wedged between the tank and the footboard. Jimmie eased him away from the boiler. The conductor stood with a broken arm directing his brakeman how to chop a crew out of the head mail-car, and the hind crews were getting out unaided. There was a quick calling back and forth, and the cry, "Nobody killed!" But the engineer and the conductor were put out of action.

There was, in fact, only one man unhurt—Jimmie Bradshaw.

The wreck of the fast mail took place just east of Crockett's siding. A west-bound freight lay at that moment on the passing track waiting for the mail to go by. Jimmie Bradshaw, the minute he righted himself, decided what must be done. Before the freight crew had reached the wreck Jimmie was telling them what he wanted. The freight conductor demurred; and the freight engineer, Kingsley, objected. "My engine won't stand it; it'll pound her to scrap," he argued. "The safest thing is to get orders."

"Get orders!" stormed Jimmie Bradshaw, pointing at the wreck. "Get orders! Are you running an engine on this line and don't know the orders for those mail-bags? The orders are to move 'em! That's orders enough. Move 'em! Uncouple three of those empty box-cars and hustle 'em back. By the Great United States, any man that interferes with moving this mail will get his time, that's what he'll get. The thing is to move the mail, not to stand here chewing about it!"

"Bucks wants the stuff hustled," put in the freight conductor, weakening before Jimmie's eloquence, "everybody knows that."

"Uncouple there!" cried Jimmie, climbing into the mogul cab. "I'll pull the bags, Kingsley; you needn't take any chances. Come back there, every one of you, and help with the transfer."

He carried his points with a rush. He was conductor

and engineer and general manager, all in one. He backed the box-cars to the curve below the spill, and set every man at work, piling the mail from the wrecked train to the freight cars. The wounded cared for the wounded, and the dead might have buried the dead; Jimmie moved the mail. Only one thing turned his hair gray; the transfer was so slow that it threatened to defeat his plan. As he stood fermenting, a stray party of Sioux Indians on a vagrant hunt rose out of the desert passes, and halted to survey the confusion. It was Jimmie Bradshaw's opportunity. He called them and talked to them for one minute; in two, he had them carrying second-class mail. The registered mail was jealously guarded by those of the mail clerks who could still hobble. The freight crews and Jimmie, dripping sweat and anxiety, handled the letter-bags; but second and third-class mail were carried for the Great White Father by his Indian children of the Rockies.

Before the disabled men could credit their senses the business was done. They were made as comfortable as possible, and, with the promise of speedy aid back to the injured, the Yellow Mail, somewhat disfigured, was heading again westward in the box-cars. This time Jimmie Bradshaw, like a dog with a bone, had the throttle. For once in his life he had the coveted fast run, and till he sighted Fort Rucker he never for a minute let up.

III

Meantime, at Medicine Bend, there was a desperate crowd around the despatcher. It was an hour and twenty minutes after Ponca Station reported the Yellow Mail out, before Fort Rucker, eighteen miles west, reported the box-cars and Jimmie Bradshaw in, and followed with a wreck report from the Crockett siding. When the wire brought word of that into the Wickiup office, Doubleday's face turned hard; the contract was lost. Then the Rucker operator began to talk about Jimmie Bradshaw. "Who's Bradshaw?" asked somebody. Rucker went on excitedly with the story of the mogul and of three box-cars, and of a war party of Sioux aboard. It came so mixed that Medicine Bend thought everybody at Rucker Station had gone mad.

While they fumed, Jimmie Bradshaw was speeding the mail through the mountains. He had Kingsley's fireman, big as an ox and full of his own enthusiasm. In no time they were flying across the flats of the Spider Water, threading the curves of the Peace River, and hitting the rails of the Painted Desert, with the mogul sprinting like a Texas steer, and the box-cars leaping at the joints like yearlings. It was no time for scientific running, no case of favoring the roadbed, of easing the strain on the machinery. Up hill and down, curve and tangent, it was all one. Never before or after was there the speed that Jimmie Bradshaw made when he ran the mail through the gorges in three box-cars. Frightened operators and paralyzed station-agents all the way up the line watched the fearful and wonderful train, with Bradshaw's red head sticking out of the cab, take the switches.

Medicine Bend couldn't understand it over the wires. There was an electric storm in the mountains, and in the midst of the confusion the wires went bad. With Doubleday frantic, the despatchers were trying to run a train down to Crockett's siding. But Jimmie Bradshaw had asked at Rucker for rights to the Bend, and in an unguarded moment they had been given. After that there was nothing to do. Nobody could get action on Jimmie Bradshaw; he took the rights. In thirty minutes the operating department were wild to kill him, but he was making such time it was concluded better to humor the lunatic than to hold him up anywhere for a parley. When this was decided, Jimmie was already reported past Bad Axe, fifteen miles below the Bend, with every truck on the box-cars smoking.

The Bad Axe run to the Bend was never done in less than fourteen minutes until Bradshaw that day brought up the mail. Between those two points the line is modeled on the curves of a ram's horn, but Jimmie with the mogul found every twist on the right of way in eleven minutes. That particular record is good yet. Indeed, before Doubleday got his men fairly on the platform to look for Jimmie, the hollow scream of the big freight engine echoed through the mountains. Shouts from below brought the operators to the upper windows. Down the Bend they saw a monster locomotive, flying from a trailing horn of smoke. As the stubby string of freight-cars slewed quartering into the lower yard, the startled officials saw them from the windows wrapped in a stream of flame. Every journal was afire, and the blaze from the boxes, rolling into the steam from the stack, curled hotly around a group of Sioux Indians, who clung sternly to the footboards and brake-wheels on top of the box-cars. It was a ride for the red men that is told around the council fires yet.

By the time Jimmie slowed up his train, the fire brigade was on the run from the roundhouse. The Sioux warriors climbed hastily down the fire-escapes, a force of bruised and bareheaded mail-clerks shoved back the box-car doors, and the car tinks tackled the conflagration. Jimmie Bradshaw, dropping from the cab with the swing of a man who has done a trick, waited at the gangway for the questions to come at him. For a minute they came hot.

"What do you mean by bringing in an engine in that condition?" choked Doubleday, pointing to the blown machine.

"I thought you wanted the mail?" winked Jimmie.

"How are we to get the mail with you blocking the track two hours?" demanded Callahan, insanely.

"Why, the mail's here, in these box-cars," answered Jimmie Bradshaw, pointing to his bobtail train. "Now don't look daffy like that; every sack is right here. I thought the best way to get the mail here was to bring it. Hm? We're forty minutes late, ain't we?"

Doubleday waited to hear no more. Orders flew from the superintendent and the master mechanic. They saw there was a life for it yet. Before the fire brigade had done with the trucks a string of new mail-cars was backed down beside the train. The relieving mail crews waiting at the Bend took hold like cats at a pudding, and a dozen extra men helped them sling the pouches. The 1014, blowing porpoisewise, was backed up, and the Yellow Mail started up the gorge for Bear Dance, only fifty-three minutes late, with Hawksworth in the cab.

"And if you can't make that up, Frank, you're no good on earth," sputtered Doubleday at the engineer he had put in for that special endeavor. And Frank Hawksworth did make it up, and the Yellow Mail went on and off the West End on the test, and into the Sierras for the coast, ON TIME.

—"*Held for Orders*" by Frank H. Spearman.

THINGS TO TALK ABOUT AND DO

1. The story of *The Yellow Mail* is presented in three divisions. Read each carefully and give each one an attractive title.

2. Make an outline of the main points in each division of the story.

3. Select one or two places where you like the description. Refer to them in class to see how many others agree with you.

4. Make a list of the words and phrases that are particularly strong for the purposes of the story. Be sure you understand the meaning of these words.

5. What would you name as the strong points in the character of Jimmie Bradshaw? How does he compare with Mr. Roosevelt's idea of an American boy? With Hamlin Garland?

6. Would you call Jimmie and Hamlin heroes in everyday work?

7. Does this story illustrate the points of a good story? Give definite instances relative to Introduction, Interesting Incidents, Turning Point, and Ending. Where is the turning point?

8. Can you tell any other good railway story?

AN INDIAN SCARE

This story is taken from a book entitled "Wells Brothers" by Andy Adams. The book tells of the experiences of two boys who became ranchmen in Kansas, about 1885.

When you have finished reading this story, compare it in your mind with the other two stories you have just read in this group. Decide which one you like best and why.

There are a few words to make sure of, if you would get the most enjoyment out of the story. Look up those you do not understand.

cavalcade	rowel	meanderings
encumbered	line-camp	coulees
lean-tos	bewilderment	baffled
tinder	mounts	reconnoiter

As you read, note what the main point of the story seems to be. Observe also how the opening sentence and first paragraph of the story picture an interesting situation, which grips your attention at the beginning of the second paragraph.

Dell and Joel had gathered together the horses wandering loose on the range. The cavalcade was drifting home at a gentle trot, but on approaching the new line-camp, where they had their winter quarters, they sighted a band of ponies forward and in a bend of the creek. The boys veered their horses, taking to the western divide, and on gaining it, saw below them and at the distance of only a quarter-mile, around the springs, an Indian encampment of a dozen tepees and lean-tos.

Dell and Joel were struck dumb at the sight. To add to

their surprise, all the dogs in the encampment set up a howling, the Indians came tumbling from their temporary shelters, many of them running for their ponies on picket, while an old, almost naked leader signaled to the brothers. It was a moment of bewilderment with the boys, who conversed in whispers, never halting on their course. When the Indians reached their ponies, every brave dashed up to the encampment. A short parley followed, during which the old Indian, evidently a chief, continued his signaling; but the boys kept edging away, and the old brave sprang on a pony and started in pursuit, followed by a number of his band.

The act was tinder to powder. The boys gave rowel to their mounts, shook out their ropes, raised the long yell, and started the loose horses in a mad dash for home. It was ten miles to headquarters, and their mounts, already fagged by carrying heavy saddles, and the day's work, were none too fresh; the Indians, on the other hand, were not encumbered by an ounce of extra clothing.

The boys led the race by fully five hundred yards. But instead of taking to the divide, the Indians bore down the valley, pursued and pursuers in plain sight of one another. For the first mile or so the loose horses were no handicap, showing clean heels and keeping clear of the whizzing ropes. But after the first wild dash, the band of relay horses began to scatter, and the Indians gained on the cavalcade, coming fairly abreast and not over four hundred yards distant.

"They're riding to cut us off!" gasped Dell. "They'll cut us off from our headquarters!"

"Our horses will outwind their ponies," shouted Joel, in reply. "Don't let the loose horses turn into the valley."

The divide was more difficult to follow than the creek. The meanderings of the latter the Indians crossed and re-crossed without halting; but the watershed zigzagged, or was broken and cut by dry washes and coulees, and thus retarded the speed of the cavalcade. The race wore on with varying advantage, and when near half way to headquarters, the Indians turned up the slope as if to verify Dell's forecast. Just then a half-dozen of the loose horses cut off from the band and turned down the slope in plain sight of the pursuers.

"If it's horses they want, they can have those," shouted Joel. "Climbing that slope will fag their ponies. Come on; here's where we have the best of it."

The Indians were not to be pacified. Without a look they swept past the abandoned horses. The boys made a clear gain along a level stretch on the divide, maintaining their first lead, when the pursuers, baffled in cutting them off, turned again into the valley.

"It isn't the horses they want," ventured Dell, with a backward glance.

"In the next dip, we'll turn the others down the western slope, and ride for our lives," answered Joel, convinced that a sacrifice of horses would not appease their pursuers.

The opportunity came shortly, when for a few minutes

the brothers dipped from the sight of the Indians. The act confused the latter, who scaled the divide only to find the objects of their chase a full half-mile in the lead, but calling on the last reserve of their fagged horses. The pursuers gradually closed the intervening gap; but with the advantage of knowing every foot of the ground, the brothers took a tack which carried them on a straight stretch homeward, and, their horses proving their mettle, the boys dashed up to the stable, where Sargent, their friend, was at work among the camp horses.

"Indians! Indians!" shouted Dell, who arrived in the lead. "Indians have been chasing us all afternoon. Run for your life, Jack!"

Joel swept past a moment later, accenting the situation, and as Sargent left the corral, he caught sight of the pursuing Indians, and he showed splendid action in reaching the dugout.

Breathless and gasping, Dell and Joel each grasped a repeating rifle, while Sargent in the excitement of the moment, unable to unearth the story, buckled on a six-shooter. The first reconnoiter revealed the Indians halted some two hundred yards distant, parleying among themselves. They seemed to be unarmed, and on Sargent's stepping outside the shack, the leader, the old brave, held up his hand.

"They must be peaceful Indians," said Sargent to the boys, and signaled in the leader.

The old Indian jogged forward on his tired pony, leaving his followers behind; as he rode up, a smile flickered on his wrinkled face. He dismounted, unearthed from his scanty breech-clout a greasy, grimy letter, and handed it to Sargent.

The latter scanned the missive, and, turning to the boys, who had ventured forth, said with a grin:

"Why, this is Chief Lone Wolf from the Pine Ridge Agency, going down to see his kinsfolk in the Indian Territory. The agent at Pine Ridge says that Lone Wolf is a peaceful Indian, and has his permission to leave the reservation. He hopes that nothing but kindness will be shown the old chief in his travels, and bespeaks the confidence of any white settlers that he may meet on the way. You boys must have been scared out of your wits. Lone Wolf only wanted to show you this letter."

Sargent conversed with the old chief in Spanish, the other Indians were signaled in, and they held a regular powwow. Dell and Joel shook hands with all the Indians, Sargent shared his tobacco with Lone Wolf, and on returning to their encampment at evening, each visitor was burdened with pickled beef and such other staples as the cow-camp afforded.

*—Adapted from "Wells Brothers,"
by Andy Adams.*

TO SEE WHAT YOU CAN DO

1. Write a different ending for this selection, beginning: "The first reconnoiter revealed the Indians halted some two hundred yards distant, and parleying among themselves." Read the six best endings to the class and vote on them.
2. Does this story illustrate the points of a good story? Give definite reasons for your answer.
3. Decide how you would rank it in a story contest with the two preceding stories.

BOOKS TO READ

If you would like to read more of ranch life, get the following books:

1. "Ranch Life and the Hunting Trail," by Theodore Roosevelt. Century.

    Describes the cowboy's life on the range, round-up, etc. 94 illustrations by Frederic Remington.

2. "Stories of the Great West," by Theodore Roosevelt. Century.

    Ten word-pictures of frontier and ranch life. Very interesting.

SUMMARY OF "THE BOY MAKES THE MAN"

It is well in one's reading to stop occasionally and sum up what one has read. It is something like the merchant taking an inventory of his goods in the store to see what he has on hand. Can you see any reason why this is important?

In this group of stories, you have had presented some fine ideals and examples of noble deeds. Which story or poem gave you the most pleasure and satisfaction? In class, take a vote to see how these several selections rank. Insist that every one give a good reason for his choice.

What ideals or traits of character pictured in this group of selections have inspired you to do in your own way as opportunity offers? What benefit have you gained from them?

Have these selections made you want to read more of the writings of these authors? If you have read more of them, report it in class. It would be interesting to make a list on the board of additional reading to see how much has been done.

It may interest you to have some two-minute talks on such topics as follow:

1. The Story in This Group I Like Best.
2. The Poem I Like Best.
3. One Trait I Have Become Interested In.
4. How the Boy Makes the Man.
5. The Value of Additional Reading.
6. How the Notes and Study Helps Have Interested Me.

The study of these selections may interest some in the class to try writing a story or poem of their own. You remember that Rudyard Kipling began his writing while a school boy. Hamlin Garland began also at an early age. If you should decide to try, remember the points of a good story.

GUIDES FOR THE STORY-TELLER

Note: To be read and discussed in class. It will make a good Speed and Comprehension Test.

A "written story-teller" is even funnier than an "oral" one.

Wherever there is a group of people the good story-teller is always welcome, because he can furnish a kind of entertainment which all the world loves. He affords amusement at the dinner-table, at a picnic, at a party, or around the evening fireside. Everything that happens is interesting to the good story-teller. That is why he knows how to tell even a commonplace happening in a way that interests his listeners.

Many of our best story writers began when schoolgirls and boys to develop their talents. To tell a story well takes interest, enthusiasm, imagination, and practice—much practice. No one knows how much he may possess of these qualities until he tries, and tries, and tries again. The finest gold and other precious metals are not commonly found on the surface of the earth, but deep down in it. The finest abilities in our natures are likewise usually found by going deep into ourselves. Training only will reveal them.

There are some rules that a story-teller or writer must follow to be successful. Here is an outline of those which are perhaps most important.

1. *Choose something interesting to tell.*

Have you ever thought that many things which occur

in your everyday life make capital stories? While fishing you are about to land a fine catch, when something happens which makes your companions laugh heartily. On a hiking trip you fail to follow the trail, and the result is an adventure. Your mother is suddenly called away to help a sick neighbor, and the responsibility of preparing the evening meal falls upon you. Very likely you will have a story to tell about your experience as a cook. A rainy day spent in the barn or in the attic may furnish a good story; a day at the circus will bring adventures worth telling.

The first questions to ask yourself, when you are thinking of telling a story of something that has happened to you, are: Will this interest other people? or, although it interested me, shall I only bore them by trying to tell it? If you cannot answer these questions, you can soon see, if you begin to tell your story, by the expressions on the faces of those who are listening, whether they like your story and the way you are telling it.

2. *Begin by rousing curiosity.*

If you wish people to listen to your stories, be sure to say something unusually interesting in the very first sentence. The easiest way to do this is to take them by surprise. Here are a good way and a bad way of beginning a story. Which is which?

a. I made a policeman jump this morning.
Jean was asking him the way to the Park when I felt the books I was carrying under my arm begin to slip. I caught at them, and

the policeman jumped back, saying indignantly: "Madam, I thought you were going to hit me!"

b. This morning as Jean and I were on our way to the library, we thought we'd go on afterward and sit in the Park a while; but we didn't know how to get there. I was carrying some heavy books under my arm. Presently we met a policeman and Jean asked him the way to the Park. Just then my books began to slip, etc.

3. *Omit what you do not need.*

In the anecdote just given, which words might have been omitted? They are not merely useless; they actually spoil the story by wearing out the listener's patience.

4. *Make the point tell.*

Many a good story is spoiled because the end is told first and the surprise is lost. The first sentence should rouse curiosity, not satisfy it. Was not this the case with the anecdote about the policeman? Did you not wonder how the speaker made a policeman jump? But you could not guess until the point of the story was reached.

So the most important thing to remember is not to give away your point until you have almost finished your story. Explanations that come after the point are never listened to; they merely spoil the impression made by the point.

SUMMARY OF THE RULES FOR STORY-TELLING

1. Ask yourself whether people will be interested in your story.
2. Cut it short if they look bored.
3. Make your first sentence rouse their curiosity.
4. Tell no more than is necessary to make your point clear.

5. Keep your point in mind from the beginning, and be careful not to give it away too soon.

6. Stop immediately after you have reached the point.

FOR CLASS DISCUSSION

1. Find in this book a story which seems to you particularly well told, and see whether every one in the class agrees with you.

2. Choose something that has happened to you lately to tell the class and see whether you can keep the rules given above.

3. Retell some story that you have read lately. Decide whether it was well told by the author.

THREE WAYS OF READING

In real life there is need of many types of reading. We need to read newspapers, magazines, time-tables, books, notices, advertisements, posters, directions. It will be worth while to stop and make a list of the types of reading you do in daily life. Bring your list to class with you.

In general, these many types of reading can be grouped into three kinds of reading.

Reading for Necessary New Information

Here is a good case: A girl hears of a new kind of homemade candy and wishes to make some of it. She finds the recipe (rĕs′ĭ-pē) and makes a careful study of it. Her reading is careful, point by point, and gives her new necessary information to enable her to do the thing she wishes.

Or it may be she wishes to make a new kind of apron. She gets the pattern and reads the directions carefully for the needed information.

Likewise a boy may desire to make a new kind of radio-receiver that he has heard about. He has not seen one of the kind, and knows nothing about it. It will be necessary for him to get the directions and drawings of the parts (the plans for construction) and make a detailed study of them—all of which is reading.

Such reading is called Study Reading. Much of this kind of reading is necessary, both in school and out of school. Here are some examples of it:

1. Taking up a new country in geography for the first time.

2. Taking up a new topic in history; a new topic in nature study or science; or in arithmetic.

3. Reading a vacation tour booklet, such as is furnished by railway and steamship companies.

Try to think of other examples or illustrations to mention in class discussion.

Reading for Additional Information

In our study of history, geography, science, and many other subjects, it is often necessary to find additional information to make the meaning as full and clear as we would like it. The knowledge we already have, and the book we are reading, have given us a good start—a beginning. But we desire to know more.

Reading for Enjoyment

There are times when one desires to read for enjoyment. Work is only a part of life. It was never intended that man should be a slave to work. Good fun, amusement, and enjoyment—what we sometimes call recreation (rĕk″rĕ-ā′shŭn)—are as necessary for a clean, strong, happy life. There are many leisure hours which one may well spend in reading a good story or a good book for the enjoyment there is in it.

Suppose, for example, because of a stormy night you were shut in with nothing to do. But there happen to be some good books at hand, like "Shen of the Sea," or "Arabian Nights," or "Child's History of the World," by V. M. Hillyer, or Kipling's "Just-So Stories"—what delightful hours are yours! Let it storm, for

"Books are magic carpets which waft us far away."

and you can go and enjoy what you will!

See if you can think of some experiences of your own when you read for enjoyment.

FOR DISCUSSION

Decide what kind of reading you believe the following to be:

1. A doctor meets a strange case which he has never had before. He desires to know the latest treatment of it.
2. A boy wishes to build a new kind of kite he has never seen.
3. A girl wishes to spend an evening reading poems from Untermeyer's "This Singing World," or from Sara Teasdale's "Rainbow Gold."
4. A mother wishes to take advantage of special sales and reads the department store "ads" on children's clothing.

5. A boy desires to know more about Edison, and takes an evening or two in reading Meadowcraft's "Boy's Life of Edison."

6. A farmer wishes to improve the soil in a certain field, and sends to the U. S. Department of Agriculture for a bulletin on soil fertility.

7. Make up a case from your own experience and see if your classmates can classify it correctly.

8. What kind of reading would the reading of crop reports be; production charts in a factory; weather and market reports?

THE USE OF REFERENCE BOOKS

Among the many kinds of reference books, there are four which persons of your age should begin to use frequently. They are the Encyclopedia, Yearbooks, Dictionary, and Atlas.

THE ENCYCLOPEDIA

The word encyclopedia (ĕn-sī″klȯ-pē′dĭ-à) has a curious origin. It comes from Greek words meaning "all-around education," or a complete circle of education. A vast amount of information is to be found in general encyclopedias. The best have something to tell you about almost any subject you can mention.

Each article in an encyclopedia is supposed to be written by some one who knows more about the subject than most other people. For this reason an encyclopedia is a useful book when we wish to find out about some particular thing.

Do you know how to find topics, subjects, or articles in the encyclopedia?

If you will look at the volumes of encyclopedias you

will find that they are arranged alphabetically like the dictionary. On the backs of good encyclopedias you will find index words which tell of the kinds of subjects treated in each volume. For example:

If you want to know what rubber is made of, you look for a volume toward the end where the letter *r* is. When you get the volume that contains articles on subjects that begin with *rub*, you will find among them an article that not only will tell you that rubber is made from the sap of a tree, but will give you a long account of the preparation and uses of rubber. A dictionary will tell you what rubber is; but if you wish to know more about it, you can read the article in a good encyclopedia.

If you can get the use of an encyclopedia, try finding the following subjects and report on one in class, telling exactly how you found it:

kite, salmon fisheries, airplane (aeroplane), Thomas Edison, paper, printing.

NOTE: Arrange for a class discussion of *The Best Way to Look Up a Topic in the Encyclopedia.*

An exercise like the following is good to give this training:

Place a set of good encyclopedias on a table so that the class may see the index words on the back of each volume. Place on the board a list of topics such as: wool, the Roosevelt Dam, forests, the Great Northern Railway, Sahara Desert, and other subjects.

Have the pupils tell in which volume a discussion of each of the topics would be found. Then assign some pupil to check the topics to see if they are found in the volumes as indicated.

Yearbooks

Other valuable reference books are the yearbooks. They are published annually and contain summaries of much valuable information that changes from year to year. For example, the value of farm products in 1920 would give us no true statement of the prosperity of farmers in the United States today. Such information is needed each year and therefore cannot be placed in encyclopedias. Many publishers of encyclopedias issue yearbooks to keep their encyclopedias up to date. Many States and some of the departments of the United States Government issue yearbooks for the same purpose. It is important for you to learn how to use such books, and to get the information they contain.

Using the Dictionary

Do you have a dictionary and the "dictionary habit"? What do you do when you meet a new word in reading, or hear a new word in conversation?

Perhaps you have not thought of it, but it is a fact that the meeting of new words is like the meeting of new friends. We have to learn them by certain characteristics if we are to be really acquainted with them.

In order to learn a word correctly you must know at least four things about it:

Its spelling; its pronunciation; its meaning; its use in the sentence.

The dictionary gives us this information about all the

words you will probably meet and need to learn. Very few people realize the variety of information contained in a dictionary. It is a wonderful book.

Make a practice of looking in the dictionary for the new words you meet in your reading, both in school and at home.

In order to use the dictionary quickly and profitably, it is necessary for you to know the following things, which you can work out in your study of English:

1. To say the alphabet forward and backward.
2. To arrange words in alphabetical order quickly.
3. To use the guide words at the top of the dictionary page to locate a word quickly in the dictionary.
4. To use diacritical marks to get the sound of the word correctly.
5. To select proper meanings to suit the use in a sentence.
6. To remember the different kinds of help that can be found in a dictionary and where each is.

There is not room here to go into a discussion of all of these points, but you can work them out in your classroom. It might be interesting to divide the class into two groups and have a contest on the following drills.

EXERCISES IN THE USE OF THE DICTIONARY

1. Say the letters of the alphabet forward and backward.
2. At a given signal open dictionaries to words beginning with L; Y; C; N.

3. Arrange the following list of words alphabetically:

home	amuse	please	baby	book-store
library	earthly	mother	country	world
India	opinion	sail	travel	silver
could	fun	joy	day	deep

4. Which letters of the alphabet are not represented as the beginning letter in the above list of words?

5. The following words begin with *d*. Arrange them alphabetically according to their second letters.

deep	decay	damp	December
doe	dungeon	dotage	dilatory
dale	divide	dogged	donate
ditch	debate	dismay	duck

6. The guide words at the top of the dictionary page tell you the first and last words of the two pages that are open before you. In the following list of words, which would come on the pages with the guide words *give—glory*?

glance	glen	glow	glacial
glare	germ	glimpse	good
George	globe	golden	glaze
ghastly	glitter	glade	gift

7. On a sheet of paper, list the following words. Look them up in the dictionary and mark them. Pronounce the words giving each syllable its proper stress. Tap the syllables with your first finger emphasizing the accented beat as you do in music.

ge og′ra phy	dis sim′i lar
in quir′y	dom′i nate
de liv′er y	em bar′go
cir′cu lar	mil′i ta ry
cler′i cal	o rig′i nal
e″lec tric′it y	ad ver′tise ment

The Atlas

While you are in school your geography will give you the location of nearly all the places you need to know, but after you have left school you will need to use a different kind of book for learning more about the geography of the world. Such a book is called an atlas.

An atlas is a collection of maps bound in one volume. The maps are usually even more complete than the maps in geography books. It is important to know how to use the atlas. One important thing about it is the index, which will save you a good deal of time. If you can get a good atlas, bring it to school to show the class what it contains, and how it can be used to advantage.

CHOOSE A MAGAZINE

Magazines form an important part of our reading. Good magazines contain the best current literature, and keep us in touch with current events. In order to get the most out of magazines we must know what type of material is offered in each, and how to use them for reference.

In reading a magazine we should first make a selection of the articles we will want to read, for, as a rule, it is unwise to read all a magazine contains for the same reasons that it is unwise to read all that a newspaper contains. One can often decide whether or not to read a magazine article by noting who wrote it. Be on the lookout to learn who are the best magazine writers.

Some magazines are devoted to *special subjects*. Among these are: *Popular Mechanics, The National Geographic Magazine, The Scientific American, The Survey,* and *The House Beautiful*. Another group of magazines deals with comments on *current events*. This group includes *Current Opinion, The Literary Digest, The Outlook, Review of Reviews, The World's Work, Collier's National Weekly*.

Magazines which feature *general articles* and *short stories* include: *Century Magazine, Atlantic Monthly, American Magazine, Harper's Magazine, Scribner's Magazine, Everybody's Magazine*.

What magazines are your favorites? Mention some magazines particularly good for children of your age.

READING THE NEWSPAPER

Roosevelt says: "Any healthy-minded American is bound to think well of his fellow-Americans if he only gets to know them." Show that your newspaper and magazine reading makes you know and understand more sympathetically the people in the different sections of our country.

Can you imagine a world without newspapers?

When Columbus discovered America, newspapers were unheard of. In the time of Queen Elizabeth, a hundred years later, they were just beginning to be printed—queer little sheets that you would not recognize as newspapers.

Until the invention of the telegraph, in 1844, newspapers could not give much except local news. They might publish letters from distant places; but as there were no trains before 1829, and no steamships before 1809, the news would be days, weeks, and even months old before it was printed.

The great development of the newspaper has been within the last fifty years. The ocean cables, as well as the telegraph, the wireless, and the telephone, help in the quick gathering of news. The little four-page sheet, published once a week, or not so often, has grown into the great newspaper of thirty-two pages or more, published several times a day as fresh news comes in. And this newspaper on Sunday becomes much larger still. There is as much reading in the Sunday newspaper of a large city as there is in a good-sized book.

Some people never learn how to read the newspaper. They begin at the left-hand upper corner of the first page and read straight through. Some of them even read the advertisements, though they may not need the things advertised. People who do this have little time to read anything else; and all their lives they miss the great pleasure that comes from reading good books.

The reason why the newspaper is so large is that there are so many different kinds of people in the world to be suited; people interested in so many different kinds of things, that the news which is dull to some is of the greatest interest to others. It is not expected that every one who takes or buys a newspaper will read it all.

The way ordinarily to begin to read a newspaper is to look first for the news that is most important for every one, and then for the news that is of special interest to you yourself. You can tell from the headlines what each news article is about. From the headline alone you can tell whether you should read the article or not.

But what news is most important? The news that concerns the welfare of the greatest number of people. A great war, an earthquake, a presidential election, an important bill discussed or passed in Congress, a discovery in science, an invention, a big political or educational meeting—these are a few of the materials for news that should be read by every one. Most intelligent people like to read also about the new books and plays, about exhibitions of pictures, about concerts and lectures.

But much space in the newspapers is given to matters that concern very few people—murders, robberies, accidents, scandals. Why should we wish to spend much time reading about such things? As long as people wish to know the details of these unpleasant things, the newspapers will make space for them, even if more important and valuable news has to be crowded out. If thousands of readers of a great newspaper stopped being interested in the horrible things that happen to only a few people in the world, the great newspapers would stop giving so much space to them. It is the people of a country who make the newspapers what they are. When the people care more about the big, important things of life, the newspapers will print more about such things.

Besides looking for the important news and that in

which you have special reason to be interested, another good plan in reading the newspaper is to allow yourself only a certain amount of time each day for doing it. Say to yourself: "I will read as much as I can in twenty minutes —or less—and let the rest go." If you read the most important news first, you will not miss much by skipping the rest. Or if you have only a little more time to give, read the headlines only.

You might have a competition in the class to see who can, for a week, read the same newspaper in the least time, and get the most news out of it.

TREASURE

O for a book and a shady nook,
Either indoors or out,
With the green leaves whispering overhead,
Or the street cries all about!
Where I may read all at my ease
Both of the New and Old,
For a jolly good book whereon to look
Is better to me than gold.

—Adapted from an Old Rhyme.

WHO HATH A BOOK

Who hath a book
  Has friends at hand,
And gold and gear[1]
  At his command;
And rich estates,
  If he but look,
Are held by him
  Who hath a book.

Who hath a book
  Has but to read
And he may be
  A king indeed;
His kingdom is
  His inglenook.[2]
All this is his
  Who hath a book.

—WILBUR DICK NESBIT.

THINGS TO TALK ABOUT

1. How would the world be different if there were nothing to read?
2. Explain: "Where I may read all at my ease
    Both of the New and Old."
3. Tell about the best friend you have met in a book.
4. What story can you recommend to your classmates in which you think they might be willing to "spend a day"?

[1] gear: tools, materials to work with.
[2] inglenook: a corner by the fireplace.

NO BOOKS

Suppose there were no books—
No books to read in cozy nooks,
No books to feed the hungry mind,
And teach the art of being kind.

No books to while an hour away,
To link today with yesterday;
No books to charm us for awhile,
To bring a tear or lure a smile.

But there are books, praise God above;
And, if we have books, and we have love,
We can dispense with other things;
For 'tis books, not crowns, that make men kings.
—STANLEY E. CRABB.

THE KEY OF STONE

Mr. Hendrik Van Loon, an historian, wrote a book for his two boys who were eight and twelve years old. He wrote what he thought they ought to know about the history of the past six thousand years. And he made ink pictures for the book with matches instead of with pens. At the beginning of the book he says to his boys:

"Wherever we go we must carry our warm cloak of human sympathy and understanding, for vast tracts of land will prove to be sterile desert—swept by storms of popular prejudice and personal greed, and unless we come well prepared we shall forsake our faith in humanity, and that, dear boys, would be the worst thing that could happen to any of us."

Mr. Van Loon doesn't wish his sons to accept all he says without weighing the ideas of others. And if, after careful study, they agree with other historians rather than with him, he is quite willing:

"Whenever you have a chance, take counsel with other travelers who have passed along the same route before. Compare their observations with mine, and if this leads you to different conclusions, I shall certainly not be angry with you."

You can get the first part of this interesting story in a book called "Ancient Man," by H. W. Van Loon, or you can get the large full history in his book, "The Story of Mankind."

Did you ever stop to think that the books we can buy so cheaply and use so commonly have taken thousands of years to be developed as we now find them?

Thousands of years ago when messages were sent to people who spoke other languages, the messengers did not carry written letters, but objects which had special meaning. When the first white man came to America the Indians were keeping their records and sending their messages in this way. You remember the story of how an unfriendly tribe of Indians sent to Miles Standish, Captain of Plymouth, a bunch of arrows, tied with a snakeskin.

Miles Standish knew that this meant the Indians intended to attack the colony; so he frightened them by sending back a snakeskin filled with bullets and powder.

But as a long message was hard to carry if many objects were necessary to tell it, gradually pictures began to take the place of objects.

These rude records and pictures are interesting to us, not only because they tell us how people lived in ancient times, but because they show us the first steps in the art of writing.

Knowing the meaning and pronunciation of these words will help you understand the following story better:

>curlicues hieroglyphics precise
>guttural re-translate phonetic
>basalt

Pronounce:

>Phœnicians: fē-nĭsh′ĭ-ans.
>Napoleon Bonaparte: nȧ-pō′lĕ-ŭn bō′nȧ-pärt.
>Jean François Champollion: zhạn frăn′swäh shon-pŏl′yon.
>King Ptolemy: tŏl′ē-mĭ.
>Cleopatra: klē″ȯ-pā′trȧ.

Fifty years before the birth of Christ, the Romans conquered Egypt. When they first set foot there, the country was already terribly old. More than six thousand and five hundred years had gone by since the history of the people of Egypt had begun. While the Romans were still savages who chased wolves and bears with clumsy stone axes, the Egyptians were writing books, were skilled doctors and surgeons, and were teaching their children multiplication tables. They had long since learned the art of writing.

We are so familiar with writing that we cannot understand how people ever managed to live without books and newspapers and magazines. But did you ever stop to think what happens when you write a letter? You put a lot of dots and dashes upon a piece of paper—you add a few more dots and dashes upon an envelope, and you carry your letter to the mailbox, together with a two-cent stamp. You have changed a number of spoken words into a number of pothooks and scrawls. But how did you know how to make your curlicues in such a fashion that both the postman and the person to whom you were writing could retranslate them into spoken words. You knew because some one had taught you how to draw the precise figures which represented the sound of your spoken words.

Just take a few letters and see how the game is played. We make a guttural noise and we write down a "G." We let the air pass through our closed teeth and we write down "S." We open our mouths wide and make a noise like a steam engine and the sound is written down "H." It took the human race thousands and thousands of years to discover how written marks could stand for sounds, and the credit for the discovery goes to the Egyptians. Of course they did not use the letters which have been used to print this book. They had a system of their own.

The Egyptian system was much prettier than ours but not so simple. It consisted of little figures of things about the house and farm, of knives and ploughs and birds and pots and pans. These little figures they scratched and painted on the walls of temples, on the coffins of dead kings, and on the dried leaves of a plant called papyrus. From papyrus they made flat sheets to write upon, something like our paper; and indeed our word *paper* comes from *papyrus*, although our paper, of course, is not made from papyrus but from grass, sawdust, and other things.

But when the Romans conquered Egypt, they were not interested in the Egyptian writing. They did not know that their own writing, which they had imitated from the Greek, came from the Phœnician writing, and that the Phœnicians had borrowed their writing from the Egyptians. So when they ruled Egypt they did not read or try to preserve the old books of the Egyptians. Later, when the Romans had gone, Egypt was in the hands of the Turks and Arabs, and they did not try to keep any writing but their own. So the Egyptian writing was forgotten.

But at the end of the eighteenth century, a French general, Napoleon Bonaparte, took an army to Egypt on his way to fight the British in India. Among his officers was one who liked to poke about among the ruins. He was stationed on the western branch of the mouth of the Nile, which is called the Rosetta.

One day he found there a strange black stone covered with picture-writing. It was a slab of black basalt, and it had on it three different kinds of writing. Of these only one was known: it was Greek. Now people could read the Greek; and they thought that the other writings would probably have the same contents as that in the Greek. So they went to work to study it. They thought that they might have on this stone the key to the old Egyptian writing. They were right. But it took more than thirty years of hard work to make the key fit the lock.

The man who gave his life to the study of this language was Jean François Champollion. At the age of nineteen he was appointed a professor of history at one of the French universities, and there he began his great work of translating the pictures on the Rosetta Stone.

After Napoleon left Egypt, the English went there. They found the Rosetta Stone and sent it home to the British Museum, where you may see it today. But the writing had been copied and taken to France where Champollion could use it.

The Greek text told about King Ptolemy V and his wife Cleopatra, the grandmother of the famous Cleopatra about whom Shakespeare wrote. One of the other inscriptions was in hieroglyphics, which was the sacred writing taught only to priests. The third was in a different kind of writing used by the common people, and called demotic. After twenty years of hard work Champollion could read only fourteen of the little figures on the stone, even though he was sure that, taken all together, they meant the same thing as he could read in the Greek. Finally, in 1823, however, he printed the first book ever written about the Egyptian hieroglyphics. Other scholars followed his methods, and today Egyptian writing can be read as certainly as we can read the print of a newspaper. When you understand how the Egyptians did their writing, you will realize what a great piece of work Champollion did.

Of course you know what a sign language is. Every Indian story has something about queer messages written in the form of little pictures. Hardly a boy has not at some time invented a sign language of his own, and all Boy Scouts are familiar with sign languages. Now suppose you were Champollion and were reading an old papyrus which told the story of a farmer living on the banks of the Nile. Suddenly you came upon the picture of a man with a saw.

"Very well," you said, "that means that the farmer went out and cut a tree down." Perhaps you were right.

Then you took another page of hieroglyphics. It told about a queen who lived to be eighty-two years old, and in the middle of the page was the same picture of the man with a saw. This was very puzzling. Queens do not go about cutting down trees—especially queens who are eighty-two years old. The picture must mean something else. But what?

Champollion found that the Egyptians used a kind of writing that we call phonetic. If we were going to use phonetic writing by means of a picture of a man with a saw, we should have two meanings for the picture: one would be a "saw," with which a tree could be cut down; the other would be the past tense of the verb "see."

At the top of page 280 is a modern English sentence done in Egyptian hieroglyphics:

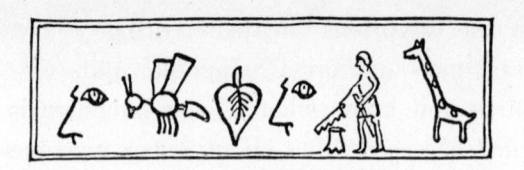

The cut at left may mean either "eye" or "I." The cut at right is either an animal which gathers honey and stings you if you touch it, or the verb "be." Or it may be the first part of a word, as in "be-come" or "be-lieve." In this case, the next picture would represent the sound of the second part of the word. So, if you put "be" and "leaf" together, you get the word "believe."

Then comes another "eye" or "I," followed by the man with the saw.

Finally, you get a picture of a giraffe. It means "giraffe" because the word has come from the old sign language in which a picture of a thing stood for the thing.

Then what does the sentence mean?

The Egyptian system, once invented, was developed during thousands of years. Gradually the most important figures came to mean single letters or sounds, which the Egyptians could use as we use our letters.

And this is the wonderful system of writing invented many thousands of years ago, which later, when it was once lost, it took men thirty years to learn how to read.

—From "Ancient Man," by Hendrik Van Loon.

TO TEST YOUR COMPREHENSION AND MEMORY

1. Did one group of people make our alphabet?
2. How long has it taken for it to be developed?
3. With what did our alphabet begin?
4. For what did these pictures stand?
5. In what way do we benefit by the work of Champollion?
6. Explain: "They thought that they might have on this stone the key to the old Egyptian writing. They were right. But it took more than thirty years of hard work to make the key fit the lock."
7. List the steps in the making of our alphabet.

VOLUNTEER WORK

1. When you have read the English sentence done in Egyptian hieroglyphics, "I believe I saw a giraffe," you may wish to try at home to make another sentence.
2. Bring it to school for the class to read if you succeed in making a clear one.
3. Divide the class into groups to look up and report on:

   a. The Phœnician Alphabet.
   b. The Indian Picture Writing.
   c. Morse Alphabet.
   d. Chinese Contribution to Writing.
   e. The First Printing Press.

4. With pictures write some picture sentences of your own.

FUN AND HUMOR IN PROSE AND VERSE

Some reading ought to be just for Fun and Pleasure, for—

> *"A little nonsense, now and then,*
> *Is relished by the best of men."*

So rules of study are now suspended, the serious affairs of classroom work are laid aside, and Fun, Humor, Wit, and Laughter are ushered in by Fool Jester. Bounding upon the stage in his motley make-up, his cap and bells a-tinkle, he bids us listen:

> *"Good people all, of every sort,*
> *Give ear unto my song;*
> *And if you find it wondrous short,*
> *It will not hold you long."*

Now let me introduce my comrades:

Fun—a comical, rollicking fellow, always ready to provoke Laughter, the pal of Mirth and friend of Drollery.

Humor—a kindly fellow, often dignified and always quite well-mannered. Sometimes whimsical and playful.

Wit—a sharp, quick, flashing fellow. Often cold and cruel. Sometimes gentle and good-natured.

Laughter—a jolly fellow, wreathed with dimpled smiles. Full of gentle merriment but sometimes loud and boisterous.

Here and there I give a quaint moral to live by; for—

> *"Though but a motley Fool am I*
> *Who lives by wit and mirth,*
> *I sometimes preach, and also teach*
> *The wiser ones of earth."*

Do you enjoy reading just for the fun, wit, humor, and drollery? If you do, you will enjoy a group of "Rhymes Without Reason," in "This Singing World," by Louis Untermeyer.

Kate Douglas Wiggin and Nora Archibald Smith have compiled "Golden Numbers," in which there is a group of poems, "In Merry Mood," full of fun and humor.

In "The Home Book of Verse for Young Folks," by Burton Stevenson, there is a group of verses called "Just Nonsense."

Bring into class some of the poems you like best in any of these volumes and talk them over. Try to explain why each is funny.

LIMERICKS

NOTE: A limerick is a nonsense poem of five lines. You will notice that lines one, two, and five rhyme and have three stresses; and that lines three and four rhyme and have two stresses.

What is the difference between *fun* and *humor?* Decide under which heading you will put each selection in this group.

There was an Old Man in a tree
Who was horribly bored by a Bee;
   When they said, "Does it buzz?"
   He replied, "Yes, it does!
It's a regular brute of a Bee."

—EDWARD LEAR.

There was a young lady of Niger
Who smiled as she rode on a tiger;
   They returned from the ride
   With the lady inside
And the smile on the face of the tiger.

—COSMO MONKHOUSE.

A tutor who tooted the flute
Tried to tutor two tooters to toot.
  Said the two to the tutor,
   "Is it harder to toot or
To tutor two tooters to toot?"

—CAROLYN WELLS.

RHYMES WITHOUT REASON

NOTE: There is a kind of nonsense verse which is funny merely because it strings together lines about things that are as unexpected as they are absurd. Often there is a surprise to make us laugh in each stanza. The following two poems are good examples of it

THE CAMEL'S PLAINT

Canary birds feed on sugar and seed,
  Parrots have crackers to crunch;
And as for the poodles, they tell me the noodles
  Have chickens and cream for their lunch.
    But there's never a question
    About my digestion—
Anything does for me!

Cats, you're aware, can repose in a chair,
  Chickens can roost upon rails;
Puppies are able to sleep in a stable,
  And oysters can slumber in pails.
    But no one supposes
    A poor camel dozes—
Any place does for me!

Lambs are inclosed where it's never exposed,
   Coops are constructed for hens;
Kittens are treated to houses well heated,
   And pigs are protected by pens.
      But a camel comes handy
      Wherever it's sandy—
   Anywhere does for me!

People would laugh if you rode a giraffe
   Or mounted the back of an ox;
It's nobody's habit to ride on a rabbit
   Or try to bestraddle a fox.
      But as for a camel, he's
      Ridden by families—
   Any load does for me!

A snake is as round as a hole in the ground,
   And weasels are wavy and sleek;
And no alligator could ever be straighter
   Than lizards that live in a creek.
      But a camel's all lumpy
      And bumpy and humpy—
   Any shape does for me!

—CHARLES EDWARD CARRYL.

Do you feel sorry for the Camel?

There follow some verses which warn us of the dangers to be encountered in the jungles.

How to Tell the Wild Animals

If ever you should go by chance
   To jungles in the East,
And if there should to you advance
   A large and tawny beast,
If he roars at you as you're dyin'
You'll know it is the Asian Lion.

Or if some time when roaming around,
   A noble wild beast greets you,
With black stripes on a yellow ground,
   Just notice if he eats you.
This simple rule may help you learn
The Bengal Tiger to discern.

If strolling forth, a beast you view,
   Whose hide with spots is peppered,
As soon as he has lept on you,
   You'll know it is the Leopard.
'Twill do no good to roar with pain,
He'll only lep and lep again.

Though to distinguish beasts of prey
   A novice might nonplus,
The Crocodiles you always may
   Tell from Hyenas thus:
Hyenas come with merry smiles;
But if they weep, they're Crocodiles.

—CAROLYN WELLS.

THE COYOTE

Samuel L. Clemens, better known as Mark Twain, was one of our most delightful humorists. Sometimes his humor was comical and rollicking; sometimes it was gentle and sly. Note how it appears in the story of the coyote.

Humor is sometimes produced by play on words, word-tricks, or by situations which perplex a person and make him seem foolish. There are other ways to arouse our sense of fun and humor, such as ridiculous situations, impossible or very unusual in ordinary life, or situations that are odd and queer. But whatever may be the source of humor, there is always in it an element of something unexpected.

1. What do you think is the most humorous point in the story?

2. By what devices does Mark Twain bring out his humor? Illustrate by selecting certain points in the story.

3. If you can find a picture of a coyote, it may help you to enjoy the description.

The coyote of the farther deserts is a long, slim, sick, and sorry-looking skeleton with a gray wolf-skin stretched over it, a tolerably bushy tail that forever sags down with a despairing expression of forsakenness and misery, a furtive and evil eye, and a long, sharp face, with slightly lifted lip and exposed teeth.

He has a genteel slinking expression all over. The coyote is a living, breathing allegory of want. He is always hungry. He is always poor, out of luck, and friendless. The meanest creatures despise him, and even the fleas would desert him for a velocipede. He is so spiritless and cowardly that, even while his exposed teeth are pretending a threat, the rest of his face is apologizing for it. And he is so homely! so scrawny, and ribby, and coarse-haired, and pitiful!

When he sees you he lifts his lip and lets a flash of his teeth out, and then turns a little out of the course he was pursuing, depresses his head a bit, and strikes a long, soft-footed trot through the sagebrush, glancing over his shoulder at you from time to time, till he is about out of easy pistol range, and then he stops and takes a deliberate survey of you. He will trot fifty yards, and stop again; another fifty, and stop again; and, finally, the gray of his gliding body blends with the gray of the sagebrush and he disappears.

But, if you start a swift-footed dog after him, you will enjoy it ever so much—especially if it is a dog that has a good opinion of himself and has been brought up to think that he knows something about speed. The coyote will go swinging gently off on that deceitful trot of his, and every little while he will smile a fraudful smile over his shoulder that will fill that dog entirely full of encouragement and worldly ambition, and make him lay his head still lower to the ground, and stretch his neck farther to the front, and pant more fiercely, and move his furious legs with a yet wilder frenzy, and leave a broader and broader and higher and denser cloud of desert sand, smoking behind, and marking his long wake across the level plain!

All this time the dog is only a short twenty feet behind

the coyote, and, to save the life of him he can not get perceptibly closer; and he begins to get aggravated, and it makes him madder and madder to see how gently the coyote glides along, and never pants or sweats, or ceases to smile; and he grows still more and more incensed to see how shamefully he has been taken in by an entire stranger, and what an ignoble swindle that long, calm, soft-footed trot is.

And next the dog notices that he is getting fagged, and that the coyote actually has to slacken speed a little, to keep from running away from him. And then that town-dog is mad in earnest, and he begins to strain, and weep, and swear, and paw the sand higher than ever, and reach for the coyote with concentrated and desperate energy.

This spurt finds him six feet behind the gliding enemy, and two miles from his friends. And then, in the instant that a wild new hope is lighting up his face, the coyote turns and smiles blandly upon him once more, and with a something about it which seems to say:

"Well, I shall have to tear myself away from you, but —business is business, and it will not do for me to be fooling along this way all day." And forthwith there is a rushing sound, and the sudden splitting of a long crack through the atmosphere; and behold, that dog is solitary and alone amidst a vast solitude!

—S. L. CLEMENS (MARK TWAIN).

THE AKOND OF SWAT

Who, or why, or which, or what,
    Is the Akond of Swat?

Is he tall or short or dark or fair?
Does he sit on a stool or a sofa or a chair,
    Or squat,
      The Akond of Swat?

Is he wise or foolish, young or old?
Does he drink his soup and his coffee cold,
    Or hot,
      The Akond of Swat?

Does he sing or whistle, jabber or talk,
And when riding abroad does he gallop or walk
    Or trot,
      The Akond of Swat?

Many stanzas follow. The author ends with:

Some one, or nobody, knows, I wot
Who, or which, or why, or what
    Is the Akond of Swat!

—EDWARD LEAR.

NOTE: Now can you tell who he is? What is the source of the humor in this selection—words or whimsical ideas? or both?

THE BLIND MEN AND THE ELEPHANT

(A Hindoo Fable)

It was six men of Indostan
  To learning much inclined,
Who went to see the Elephant
  (Though all of them were blind).
That each by observation
  Might satisfy his mind.

The *First* approached the Elephant,
  And happening to fall
Against his broad and sturdy side,
  At once began to bawl:
"God bless me! but the Elephant
  Is very like a wall!"

The *Second*, feeling of the tusk,
  Cried, "Ho! what have we here
So very round and smooth and sharp?
  To me 'tis mighty clear
This wonder of an Elephant
  Is very like a spear!"

The *Third* approached the animal,
  And happening to take
The squirming trunk within his hands,
  Thus boldly up and spake:
"I see," quoth he, "the Elephant
  Is very like a snake!"

The *Fourth* reached out an eager hand,
　And felt about the knee.
"What most this wondrous beast is like
　Is mighty plain," quoth he;
"'Tis clear enough the Elephant
　Is very like a tree!"

The *Fifth*, who chanced to touch the ear,
　Said: "E'en the blindest man
Can tell what this resembles most;
　Deny the fact who can,
This marvel of an Elephant
　Is very like a fan!"

The *Sixth* no sooner had begun
　About the beast to grope,
Than, seizing on the swinging tail
　That fell within his scope,
"I see," quoth he, "the Elephant
　Is very like a rope!"

And so these men of Indostan
　Disputed loud and long,
Each in his own opinion
　Exceedingly stiff and strong,
Though each was partly in the right,
　And all were in the wrong!

Moral

So oft in disputatious wars,
  The disputants, I ween,
Rail on in utter ignorance
  Of what the others mean,
And prate about an Elephant
  Not one of them has seen!

—JOHN GODFREY SAXE.

1. Does this poem amuse you? Why?
2. Read the stanza that tells the real point of the poem.
3. When people are disputing about something, what is it wise to do?

THEIR NEIGHBORS' FAULTS

Why human kind should ever be
So keen their neighbors' faults to see,
While (wonderful to tell!) their own
Are to themselves almost unknown,
This ancient fable clearly shows:
Once on a time—the story goes—
Great Jove, the wise Olympian King,
Proclaimed to each created thing,
That he would hold a special court
Where all might come and make report
Of aught that each might deem it wise
To change in feature, form, or size.
He promised quickly to redress
All imperfections, large or less;

Whatever error or defect
Each in his person might detect.
First came the *Monkey*. Naught had he
Of special fault—that *he* could see!
A paragon of wit and grace,
Who had—almost—a human face!
One seeks a finer form in vain,
Pray, why should such as *he* complain?
"But look at Bruin!" cried the ape:
Was ever such a clumsy shape?
And then, for life, condemned to wear
That ugly suit of shaggy hair!"
"Nay," said the bear, "I find my form
As I could wish. My fur is warm,
And looks, I think, extremely fine,
Good Master Ape, compared with thine!
But see the *Elephant!* his size
Is much too huge!—and I advise
(So ludicrous the beast appears)
To stretch his tail and crop his ears!"
"Nay," quoth the Elephant, who deems
His figure clear of all extremes,
"I can't complain—I'm quite content!"
But then he marveled what it meant
The *Whale* should be so huge and fat!
The *Ant* was sorry for the *Gnat!*
The *Gnat* reproached the tiny *Flea!*
How could one live so small as she?

Thus all the animals, in turn,
The faults of others could discern;
But not a creature, large or small,
His own defects could see at all!

—JOHN GODFREY SAXE.

1. Do you like this poem?
2. What other animals might have been included?
3. What is the main point of the poem?
4. Robert Burns, the Scottish poet, once said:

> "Oh, wad some power the giftie gie us
> To sae oursels as ithers sae us!
> It wad frae mony a blunder free us,
> And foolish notion!"

HOW PIGS WERE FIRST ROASTED

Charles Lamb, the author of the essay from which the following passage is taken, pretended that his account came from an old Chinese manuscript. His pretence of solemnity and authority adds to the fun. Select what you feel is the most humorous point in the story. Why? How does the author produce his humor—by word-play or situations?

Mankind, says a Chinese manuscript, for the first seventy thousand ages ate their meat raw; but the art of roasting, or rather broiling, was accidentally discovered in the manner following:

The swineherd Ho-ti, having gone out into the woods one morning, as his manner was, to collect mast[1] for his

---
[1] mast: nuts of the oak, beech, or chestnut, especially when used as food for swine.

hogs, left his cottage in the care of his eldest son, Bo-bo. The boy, being fond of playing with fire, as youngsters of his age commonly are, let some sparks escape into a bundle of straw. This kindled quickly and spread the conflagration[1] over every part of their poor house till it was reduced to ashes. Together with the cottage, a fine litter of young pigs perished.

Bo-bo was terribly frightened, not so much for the loss of the house, which he and his father could easily build up again from a few dry branches, but for the loss of the pigs.

While he was thinking what he should say to his father and wringing his hands over the smoking remnants of one of the pigs, he smelled something unlike any odor that had ever reached his nostrils before. What could it be from? Not from the cottage; he had smelled that before when it was burned. Not from any known herb, weed, or flower. At the same time his mouth began to water. He did not know what to think of this new experience.

[1] conflagration: a very destructive fire.

He next stooped to feel whether there were any signs of life in the pig at his feet. He burned his fingers, and to cool them he placed them, in his booby fashion, in his mouth. Some of the crumbs of the scorched skin had come away on his fingers, and for the first time in his life, he tasted—crackling!

Again he felt and fumbled at the pig. It did not burn him so much now. Still he licked his fingers. At length he understood that it was the pig he smelled, and the pig that tasted so delicious. He fell to tearing away handfuls of the scorched skin and of the flesh next it, and was cramming it down his throat when his father returned.

Finding the house burned down, Ho-ti began to beat his son, but could not drive him from the pig he was devouring until he had finished it.

"You graceless whelp, what are you devouring? Is it not enough that you have burned down three of my houses with your tricks, but you must be eating fire and I know not what— What have you there, I say?"

"O father, the pig, the pig! Do come and taste how nice the burnt pig eats."

The ears of Ho-ti tingled with horror that he should have a son who ate burnt pig instead of pig in its natural state. But Bo-bo soon raked another little pig out of the ashes and, pulling it apart, thrust the pieces into his father's hands, shouting: "Eat, eat, eat the burnt pig, father. Only taste it!" he went on, eating as fast as he could.

Ho-ti, still angry to see his son eating such unnatural

food, burned his fingers on the hot skin, and he also put his fingers into his mouth to ease the pain. As soon as he had tasted, he too set to eating. Between the two of them they ate the whole litter of nine little pigs.

Bo-bo was told that he must not let the secret be known among the neighbors; they would stone people who were

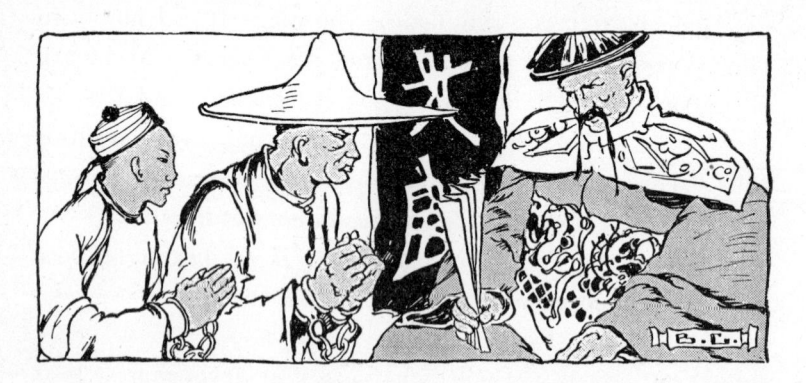

trying to improve upon their good, natural food. But it was soon observed that Ho-ti's cottage was burned down whenever he had a litter of little pigs.

At length Ho-ti and Bo-bo were watched and their terrible secret was discovered. They were arrested and taken to Pekin to be tried for the crime of eating unnatural food. The verdict was about to be given when the foreman of the jury asked that some of the food offered as evidence should be passed to the jury. It was offered, still hot, and burned the fingers of the jurymen. Immediately they all licked their fingers, and without another word, they brought in a verdict of "Not Guilty."

298

The judge was a shrewd fellow, and as soon as court was dismissed, he went out and bought all the pigs he could. In a few days his town house was observed to be on fire. The idea spread and soon there were fires in all directions. Fuel and pigs grew enormously dear all over the district. People built their houses slighter and slighter every day until it began to be feared that the art of architecture would be lost to the world. This custom of setting houses on fire continued until in the course of time some wise man discovered that the flesh of swine, or indeed of any other animal, might be cooked (*burnt*, they called it), without burning down a whole house. Then began the rude form of the gridiron. Roasting by the string or spit came in a century or two later. By such slow degrees, concludes the manuscript, do the most useful and seemingly the most obvious arts make their way among mankind.

—*Abridged from "A Dissertation Upon Roast Pig," by Charles Lamb.*

NOTE: If you wish to read more stories by Charles Lamb, there is a volume of "Tales from Shakespeare" which he wrote with his sister, Mary Lamb; and later on, you will wish to read some of his essays and letters.

If this story from old Chinese folk-tales should interest you, you may want to read "Shen of the Sea," by Arthur Chrisman. This book was awarded the John Newberry Medal, October, 1926, as being the most distinguished children's book during the year 1925.

A RILL FROM THE TOWN PUMP

Hawthorne is a great story-writer of New England. If he had not written his novels and short stories, we should know much less than we do about the lives and thoughts of our forefathers in New England. In this sketch he describes a scene in the old town of Salem such as few if any of us have ever known. It is not only interesting; it is amusing.

1. Select what seems to you the most amusing part.
2. If you wished to make the story serious, how could you do so?

(*Scene*—the corner of two principal streets—Essex and Washington Streets, Salem. The Town Pump talking through its nose.)

Noon, by the north clock! Noon, by the east! High noon, too, by these hot sunbeams which fall, scarcely aslope, upon my head, and almost make the water bubble and smoke in the trough under my nose. Summer or winter, nobody seeks me in vain; for, all day long, I am seen at the busiest corner, just above the market, stretching out my arms to rich and poor alike; and at night, I hold a lantern over my head, both to show where I am, and keep people out of the gutters.

At this sultry noontide, I am cupbearer to the parched populace, for whose benefit an iron goblet is chained to my waist. I cry aloud to all and sundry, in my plainest accents, and at the very tiptop of my voice: Here it is, gentlemen! Walk up, walk up, gentlemen. Here is the superior stuff! Here is the unadulterated ale of father Adam—better than strong beer, or wine of any price; here it is, by the hogshead or the single glass, and not a cent to pay! Walk up, gentlemen, walk up, and help yourselves!

It were a pity if all this outcry should draw no customers. Here they come. A hot day, gentlemen! Quaff and away again, so as to keep yourselves in a nice cool sweat. You, my friend, will need another cupful, to wash the dust out of your throat, if it be as thick there as it is on your cowhide shoes. I see that you have trudged half a score of miles today; and, like a wise man, have passed by the taverns, and stopped at the running brooks and well curbs. Otherwise, betwixt heat without and fire within, you would have been burned to a cinder, or melted down to nothing at all, in the fashion of a jellyfish. Drink, and make room for that other fellow. Who next? O, my little friend, you are let loose from school, and come hither to scrub your blooming face, and drown the memory of certain taps of the ferule,[1] and other schoolboy troubles, in a draught

---

[1] ferule: a rod or flat stick, like a pointer or ruler; sometimes used in older days to punish children—as in the days of "lickin' and larnin'."

from the Town Pump? Take it, pure as the current of your young life. Take it, and may your heart and tongue never be scorched with a fiercer thirst than now! There, my dear child, put down the cup, and yield your place to this elderly gentleman, who treads so tenderly over the paving-stones, that I suspect he is afraid of breaking them. What! he limps by, without so much as thinking of me. The thirsty dog, with his red tongue lolling out, does not scorn my hospitality, but stands on his hind legs, and laps eagerly out of the trough. See how lightly he capers away again!

Are you all satisfied? Then wipe your mouths, my good friends; and, while my spout has a moment's leisure, I will delight the town with a few historical reminiscences.[1] In far antiquity, a spring bubbled out of the leaf-strewn earth in the very spot where you now behold me on the sunny pavement. The water was as bright and clear, and deemed as precious, as liquid diamonds. The Indian sagamores[2] drank of it from time immemorial, till the fatal deluge of the fire-water burst upon the red men, and swept their whole race away from the cold fountains. Endicott and his followers came next, and often knelt down to drink, dipping their long beards in the spring. The richest goblet then was of birch bark. Governor Winthrop, after a journey afoot from Boston, drank here out of the hollow of his hand. The elder Higginson here wet his palm, and laid

---

[1] reminiscences: calling back to the mind past experiences; memories.
[2] sagamores: Indian chieftains among certain North American tribes.

it on the brow of the first town-born child. For many years it was the watering place, and, as it were, the washbowl of the vicinity—whither all decent folks resorted, to purify their visages and gaze at them afterward—at least the pretty maidens did—in the mirror it made. On Sabbath days, whenever a babe was to be baptized, the sexton filled his basin here, and placed it on the communion-table of the humble meetinghouse, which partly covered the site of yonder stately brick one. Thus, one generation after another was consecrated by its waters. Finally the fountain vanished. Cellars were dug on all sides, and cartloads of gravel flung upon its source, whence oozed a turbid stream, forming a mud puddle, at the corner of two streets. In the hot months, when its refreshment was most needed, the dust flew in clouds over the forgotten birthplace of the waters, now their grave. But, in the course of time, a town pump was sunk into the source of the ancient spring; and when the first decayed, another took its place—and then another, and still another—till here stand I, gentlemen and ladies, to serve you with my iron goblet. Drink and be refreshed! The water is as pure and cold as that which slaked the thirst of the red sagamore beneath the aged boughs, though now the gem of the wilderness is treasured under these hot stones, where no shadow falls but from the brick buildings. And be it the moral of my story, that, as this wasted and long-lost fountain is now known and prized again, so shall the virtues of cold water, too little valued since your fathers' days, be recognized by all.

Your pardon, good people! I must interrupt my stream of eloquence, and spout forth a stream of water, to replenish the trough for this teamster and his two yoke of oxen, who have come from Topsfield, or somewhere along that way. No part of my business is pleasanter than the watering of cattle. Look! how rapidly they lower the watermark on the sides of the trough, till their capacious stomachs are moistened with a gallon or two apiece, and they can afford time to breathe it in, with sighs of calm enjoyment. Now they roll their quiet eyes around the brim of their monstrous drinking vessel. An ox is your true toper.

I shall say nothing of my all-important aid on washing-days; though, on that account alone, I might call myself the household god of hundreds of families. Far be it from me also to hint, my respectable friends, at the show of dirty faces which you would present, without my pains to keep you clean. Nor will I remind you how often, when the midnight bells make you tremble for your combustible town, you have fled to the Town Pump, and found me always at my post, firm amid the confusion, and ready to drain my vital current in your behalf.

From my spout, and such spouts as mine, must flow the stream that shall cleanse our earth of the vast portion of its crime and anguish, which has gushed from the fiery fountains of the still. In this mighty enterprise, the cow shall be my great confederate. Milk and water! The Town Pump and the Cow! Such is the glorious copartnership that shall tear down the distilleries and brewhouses, uproot the vineyards, shatter the cider-presses, ruin the tea and coffee trade, and, finally, monopolize the whole business of quenching thirst. Then, Poverty shall pass away from the land, finding no hovel so wretched where her squalid form may shelter itself. Then Disease, for lack of other victims, shall gnaw its own heart, and die. Then Sin, if she do not die, shall lose half her strength. When that inward fire shall be extinguished, the heat of passion cannot but grow cool, and war—the drunkenness of nations—perhaps will cease. At least there will be no war of households.

Ahem! Dry work, this speechifying; especially to an unpracticed orator. Do, some kind person, pump a stroke or two, just to wet my whistle. Thank you, sir!

One o'clock! Nay, then, if the dinner bell begins to speak, I may as well hold my peace. Here comes a pretty young girl of my acquaintance, with a large stone pitcher for me to fill. Hold out your vessel, my dear! There it is, full to the brim; so now run home, peeping at your sweet image in the pitcher as you go; and forget not, in a glass of my own liquor, to drink—"SUCCESS TO THE TOWN PUMP!"

—*Adapted from Nathaniel Hawthorne.*

FOR MORE FUN

This story is excellent for both oral and silent reading. Read it silently first for your own enjoyment. Then prepare what you think is one of the most interesting parts in it for oral reading to the class. In your oral reading, try to put yourself in the place of the town pump and speak in the same manner that you think the pump did.

TO SEE WHICH STORY IS LIKED BEST

1. Which do you like the best: "The Coyote," "How Pigs Were First Roasted," or "A Rill from the Town Pump"?
2. In which of the stories is a great fuss made about a very simple matter? Is it always funny to read about or to see such a thing? Should you have been amused to have watched what happened in this story?
3. In which story is the fun more in the use of unexpected words? Could you describe a dog or a cat in the way words are used in this story?
4. In which story does the fun come from a pretence that one thing is another? What is the speaker like? Show how the comparison is carried out.

NOTE: If you wish to read more by Hawthorne, there is a volume called "Tanglewood Tales," in which he retells many old Greek myths about gods and goddesses in a way that most people like very much.

Perhaps some one in the class will volunteer to look up something about his life and report it in class.

SUMMARY

Now that we have finished this group of *Fun and Humor in Prose and Verse*, let us compare our ideas about them.

Discuss and vote on the following questions in class:

1. Which poem do you like best? Give specific reasons.
2. Which prose selection do you like best? Why?
3. What similar selections, in prose or poetry, have you read?
4. What was the best supplementary selection brought to class?
5. Have these selections given you a better idea of humor and how it is developed in writing?
6. What differences have you noticed between *fun* and *humor?*

FRIENDS AND NEIGHBORS

Men are social beings. They do not like to live alone. They form themselves into groups, into families, into tribes, and into nations, for enjoyment and for protection. They build houses and towns and cities.

They make laws to live by and houses to live in, churches for worship, and public buildings for business and for the making of laws.

One of the ways in which we can all have a part is to be a good citizen and a good neighbor. To live happily with our friends and neighbors is something we can all try to do.

In our own homes are other friends. These friends are books. They help us to understand the people we meet every day. And he who understands will be a good neighbor, and a good neighbor will never lack a friend.

NEIGHBORS AND FRIENDS

So long as we love, we serve. So long as we are loved by others, I would almost say that we are indispensable: and no man is useless while he has a friend.

—ROBERT LOUIS STEVENSON.

BEING NEIGHBORLY

Louisa M. Alcott (1832–88) was one of the best story-writers for young people. This story is taken from her book "Little Women." It is interesting to know that Miss Alcott began writing the book under great discouragement. She did not think the story worth while. Her publishers thought it dull. But the book was a great success from the first. In two months the first edition was exhausted and many, very many editions have been printed since that time.'

"Jo" in the story is Miss Alcott herself. The other girls are her sisters. Mrs. March is her mother.

As you read, notice the beautiful home life, and the fine character of Jo and of Laurie.

Read silently and rapidly.

"What in the world are you going to do now, Jo?" asked Meg, one snowy afternoon, as her sister came tramping through the hall, in rubber boots, old sack and hood, with a broom in one hand and a shovel in the other.

"Going out for exercise," answered Jo, with a mischievous twinkle in her eyes.

"I should think two long walks this morning would have been enough! It's cold and dull out; and I advise you to stay, warm and dry, by the fire, as I do," said Meg, with a shiver.

"Never take advice! Can't keep still all day, and, not being a pussy-cat, I don't like to doze by the fire. I like adventures, and I'm going to find some."

Meg went back to toast her feet and read "Ivanhoe"; and Jo began to dig paths with great energy. The snow was light, and with her broom she soon swept a path all round the garden, for Beth to walk in when the sun came out, and the invalid dolls needed air. Now, the garden separated the Marches' house from that of Mr. Laurence. Both stood in a suburb of the city, which was still country-like, with groves and lawns, large gardens, and quiet streets. A low hedge parted the two estates. On one side was an old, brown house, looking rather bare and shabby, robbed of the vines that in summer covered its walls, and the flowers which then surrounded it. On the other side was a stately stone mansion suggesting every sort of comfort and luxury, from the big coach-house and well-kept grounds to the conservatory and the glimpses of lovely things one caught between the rich curtains. Yet it seemed a lonely, lifeless sort of house; for no children frolicked on the lawn, no motherly face ever smiled at the windows, and few people went in and out, except the old gentleman and his grandson.

To Jo's lively fancy, this fine house seemed a kind of enchanted palace, full of splendors and delights, which no one enjoyed. She had long wanted to behold these hidden glories, and to know the "Laurence boy," who looked as if he would like to be known, if he only knew how to begin. She had not seen him since she met him at their neighbor's party. Jo began to think he had gone away, when one day she spied a brown face at an upper window, looking wistfully down into their garden, where Beth and Amy were snowballing one another.

"That boy is suffering for society and fun," she said to herself. "His grandpa does not know what's good for him, and keeps him shut up all alone. He needs a party of jolly boys to play with, or somebody young and lively. I've a great mind to go over and tell the old gentleman so!"

The idea amused Jo, who liked to do daring things, and was always scandalizing Meg. The plan of "going over" was not forgotten; and when the snowy afternoon came, Jo resolved to try what could be done. But she saw Mr. Laurence drive off, as she sallied out to dig her way down to the hedge; she paused, and took a survey. All quiet,—curtains down at the lower windows; servants out of sight, and nothing human visible but a curly black head leaning on a thin hand at the upper window.

"There he is," thought Jo, "poor boy! all alone and sick this dismal day. It's a shame! I'll toss up a snowball, make him look out, and then say a kind word to him."

Up went a handful of soft snow, and the head turned at once, showing a face which lost its listless look in a minute, as the big eyes brightened and the mouth began to smile. Jo nodded and laughed, and flourished her broom as she called out:

"How do you do? Are you sick?"

Laurie opened the window, and croaked out as hoarsely as a raven:

"Better, thank you. I've had a bad cold, and been shut up a week."

"I'm sorry. What do you amuse yourself with?"

"Nothing; it's as dull as tombs up here."

"Don't you read?"

"Not much; they won't let me."

"Can't somebody read to you?"

"Grandpa does, sometimes; but my books don't interest him, and I hate to ask Brooke all the time."

"Have some one come and see you, then."

"There isn't any one I'd like to see. Boys make such a row, and my head is weak."

"Isn't there some nice girl who'd read and amuse you? Girls are quiet, and like to play nurse."

"Don't know any."

"You know us," began Jo, then laughed, and stopped.

"So I do! Will you come, please?" cried Laurie.

"I'm not quiet and nice; but I'll come, if mother will

let me. I'll go and ask her. Shut that window, like a good boy, and wait till I come.''

With that, Jo shouldered her broom and marched into the house, wondering what they would all say to her. Laurie was in a flutter of excitement at the idea of having company, and flew about to get ready; for, as Mrs. March said, he was "a little gentleman," and did honor to the coming guest by brushing his curly pate, putting on a fresh collar, and trying to tidy up his parlor, which, in spite of half a dozen servants, was anything but neat. Presently there came a loud ring, then a decided voice, asking for "Mr. Laurie," and a surprised-looking servant came running up to announce "a young lady."

"All right, show her up, it's Miss Jo," said Laurie, going to the door of his little parlor to meet Jo, who appeared, looking rosy and kind, and quite at her ease, with a covered dish in one hand, and Beth's three kittens in the other.

"Here I am, bag and baggage," she said briskly. "Mother sent her love, and was glad if I could do anything for you. Meg wanted me to bring some of her blancmange; she makes it very nicely, and Beth thought her cats would be comforting. I knew you'd laugh at them, but I couldn't refuse, she was so anxious to do something."

It so happened that Beth's funny loan was just the thing; for, in laughing over the kits, Laurie forgot his bashfulness, and grew sociable at once.

"That looks too pretty to eat," he said, smiling with

pleasure, as Jo uncovered the dish, and showed the blancmange, surrounded by a garland of green leaves, and the scarlet flowers of Amy's pet geranium.

"It isn't anything, only they all felt kindly, and wanted to show it. Tell the girl to put it away for your tea; it's so simple, you can eat it; and, being soft, it will slip down without hurting your sore throat. What a cosey room this is!"

"It might be if it was kept nice; but the maids are lazy, and I don't know how to make them mind. It worries me, though."

"I'll right it up in two minutes; for it only needs to have the hearth brushed, so—and the things made straight on the mantelpiece, so—and the books put here, and the bottles there, and your sofa turned from the light, and the pillows plumped up a bit. Now, then, you're fixed."

And so he was; for, as she laughed and talked, Jo had whisked things into place, and given quite a different air to the room. Laurie watched her in respectful silence; and when she beckoned him to his sofa, he sat down with a sigh of satisfaction, saying gratefully:

"How kind you are! Yes, that's what it wanted. Now please take the big chair, and let me do something to amuse my company."

"No; I came to amuse you. Shall I read aloud?" and Jo looked affectionately toward some inviting books near by.

"Thank you; I've read all those, and if you don't mind, I'd rather talk," answered Laurie.

"Not a bit; I'll talk all day if you'll only set me going. Beth says I never know when to stop."

"Is Beth the rosy one, who stays at home a good deal, and sometimes goes out with a little basket?" asked Laurie, with interest.

"Yes, that's Beth; she's my girl, and a regular good one she is, too."

"The pretty one is Meg, and the curly-haired one is Amy, I believe?"

"How did you find that out?"

Laurie colored up, but answered frankly, "Why, you see, I often hear you calling to one another, and when I'm alone up here, I can't help looking over at your house, you always seem to be having such good times. I beg your pardon for being so rude, but sometimes you forget to put down the curtain at the window where the flowers are; and when the lamps are lighted, it's like looking at a picture to see the fire, and you all round the table with your mother; her face is right opposite, and it looks so sweet behind the flowers, I can't help watching it. I haven't got any mother, you know"; and Laurie poked the fire to hide the little twitching of the lips that he could not control.

The solitary, hungry look in his eyes went straight to Jo's warm heart. She had been so simply taught that there was no nonsense in her head, and at fifteen she was as innocent and frank as any child. Laurie was sick and lonely; and, feeling how rich she was in home-love and happiness, she gladly tried to share it with him. Her face was friendly and her sharp voice unusually gentle as she said:

"We'll never draw that curtain any more, and I give you leave to look as much as you like. I just wish, though, instead of peeping, you'd come over and see us. Mother is so splendid, she'd do you heaps of good, and Beth would sing to you if *I* begged her to, and Amy would dance; Meg and I would make you laugh over our funny stage properties, and we'd have jolly times. Wouldn't your grandpa let you?"

"I think he would, if your mother asked him. He's very kind, though he does not look so; and he lets me do what I like, pretty much, only he's afraid I might be a bother to strangers," began Laurie, brightening more and more.

"We are not strangers, we are neighbors, and you needn't think you'd be a bother. We *want* to know you, and I've been trying to do it this ever so long. We haven't been here a great while, you know, but we have got acquainted with all our neighbors but you."

"You see grandpa lives among his books, and doesn't mind much what happens outside. Mr. Brooke, my tutor, doesn't stay here, you know, and I have no one to go about with me, so I just stop at home and get on as I can."

"That's bad. You ought to make an effort, and go visiting everywhere you are asked; then you'll have plenty of friends, and pleasant places to go to. Never mind being bashful; it won't last long if you keep going."

Laurie turned red again, but wasn't offended at being

accused of bashfulness; for there was so much good will in Jo, it was impossible not to take her blunt speeches as kindly as they were meant.

"Do you like your school?" asked the boy, changing the subject, after a little pause, during which he stared at the fire, and Jo looked about her, well pleased.

"Don't go to school; I'm a business man—girl, I mean. I go to wait on my great-aunt, and a dear, cross old soul she is, too," answered Jo.

Laurie opened his mouth to ask another question; but remembering just in time that it wasn't manners to make too many inquiries into people's affairs, he shut it again, and looked uncomfortable. Jo liked his good breeding, and didn't mind having a laugh at Aunt March, so she gave him a lively description of the fidgety old lady, her fat poodle, the parrot that talked Spanish, and the library where she revelled. Laurie enjoyed that immensely; and when she told about the prim old gentleman who came once to woo Aunt March, and, in the middle of a fine speech, how Poll had tweaked his wig off to his great dismay, the boy lay back and laughed till the tears ran down his cheeks, and a maid popped her head in to see what was the matter.

"Oh! that does me no end of good. Tell on, please," he said, taking his face out of the sofa-cushion, red and shining with merriment.

Much elated with her success, Jo did "tell on," all about their plays and plans, their hopes and fears for father on the battlefields, and the most interesting events of the little world in which the sisters lived. Then they got to talking about books, and to Jo's delight, she found that Laurie loved them as well as she did, and had read even more than herself.

"If you like them so much, come down and see ours. Grandpa is out, so you needn't be afraid," said Laurie, getting up.

"I'm not afraid of anything," returned Jo, with a toss of her head.

"I don't believe you are!" exclaimed the boy, looking at her with much admiration, though he privately thought she would have good reason to be a trifle afraid of the old gentleman, if she met him in some of his moods.

The atmosphere of the whole house being summer-like, Laurie led the way from room to room, letting Jo stop to examine whatever struck her fancy; and so at last they came to the library, where she clapped her hands, and pranced, as she always did when especially delighted. It was lined with books, and there were pictures and statues, and distracting little cabinets full of coins and curiosities, and sleepy-hollow chairs, and queer tables, and bronzes; and, best of all, a great open fireplace, with quaint tiles all around it.

"What richness!" sighed Jo, sinking into the depth of a velvet chair, and gazing about her with an air of intense satisfaction. "Theodore Laurence, you ought to be the happiest boy in the world," she added impressively.

"A fellow can't live on books," said Laurie, shaking his head, as he perched on a chair opposite.

Before he could say more, a bell rang, and Jo flew up, exclaiming with alarm, "Mercy me! it's your grandpa!"

"Well, what if it is? You are not afraid of anything, you know," returned the boy, looking wicked.

"I think I am a little bit afraid of him, but I don't know why I should be. Mother said I might come, and I don't think you're any the worse for it," said Jo, composing herself, though she kept her eyes on the door.

"I'm a great deal better for it, and ever so much obliged. I'm only afraid you are very tired talking to me; it was *so* pleasant, I couldn't bear to stop," said Laurie gratefully.

"The doctor to see you, sir," and the maid beckoned as she spoke.

"Would you mind if I left you for a minute? I suppose I must see him," said Laurie.

"Don't mind me. I'm as happy as a cricket here," answered Jo.

Laurie went away, and his guest amused herself in her own way. She was standing before a fine portrait of the old gentleman, when the door opened again, and, without turning, she said decidedly, "I'm sure now that I shouldn't be afraid of him, for he's got kind eyes, though his mouth is grim, and he looks as if he had a tremendous will of his own. He isn't as handsome as *my* grandfather, but I like him."

"Thank you, ma'am," said a gruff voice behind her; and there, to her great dismay, stood old Mr. Laurence.

Jo blushed till she couldn't blush any redder, and her heart began to beat uncomfortably fast as she thought what she had said. For a minute a wild desire to run away possessed her; but that was cowardly, and the girls would laugh at her: so she resolved to stay, and get out of the scrape as she could. A second look showed her that the living eyes, under the bushy gray eyebrows, were kinder even than the painted ones; and there was a sly twinkle in them, which lessened her fear a good deal. The gruff voice was gruffer than ever, as the old gentleman said abruptly, after that dreadful pause, "So you're not afraid of me, hey?"

"Not much, sir."

"And you don't think me as handsome as your grandfather?"

"Not quite, sir."

"And I've got a tremendous will, have I?"

"I only said I thought so."

"But you like me, in spite of it?"

"Yes, I do, sir."

That answer pleased the old gentleman; he gave a short laugh, shook hands with her, and, putting his finger under her chin, turned up her face, examined it gravely, and let it go, saying with a nod, "You've got your grandfather's spirit, if you haven't his face. He *was* a fine man, my dear; but, what is better, he was a brave and honest one, and I was proud to be his friend."

"Thank you, sir"; and Jo was quite comfortable after that, for it suited her exactly.

"What have you been doing to this boy of mine, hey?" was the next question, sharply put.

"Only trying to be neighborly, sir"; and Jo told how her visit came about.

"You think he needs cheering up a bit, do you?"

"Yes, sir; he seems a little lonely, and young folks would do him good perhaps. We are only girls, but we should be glad to help if we could, for we don't forget the splendid Christmas flowers you sent us," said Jo eagerly.

"Tut, tut, tut, that was the boy's affair. How is the poor woman?"

"Doing nicely, sir"; and off went Jo, talking very fast, as she told all about the Hummels, in whom her mother had interested richer friends than they were.

"Just her father's way of doing good. I shall come and see your mother some fine day. Tell her so. There's the tea-bell; we have it early, on the boy's account. Come down, and go on being neighborly."

"If you'd like to have me, sir."

"Shouldn't ask you, if I didn't"; and Mr. Laurence offered her his arm with old-fashioned courtesy.

"What *would* Meg say to this?" thought Jo, as she was marched away, while her eyes danced with fun as she imagined herself telling the story at home.

"Hey! Why, what the dickens has come to the fellow?" said the old gentleman, as Laurie came running downstairs, and brought up with a start of surprise at the astonishing sight of Jo arm-in-arm with his redoubtable grandfather.

"I didn't know you'd come, sir," he began, as Jo gave him a triumphant little glance.

"That's evident, by the way you racket downstairs. Come to your tea, sir, and behave like a gentleman"; and having pulled the boy's hair by way of a caress, Mr. Laurence walked on.

The old gentleman did not say much as he drank his four cups of tea, but he watched the young people, who soon chatted away like old friends, and the change in his grandson did not escape him. There was color, light, and life in the boy's face now, vivacity in his manner, and genuine merriment in his laugh.

"She's right; the lad *is* lonely. I'll see what these little girls can do for him," thought Mr. Laurence, as he looked and listened. He liked Jo, for her odd, blunt ways suited him; and she seemed to understand the boy almost as well as if she had been one herself.

If the Laurences had been what Jo called "prim and poky," she would not have got on at all, for such people always made her shy and awkward; but finding them free and easy, she was so herself. When they rose she proposed to go, but Laurie said he had something more to show her, and took her away to the conservatory, which had been lighted for her benefit. It seemed quite fairylike to Jo, as she went up and down the walks, enjoying the blooming walls on either side, the soft light, the damp sweet air, and the wonderful vines and trees that hung above her,—while her new friend cut the finest flowers till his hands were full; then he tied them up, saying, with the happy look Jo liked to see: "Please give these to your mother, and tell her I like the medicine she sent me very much."

They found Mr. Laurence standing before the fire in the great drawing-room, but Jo's attention was entirely absorbed by a grand piano, which stood open.

"Do you play?" she asked, turning to Laurie.

"Sometimes," he answered modestly.

"Please do now. I want to hear it, so I can tell Beth."

So Laurie played, and Jo listened, with her nose luxuriously buried in heliotrope and tea-roses. Her respect and regard for the "Laurence boy" increased very much, for he played remarkably well, and didn't put on any airs. She wished Beth could hear him, but she did not say so; only praised him till he was quite abashed, and his grandfather came to the rescue. "That will do, that will do, young lady. Too many sugar plums are not good for him. His music isn't bad, but I hope he will do as well in more important things. Going? Well, I'm much obliged to you, and I hope you'll come again. My respects to your mother. Good-night, Doctor Jo."

He shook hands kindly, and Laurie went with her into the hall. "John is going home with you, as I can't."

"No need of that; I am not a young lady, and it's only a step. Take care of yourself, won't you?"

"Yes; but you will come again, I hope?"

"If you promise to come and see us after you are well."

"I will."

"Good-night, Laurie!"

"Good-night, Jo, good-night!"

When all the afternoon's adventures had been told, the family felt inclined to go visiting in a body, for each found something very attractive in the big house on the other side of the hedge. Mrs. March wanted to talk of her father with the old man who had not forgotten him; Meg longed to walk in the conservatory; Beth sighed for the grand piano; and Amy was eager to see the fine pictures and statues.

—From "Little Women," by Louisa M. Alcott.

BOOKS TO READ

1. "Louisa Alcott," by Sara K. Bolton. Crowell.
   In "Lives of Girls Who Became Famous."
2. "Louisa Alcott," by E. D. Cheney. Little, Brown.
   Her life, letters, and journals.
3. "Louisa Alcott," by Belle Moses. Appleton.
   By reading this you can find out how Miss Alcott used her own experiences in her stories.
4. Best Books by Miss Alcott:
   "Little Women." This book always interests girls.
   "Little Men." About the same people—and some lively boys.
   "An Old-Fashioned Girl." City life through a country girl's eyes.

CHRISTMAS AT BRACEBRIDGE HALL

Every country has its Christmas customs, many of which can be traced back for hundreds of years. In Germany, Christmas would not be Christmas without a Christmas tree; in Holland, children must put out their wooden shoes for St. Nicholas to fill; in Norway, the birds must have their Christmas sheaf. These are only three of the many Christmas customs about which you may be interested to read.

Many of the old Christmas customs we have never adopted, and many have died out in the countries from which they come. In England particularly, very few of the good times described by Washington Irving, a hundred years ago, now exist. You might make a list of the Christmas customs he describes and compare them with others that you know.

I

It was delightful to see the Squire[1] in his elbow-chair, by the hospitable fireside of his ancestors, beaming warmth and gladness to every heart. Even the dog at his feet, as he lazily shifted his position and yawned, would look up in his master's face, wag his tail against the floor, and stretch himself again to sleep, confident of kindness and protection. I had not been seated many minutes by the comfortable hearth before I found myself as much at home as if I had been one of the family.

[1] squire: an English landowner; the chief landowner of a district.

Soon supper was served in a spacious oaken chamber, the panels of which shone with wax and made a background for the family portraits decorated with holly and ivy. Besides the usual lights, two great wax tapers called Christmas candles, wreathed with greens, were placed on a polished buffet among the family plate. The table was abundantly spread with substantial fare; but the Squire made his supper of frumenty, a dish of wheat boiled in milk with rich spices, which was always served on Christmas Eve.

After supper Master Simon was called on for a Christmas song. He thought a moment, and then began the quaint old ditty:

> "Now Christmas is come
> Let us beat up the drum,
> And call all our neighbors together,
> And when they appear,
> Let us make them such cheer
> As will keep out the wind and the weather."

Then an old harper, who had been strumming all evening by the kitchen fire, was called in, and we had a dance, followed by more songs; and we broke up for the night with the kind-hearted old custom of shaking hands, when the dying embers of the Yule log[1] sent forth a dusky glow.

I had scarcely got into bed when a strain of music broke

[1] Yule log: a huge log for the Christmas hearth.

forth in the air just below the window. It was the waits[1] from the neighboring village. They went round the house, playing under the windows. As the sounds receded, they became more soft and aerial and accorded well with the quiet and moonlight.

As I awoke in the morning, I heard the sound of little feet pattering outside my door, and then children's voices singing an old Christmas carol. After breakfast I walked about the grounds with Frank Bracebridge and Master Simon, escorted by a number of gentlemanlike dogs, that seemed loungers about the establishment, from the frisking spaniel to the steady old staghound. While we were talking, we heard the distant tolling of the village bell, and I was informed that the Squire was a little particular about having his household at church on a Christmas morning, for he agreed with the old poet who wrote:

"At Christmas be merry, *and thankful withal*,
And feast thy poor neighbors, the great with the small."

The parson gave us a sermon on Christmas, on the propriety of observing it not merely as a day of thanksgiving but of rejoicing. He concluded by urging his hearers to stand by the customs of their fathers, and to feast and make merry on this joyful anniversary of the church.

On leaving the church, the congregation one and all seemed possessed with the gayety of spirit so earnestly enjoined by their pastor. The elder folk gathered in knots

[1] waits: a band of musicians who play and sing carols in the streets at Christmas time.

in the churchyard, greeting and shaking hands; and the children ran about singing:

> "Ule! Ule!
> Three puddings in a pule;
> Crack nuts and cry ule!"

This, the parson told us, was a very old rhyme handed down for generations.

II

On the way homeward, sounds of rustic merriment now and then reached our ears. "I love," said the Squire, "to see this day well kept by rich and poor; it is a great thing to have one day in the year, at least, when you are sure of being welcome wherever you go, and of having, as it were, the world all thrown open to you. I join with Poor Robin when he says:

> "Those who at Christmas do repine
> And would fain hence dispatch him,
> May they with old Duke Humphrey dine,
> Or else may Squire Ketch catch 'em."

So on Christmas day he always invited all the better part of the neighboring country folk to come to the hall, and he distributed beef, bread, and ale among the poor that they might be merry in their own homes.

We had not been long home when we heard music from a distance. A band of country lads, without coats, their shirtsleeves fancifully tied with ribbons, their hats decorated with greens, and clubs in their hands, advanced up the avenue, followed by a crowd of villagers and country folk. They stopped before the hall door, where the music struck up a peculiar air, and the lads performed a curious and intricate dance, advancing, retreating, and striking their clubs together, keeping exact time to the music; while one, whimsically crowned with a fox's skin, the tail of which flaunted down his back, capered round the skirts of the dance, and rattled a Christmas box with many antic gesticulations. After the dance, the whole party was entertained with brawn and beef and homebrew. Everywhere there was good cheer and joking.

The dinner was served in the great hall. A blazing, crackling fire of logs warmed the spacious apartment, and the flame went sparkling and wreathing up the wide-mouthed chimney. The walls were wreathed with holly and ivy. A sideboard was gleaming with flagons, cans, cups, beakers, goblets, basins, and ewers—gorgeous utensils of good companionship that had gradually accumulated through many generations of good housekeepers. Before these stood the two Yule candles and others were distributed here and there in branched candlesticks. On a stool beside the fireplace sat the old harper, twanging his instrument with more power than melody.

The parson said grace. There was a pause; then the butler entered the hall, attended by a servant on each side with a large wax-light. He bore a silver dish, on which was an enormous pig's head, decorated with rosemary, and having a lemon in its mouth. The harper struck up a flourish, and the Oxford student began to sing an old carol, half English and half Latin, part of which went:

> "The boar's head in hand bring I
> With garlands gay and rosemary,
> I pray you all sing merrily. . . ."

The table was loaded with good cheer. Among other curiously adorned dishes was a pheasant pie magnificently decorated with peacock feathers, in imitation of the tail of that bird. Formerly, the pie itself was made of peacock, which was thought a delicacy.

When the cloth was removed, the butler brought in a huge silver vessel of rare and curious workmanship, which was called the wassail bowl. It contained a drink called lamb's wool, composed of ale mixed with sugar, nutmeg, and ginger, and with roasted crabapples floating on the surface. The Squire drank first, with a hearty wish of merry Christmas to all present. He then sent the bowl round the board for every one to follow his example. The word *wassail* means "Health to you."

After the dinner table was removed, the hall was given up to the younger members of the family, who played at romping games, especially blind man's buff. In the drawing-room the company sat round the fire while the parson told strange stories of the popular superstitions and legends of the surrounding country.

Suddenly there came from the hall sounds like the clang

of rude minstrelsy, the uproar of many small voices, and girlish laughter. The door flew open and a train came in that might almost have been mistaken for the breaking up of the court of Fairy. Master Simon, who was acting as Lord of Misrule in that merry house, had taken upon himself to devise a Christmas mummery or masking. Antique clothes-presses and wardrobes had been rummaged, and all the young people were bedizened into a burlesque of an antique mask.

Master Simon led the van as "Father Christmas," in a ruff, a great cloak, and a hat tall enough to be a village steeple, from under which curved out a great nose with a frost-bitten bloom. He was accompanied by "Dame Mince Pie" in a faded brocade, with a long stomacher, and high-heeled shoes. With them were Robin Hood, in Kendal Green and a gold-tasseled cap, on his arm Maid Marian in rustic dress. The other girls were all trussed up in the finery of ancient Bracebridge belles, and the striplings were bewhiskered with burnt cork, and clad in broad skirts, hanging sleeves, and full-bottomed wigs, to represent "Roast Beef," "Plum Pudding," and the other worthies of a Christmas masque.

This motley crew, brought in according to custom with beat of drum, at once began to dance the minuet and other ancient dances; and as the old manor house almost reeled with mirth and wassail, it seemed to be echoing the joviality of long-departed years.

—Adapted from Washington Irving.

INTERESTING POINTS TO WORK OUT

1. How does Irving put us at ease with the Squire in paragraph one? Is it an artistic introduction? What details are used to furnish a fine situation or setting for the story? Write them down for class discussion.
2. Select words to describe the neighborly characteristics of the old Squire. Have them written on the board.
3. What Christmas customs in your home would go into the making of an interesting account of Christmas celebration? How would it differ from Christmas at Bracebridge Hall?

WASHINGTON IRVING

Washington Irving (1783-1859) will always be remembered as one of our prominent writers. He was born in New York the year our War of the Revolution came to an end. His mother said: "Washington's work is ended and the child shall be named after him." One day six years later, when General Washington had become the first President of the new nation, a Scotch maidservant of the Irving family saw the President go into a shop. She followed him with the little boy and said: "Please, your honor, here's a bairn was named after you." "The bairn" never forgot the touch of Washington's kind hand on his head.

Irving's life was full of many interesting experiences. He traveled much in Europe.

You will find good accounts of his life in:

1. "Famous American Authors," S. K. Bolton.
2. "Four Famous American Writers," S. Cody.
3. "Story of American Literature," Tassin and Maurice.

Among his writings you will find his "Tales of the Alhambra," "The Legend of Sleepy Hollow," and "Knickerbocker's History of New York" most fascinating. The first book gives us a picture of Moorish life in Spain.

KIDNAPPED

In a good story the reader is made to wonder all the time what is coming next; he is made to hope that things will turn out in a certain way, to think that they cannot turn out as he wishes them to do; and to be delightfully surprised when an unexpected means of bringing the ending he desires is found.

The story "Kidnapped," by Robert Louis Stevenson, is full of surprising adventures. They begin in the very first chapter. You will be greatly surprised by the behavior of the old woman in the first paragraph—more surprised by the behavior of David's uncle at Shaws. And if you want to know what happened to David, there is not only "Kidnapped," to read, but its sequel, "David Balfour."

It was drawing on to sundown of the second day when I met a stout, dark, sour-looking woman coming trudging down a hill; and she, when I put my usual question, if she had ever heard tell of the house they called the house of Shaws, turned sharp about, accompanied me back to the summit she had just left, and pointed to a great bulk of building standing very bare upon a green in the bottom of the next valley. The country was pleasant round about, running in low hills, pleasantly watered and wooded, and the crops, to my eyes, wonderfully good; but the house itself appeared to be a kind of ruin; no road led up to it; no smoke arose from any of the chimneys; nor was there any semblance of a garden. My heart sank. "That!" I cried.

The woman's face lit up with a malignant anger. "That is the house of Shaws!" she cried. "Blood built it; blood stopped the building of it; blood shall bring it down. See here!" she cried again—"I spit upon the ground, and crack my thumb at it! Black be its fall! If ye see the laird, tell him what ye hear; tell him this makes the twelve hunner and nineteenth time that Jennet Clouston has called down the curse on him and his house, and stable, man, guest, and master, wife, miss, or child—black, black be their fall!"

And the woman, whose voice had risen to a singsong, turned with a skip, and was gone. I stood where she left me, with my hair on end. In those days folk still believed in witches and trembled at a curse; and this one, like an omen, to stop me ere I carried out my purpose, took the pith out of my legs.

I sat me down and stared at the house of Shaws. The more I looked, the pleasanter that countryside appeared; being all set with hawthorn bushes full of flowers; the fields dotted with sheep; a fine flight of rooks in the sky; and every sign of a kind soil and climate; and yet the barrack in the midst of it went sore against my fancy.

Country folk went by from the fields as I sat there on the side of the ditch, but I lacked the spirit to give them a good-e'en. At last the sun went down, and then, right up against the yellow sky, I saw a scroll of smoke go mounting, not much thicker, as it seemed to me, than the smoke of a candle; but still there it was, and meant a fire, and warmth, and cookery, and some living inhabitant that must have lit it. And this comforted my heart wonderfully.

So I set forward by a little faint track in the grass that

led in my direction. It was very faint indeed to be the only way to a place of habitation; yet I saw no other. Presently it brought me to stone uprights with an unroofed lodge beside them, and coats of arms upon the top. A main entrance, it was plainly meant to be, but never finished; instead of gates of wrought iron, a pair of hurdles were tied across with a straw rope; and the track that I was following went wandering on toward the house.

The nearer I got to that, the drearier it appeared. It seemed like the one wing of a house that had never been finished. The upper floors stood open, and showed against the sky with steps of uncompleted masonry. Many of the windows were unglazed, and bats flew in and out like doves at a dovecote.

The night had begun to fall as I got close; and in three of the lower windows, which were very high up, and narrow, and well barred, the changing light of a little fire began to glimmer.

Was this the palace I had been coming to? Was it within these walls that I was to seek new friends and begin great fortunes? Why, in my father's house which I had left, the fire and the bright lights would show a mile away, and the door open to a beggar's knock.

I came forward cautiously, and giving ear as I came, heard some one rattling the dishes, and a little dry, eager cough that came in fits; but there was no sound of speech, and not a dog barked. The door, as well as I could see in the dim light, was a great piece of wood all studded with nails; and I lifted my hand with a faint heart under my jacket, and knocked once. Then I stood and waited. The house was fallen into a dead silence; a whole minute passed, and nothing stirred but the bats overhead. I knocked again and hearkened again. By this time my ears had grown so accustomed to the quiet, that I could hear the ticking of the clock inside as it slowly counted out the seconds; but whoever was in that house kept deadly still, and must have held his breath.

I was two minds whether to run away; but anger got the upper hand, and I began instead to rain kicks and buffets on the door, and to shout out aloud for Mr. Balfour. I was in full career, when I heard a cough right overhead, and jumping back and looking up, beheld a man's head in a tall nightcap, and the mouth of a blunderbuss, at one of the first-story windows.

"It's loaded," said a voice.

"I have come here with a letter," I said, "to Mr. Ebenezer Balfour of Shaws. Is he here?"

"From whom is it?" asked the man with the blunderbuss.

"That is neither here nor there," said I, for I was growing very wroth.

"Well," was the reply, "ye can put it down upon the doorstep, and be off with ye."

"I will do no such thing," I cried. "I will deliver it into Mr. Balfour's hands, as it was meant I should. It is a letter of introduction."

"A what?" cried the voice, sharply.

I repeated what I had said.

"Who are ye, yourself?" was the next question, after a considerable pause.

"I am not ashamed of my name," said I. "They call me David Balfour."

At that, I made sure the man started, for I heard the blunderbuss rattle on the window-sill; and it was after quite a long pause, and with a curious change of voice, that the next question followed:

"Is your father dead?"

I was so much surprised at this, that I could find no voice to answer, but stood staring.

"Ay," the man resumed, "he'll be dead, no doubt; and that'll be what brings ye chapping to my door." Another pause, and then, defiantly, "Well, man," he said, "I'll let ye in"; and he disappeared from the window.

—*From "Kidnapped," by Robert Louis Stevenson.*

OBSERVING THE FINE POINTS OF GOOD DESCRIPTION

1. Read the first paragraph carefully to note the vivid description. Note especially the last half of the paragraph.
2. Select other impressive passages.
3. Could an artist draw a good picture of Shaw house from Stevenson's description of it? What details would you point out as valuable to an artist? Make a list of them.
4. What do you suppose happened when David Balfour was let into the house? Write a description of what you imagine and then get the book, "Kidnapped," and compare it with what did happen.

THINGS TO TALK ABOUT AND DO

1. Have you read Stevenson's "Treasure Island"? It is one of the best stories of piracy and concealed treasure ever written for children. Published by Scribners.
2. Give a two-minute talk on Robert Louis Stevenson. In Ariadne Gilbert's "More Than Conquerors," chapter XII is called "The Lighthouse-Builder's Son." It is about R. L. Stevenson.
3. It might be interesting to take a speed test on this section.
4. Prepare some good questions to test the accuracy of reading in the class.

WORDS

FOUR POEMS

When short poems give a real idea in a few words, we can easily learn them and so have the idea always with us.

The first poem in this group is by one of our good American poets. He is good especially because he does not copy other poetry but works out his own ideas in his own way. His "Primer Lesson" is one that most grown people ought to learn. Why?

The other three poems are by Indians. In each of the first two you can find one word that gives the idea of the poem. In the third, you have to put the idea in your own words. What is it?

PRIMER LESSON

Look out how you use proud words.
When you let proud words go, it is not
  easy to call them back.
They wear long boots, hard boots;
  they walk off proud; they can't
  hear you calling—
Look out how you use proud words.

—CARL SANDBURG.

WAWAN SONG (Omaha)

The clear sky,
The green fruitful earth is good;
But peace among men is better.

SONG TO THE PLEIADES (Pawnee)

Look as they rise, rise
Over the line where sky meets the earth;
Pleiades!
Lo! They ascending, come to guide us,
Leading us safely, keeping us one;
Pleiades,
Teach us to be, like you, united.

WAR SONG (Dakota)

Friend, whatever hardships threaten,
If thou call me,
I'll befriend thee;
All enduring fearlessly,
I'll befriend thee.

—*From "American Indian Lyrics,"*
selected by Nellie Barnes.

HOW BIRDS HELP MAN

Perhaps you have read that there is no part of a tree that insects may not harm. Roots, trunks, branches, twigs, leaves, and fruit all have their insect enemies. These bore into a tree; they sting and girdle and excavate and mine; they infest trees and feed upon all parts. Oaks alone are prey to more than 500 different kinds of insects, with countless millions of eggs and insects in each of the 500 kinds. If it were not that other insects and birds destroy in great numbers these enemies of the oak, there would soon be no oak trees in the world.

As it is with trees, so it is with other plants, especially those in cultivation. They are beset with enemies which it is to our interest to hold in check. Fortunately, there are birds that, in their search for food, can help us.

If we are wise, we will encourage and protect the birds for their services to our vegetation. For they not only help plant forests by dropping seeds and by hiding and forgetting them, but they destroy billions of weed seeds, and they feed upon insects injurious to trees and to other plants that we want and need.

THE BLACKBIRD

In the far corner
close by the swings
every morning
a blackbird sings.

His bill's so yellow,
his coat's so black
that he makes a fellow
whistle back.

Ann, my daughter,
thinks that he
sings for us two
especially.

—HUMBERT WOLFE.

LITTLE TROTTY WAGTAIL

Little trotty wagtail, he went in the rain,
And tittering, tottering sideways he ne'er got straight again,
He stooped to get a worm, and looked up to get a fly,
And then he flew away before his feathers all were dry.

Little trotty wagtail, he waddled in the mud,
And left his little footmarks, trample where he would.
He waddled in the water-pudge, and waggle went his tail,
He chirrupt up his wings to dry upon the garden rail.

Little trotty wagtail, you nimble all about,
And in the dimpling water-pudge you waddle in and out;
Your home is near at hand, and in the warm pig-stye,
So little Master Wagtail, I'll bid you a good-bye.
—JOHN CLARE.

Write a different ending for this poem.

WHEN ON A SUMMER'S MORN

When on a summer's morn I wake,
    And open my two eyes,
Out to the clear, born-singing rills
    My bird-like spirit flies;

To hear the blackbird, cuckoo, thrush,
    Or any bird in song;

And common leaves that hum all day,
  Without a throat or tongue.

And when Time strikes the hour for sleep,
  Back in my room alone,
My heart has many a sweet bird's song—
  And one that's all my own.
                              —W. H. DAVIES.

TO THINK ABOUT

1. Compare this poem with Davies's "Nature's Friend." Which do you like best?
2. Explain: (a) "And common leaves that hum all day."
  (b) "My heart has many a sweet bird's song."
3. What song do you think is the "one that's all my own"?

THE ECONOMIC VALUE OF BIRDS TO MAN

Intelligent people in almost every country are trying to protect birds. In nearly every State in our country, laws have been passed for bird protection. We have begun to realize that birds not only make the world a happier place with their beauty and song, but are of infinite value in destroying injurious insects and animals.

When you come to paragraph two, see if you can name one bird that is of value for its beauty, one for its music, one for the insects it eats, and so on.

Notice how careful ornithologists[1] have to be in their decisions.

All over our country people are beginning to realize that birds are of great importance to us. Not only do their song and beauty give us pleasure, but their habits of feed-

[1] ornithologist: (ôr″nĭ-thŏl′ ŏ-jĭst) one who makes a special study of birds.

ing and living may be of benefit or harm to man. It is necessary that we know which birds to protect and which to get rid of.

Birds are of value not only because of our joy in their beauty and music, but also because (1) they eat harmful insects; (2) they eat the eggs and larvæ of harmful insects; (3) they eat weed seeds which men want destroyed; (4) they kill mice and small animals that injure crops; (5) they act as scavengers by eating refuse and thus prevent disease. In these ways they help foresters, fruit-growers, farmers, and people in cities and towns.

There are persons who make a study of birds and who are able to give us exact information regarding the helpful or injurious habits of birds. We call them ornithologists. If they wish to know the food of a certain kind of bird, let us say the screech owl, they examine the contents of the stomachs of many screech owls, and the pellets of fur and bones that the owls have cast up. They call upon insect and mammal experts to help them. Such men often can identify an animal by seeing one bone of its body; they can name an insect by seeing some small part of it, such as a wing-cover or a mouth-part. They can tell with certainty whether a bird has eaten seeds or insects or something else.

A bird may look as if he were eating seeds and yet he may feed only upon insects he finds among the seeds. He may even crack open seeds for insects he finds within. If once an expert study is made of him, we know what his food is. The only way for the ornithologist to make sure is to examine the contents of many stomachs of that kind of bird at different seasons of the year, and in different localities. If, for example, no cuckoo of the many examined is ever found to have eaten seeds, it is safe to say that under ordinary conditions cuckoos do not eat seeds. And so with all other birds examined.

Again, in some places a bird may be harmful one month of the year and useful the other eleven months. The robin, for example, feeds upon cherries and strawberries, but on the whole is more valuable than harmful. Or, like the bobolink, a bird may be destructive while he is in the South, and serviceable during his stay in the North. Or, like the hawks, some members of a family may be harmful, and others very helpful and necessary to man.

Ornithologists take all these matters into consideration and keep records to show on what they base their judgments. In the following pages are different kinds of reports made by ornithologists. One report was made as long ago as 1885; but farmers today can learn a lesson from it.

Hawks and Owls

Because a hawk carries off a chicken now and then, farmers and others have come to believe that all hawks are "chicken hawks" and should be killed. Owls, too, have a bad name, although they are particularly valuable as mousers and eaters of insects.

That we might know with certainty whether, on the

whole, hawks and owls are helpful or harmful, our government employed Doctor Fisher, an expert ornithologist, to make a study of their food. He spent several years collecting and examining the contents of the stomachs of nearly 2,700 hawks and owls. His records show that all but two kinds of hawks and most owls are of particular service to man. The stomachs examined contained very little poultry, a few other birds, many mice and other mammals and insects, besides reptiles, frogs, lizards, spiders, crawfish, earthworms, and offal. Experts suggest that we do not kill these birds unless we actually see them taking our chickens.

The hawks that do the great mischief for which all hawks are blamed are not the kind that scream and soar. They are the long, slim birds which lurk under cover, the Cooper's hawk, and the sharp-shinned hawk. Their chief food is poultry and other birds, and they do very little in ridding men of pests.

—Adapted from "*The Economic Value of Birds to the State,*" by F. M. Chapman.

FOR DISCUSSION

1. How can you help the farmers understand how necessary most hawks are to farms? If you have a farmer friend, what can you tell him about helpful hawks?

2. What are the field marks of the mischief-makers among hawks? How else may they be known?

3. What posters can you plan to help people know which hawks are valuable to us and which should be destroyed?

$2,105 SPENT TO SAVE A DOLLAR

See who can write the best sentence giving the main point in the following article.

In 1885 a law was passed in Pennsylvania "for the benefit of agriculture." It provided a bounty of fifty cents each on hawks, owls, weasels, and minks killed in that State, and a fee of twenty cents to the notary or justice to whom the heads were brought.

As a result, $90,000 was paid in bounties in a year and a half. This meant the destruction of at least 128,571 of the animals named above, most being hawks and owls.

If we grant that 5,000 chickens were killed yearly in Pennsylvania by hawks and owls, and that they were worth twenty-five cents each (which is not likely, because most of those killed were very young), the total loss would be $1,875. Hence in eighteen months the State of Pennsylvania spent $90,000 to save its farmers a loss of $1,875. But this is not all. It is safe to say that in the course of a year, every hawk and owl destroys at least a thousand mice or their equivalent in insects, and that each mouse or its equivalent so destroyed would cause the farmer a loss of two cents a year. Now, the increase in numbers of the mice and insects would be enormous when their natural check, the hawks and owls, would be removed. But without considering this, the lowest possible estimate of the value to the farmer of each hawk, owl, and weasel would be $30 in a year and a half.

Hence, the State not only spent $90,000 to destroy 128,571 of its benefactors; but in that year and a half it caused a loss of $3,947,130 to its farming interests. In other words, the State threw away $2,105 for every dollar saved! And even this did not represent fairly the full loss; for with the removal of so many hawks and owls, the mice and insects would increase in such numbers that it would take years to restore the balance between these pests and their enemies. It would be years before there would be enough hawks and owls to hold mice and insects in check.

*—Adapted from C. Hart Merriam's Report,
Department of Agriculture.*

THINGS TO DO

1. State briefly, without giving figures, what Doctor Merriam wishes to emphasize in his report.
2. Bring to class pictures of the birds and animals mentioned.
3. Look up additional facts about these birds and animals.
4. Make up five problems using the statistics given here.

A REMINDER

I

What Birds Do for Us

Birds gladden us with their beauty, their song, and their interesting ways. They destroy weed seeds that we are glad to be rid of. They destroy insects that threaten our vegetation. They destroy small animals that are harmful to man. They act as scavengers, and thus lessen disease.

II
WHAT WE CAN DO FOR BIRDS

We can make and enforce laws for the protection of birds.

We can compel the licensing of cats, the same as dogs.

We can create a sentiment against the killing of birds or the taking of eggs.

We can provide nesting-boxes and sites for those that will use them; and also nesting materials, such as straw, hair, string, and lint.

We can plant extra fruit trees (mulberry, cherry, etc.) and berry bushes to supply their needs.

We can set out bird baths, food tables, suet cages, and bird shelters. We can put cat shields on nesting trees.

We can spread information as to the importance of birds to man.

THINGS TO DO

1. Name the birds you know that destroy weed seeds; that destroy insects; that destroy small animals; that act as scavengers. Which have you seen? Which have you heard? What was the most beautifully colored bird you have seen?

2. Write a paragraph about a bird you have observed. Do not write the paragraph, however, until you have read all the selections in this group; bring the paragraph to class within a week of that time.

3. Organize a Bird Club. If you really want to know birds and bird ways you must observe what you can, first-hand—learn where they build their nests, what they eat, and all about their habits.

WHAT JAMES RUSSELL LOWELL THOUGHT OF ANIMALS AND BIRDS

Lowell was a man of wide interests. In his book of essays called ''My Study Windows,'' you might suppose that he is going to be very learned and even dull; but actually the book is full of interesting talk about the birds and animals that he watched. By reading what follows you can catch a glimpse of what he sees.

Of his various garden acquaintance, to give a single quotation, he says: ''If they will not come near enough to me (as most of them will), I bring them close with an opera glass—a much better weapon than a gun. I would not, if I could, convert them from their pretty pagan ways. The only one I sometimes have savage doubts about is the red squirrel. I think he eats eggs. I know he eats cherries (we counted five of them at one time in a single tree, the stones pattering down like the sparse hail that preludes a storm), and that he gnaws off the small ends of pears to get at the seeds. He steals the corn from under the noses of my poultry. But what would you have? He will come down upon the limb of the tree I am lying under till he is within a yard of me. He and his mate will scurry up and down the great black walnut for my diversion, chattering like monkeys. Can I sign his death-warrant who has tolerated me about his grounds so long? Not I. Let them steal. I am sure I should, had I had the same bringing-up. As for the birds, I do not believe there is one of them but does more good than harm; and of how many featherless bipeds can this be said?''

CHICKADEE AND TITMOUSE

I

The chickadee and the tufted titmouse belong to the same family. Both of them are too busy hunting food to be very timid of us; so we often get a close look at them. Both of them have calls that are unforgettable.

"Chickadee-dee-dee, chick-a, chick-a-dee-dee," says chickadee in a businesslike manner. His voice is husky and surprisingly loud.

Upside down or right side up he swings and teeters on twigs and branches. He tears away the bark and finds a hidden grub. "Dee-dee," he says, and looks for more. Men who make a study of birds in their relation to man say that farmers have no better friend among birds than the chickadee. He eats injurious insects and their eggs in astonishing numbers, and he is on the farm the year round. Cankerworm moths, beetles and the eggs of these, and plant lice—all of them enemies to plants—are his food. It is said by authorities that one chickadee eats on the average thirty female cankerworms a day when they are to be had, and thus destroys 5,550 cankerworm eggs daily for almost a month.

The cheeriness and friendliness of the chickadee, his husky call which tells us his name, and his great service to man make him one of the best beloved of birds.

II

Chickadee's relative, the tufted titmouse, whistles like a boy. "Peto, peto, peto, peto," he says. Sometimes he trills, and once in a while he calls a hoarse *de-de-de-de*. He is easily identified by his conspicuous tuft or crest, and by his clear *peto* whistle. I have seen him pick up winged seeds, and with his bill hammer and hatch away at the seed part. Whether he found grubs in the seeds as well as kernels, I could not tell. He varies his diet with the season; berries, nuts, and other seeds and countless insects injurious to plant life are his food.

—NINA LEUBRIE.

ROBINS

READING AIMS: Read silently and rapidly the first time to get the meaning. Then re-read and work out the following points:

List the things harmful to us that robins eat:	List things helpful to us that robins eat:
1.	1.
2.	2.
	3., etc.

SUBJECT FOR DEBATE: Resolved, that robins are more helpful than harmful. Let this selection help you to prove your points.

Our robin is not much like an English robin, except that both have red breasts. Our robin is really a thrush. The baby robins have speckled breasts like those of thrushes; but when they grow up their breasts turn red.

The poet Lowell was a great bird-lover. This is what he wrote about our robins:

"In spite of his name of migratory thrush, our robin stays with us all winter. I have seen him when the thermometer marked fifteen degrees below zero, as cheerful as could be.

"The robin has a bad reputation among people who are fond of cherries, but I would not exchange him for all the cherries that ever were. He has a finer taste in fruit than many committees of Horticultural Societies, and he eats with a relishing gulp. He feels and freely exercises his right to the whole garden. His is the earliest mess of green peas; his are all the mulberries I had fancied mine. But if he gets the lion's share of the raspberries, he is also a great planter and sows wild ones in the woods.

"He keeps a strict eye over your fruit and knows to a shade of purple when your grapes have cooked long enough in the sun. During a recent drought, all the robins vanished from my garden. Meanwhile, a small foreign grapevine seemed to like the dusty air and somehow ripened its bunches. I watched them from day to day till I thought the grapes were ripe and then went out with a basket to gather the score or so of bunches that I had seen on the vines. But the robins also had been watching. They must have sent out spies before I was up. When I arrived, at least a dozen of them bustled out from among the leaves and, alighting on the nearest trees, exchanged shrill remarks about me that were by no means polite. The tattered scrap of a single bunch was all they had left on the grapevine. I could not help laughing, and the robins seemed to laugh with me. There was a common grapevine near, loaded with blue grapes, but my thieves preferred the foreign flavor. Could I say they had not good taste?

"The robins are not good solo singers, but their chorus, when they are singing the return of light and warmth to the world, is unrivalled. There are a hundred singing like one. But when they come after cherries to the tree near my window, they muffle their voices. Their faint *pip-pip-pop!* sounds far away at the bottom of the garden. There is only a great black walnut with bitter-rinded nuts, which I know they cannot eat.

"But fraud as the robin is, how brightly his breast, which looks rather shabby in the sunlight, shines in a rainy day against the dark green of the fringe-tree! After he has pinched and shaken all the life out of an earthworm and then gulped him, how a robin stands up in honest self-confidence! How he expands his red waistcoat with an air that seems to say, 'Do I look like a bird that knows the flavor of raw vermin? Ask any robin if he ever ate anything richer than juniper berries!' I have no doubt that at that very moment his breast is redder with the blood of my raspberries.

"But when we remember how omnivorous the robin is, and that he in a short time eats as much as he weighs, and when we remember that Nature seems always to be inventing new insects that harm fruits and vegetables, we may reckon that he does more good than harm. For my own part I would rather have his cheerfulness and kind neighborhood than many berries."

Note: In a two-minute talk give Lowell's arguments for protecting the robin.

THE MOCKING-BIRD

The song of the mocking-bird is celebrated in verse and in prose.

After reading the selection list the essential differences in the "mounting song" and the "dropping song." This will help you to recognize each, should you have the good fortune to see a mocking-bird.

Whoever has closely observed the mocking-bird has noted its "mounting song," a very frequent performance, wherein the songster begins on the lowest branch of a tree and appears literally to mount on its music, from bough to bough, until the highest spray of the top is reached, where it will sit for many minutes flinging upon the air a stream of infinitely varied song. But he who has never heard the "dropping song" has not discovered the last possibility of the mocking-bird's voice.

I have not kept the date of my first actual observation, but it was late in April or very early in May; for the crab-apple trees, growing wild in the Georgian hills, were in full bloom. I had been out since the first sparkle of daylight.

The sun was rising, and I had been standing quite still for some minutes, watching a mocking-bird that was singing in a snatchy, broken way, as it fluttered about in a thick-topped crabapple-tree, thirty yards distant from me. Suddenly the bird, a fine specimen, leaped like a flash to the highest spray of the tree and began to flutter in a trembling, peculiar way, with its wings half spread, and its feathers puffed out.

Almost immediately there came a strange, gurgling series of notes, liquid and sweet, that seemed to express utter rapture. Then the bird dropped with a backward motion, from the spray, and began to fall slowly and somewhat spirally down through the bloom-covered boughs. Its progress was quite like that of a bird wounded to death by a shot, clinging here and there to a twig, quivering and weakly striking with its wings as it fell, but all the time it was pouring out the most exquisite gushes and trills of song, not at all like its usual medley of improvised imitations, but strikingly individual and unique. The bird appeared to be dying of an ecstasy of musical inspiration. The lower it fell the louder and more rapturous became its voice, until the song ended on the ground in a burst of incomparable power. It remained for a short time, after its song was ended, crouching where it had fallen, with its wings outspread, and quivering and panting as if utterly exhausted; then it leaped boldly into the air and flew away into a near thicket. —*Adapted from Maurice Thompson.*

THE MOCKING-BIRD

Can you tell whether this poem refers to the "mounting song" or to the "dropping song" described by Maurice Thompson?

Hear! hear! hear!
Listen! the word
Of the mocking-bird!
Hear! hear! hear!
I will make all clear;
I will let you know
Where the footfalls go
That through the thicket and over the hill
Allure, allure.
How the bird-voice cleaves
Through the weft of leaves
With a leap and a thrill
Like the flash of a weaver's shuttle, swift and sudden and sure!

And lo, he is gone—even while I turn
The wisdom of his runes to learn.
He knows the mystery of the wood,
The secret of the solitude;
But he will not tell, he will not tell,
For all he promises so well.
—RICHARD HOVEY.

NOTE: Make sure of the meaning of "weft" and "runes."

THE THROSTLE

After you have read the poem, again read the lines which tell —according to Tennyson—what the thrush sings. Then read the lines which tell what the poet says to the thrush.

"Summer is coming, summer is coming.
   I know it, I know it, I know it.
Light again, leaf again, life again, love again!"
   Yes, my wild little poet.

Sing the new year in under the blue.
   Last year you sang it as gladly.
"New, new, new, new!" Is it then so new
   That you should carol so madly?

"Love again, song again, rest again, young again,"
   Never a prophet so crazy!
And hardly a daisy as yet, little friend,
   See, there is hardly a daisy.

"Here again, here, here, here, happy year!"
   O warble unchidden, unbidden!
Summer is coming, is coming, my dear,
   And all the winters are hidden.

—ALFRED, LORD TENNYSON.

NOTE: For the following poem make sure of the meaning of these words: quirk, pirouette, to vault, demure, iridescent, prate, eloquence.

TO A PHŒBE BIRD

Under the eaves, out of the wet,
   You nest within my reach;
You never sing for me and yet
   You have a golden speech.

You sit and quirk a rapid tail,
   Wrinkle a ragged crest,
Then pirouette from tree to rail
   And vault from rail to nest.

And when in frequent, dainty fright
   You grayly slip and fade,
And when at hand you re-alight
   Demure and unafraid,

And when you bring your brood its fill
   Of iridescent wings
And green legs dewy in your bill,
   Your silence is what sings.

Not of a feather that enjoys
   To prate or praise or preach,
O phœbe, with so little noise,
   What eloquence you teach!

—WITTER BYNNER.

FOR DISCUSSION

How does the phœbe teach eloquence without singing?

OFF THE COAST

Far off the petrel in the troubled way
Swims with her brood, or flutters in the spray;
She rises often, often drops again,
And sports at ease on the tempestuous main.
High o'er the restless deep, above the reach
Of gunners' hope, vast flocks of wild ducks stretch;
Far as the eye can glance on either side,
In a broad space and level line they glide;
All in their wedge-like figures from the north
Day after day, flight after flight, go forth.
In-shore their passage tribes of sea gulls urge,
And drop for prey within the sweeping surge;
Oft in the rough opposing blast they fly
Far back, then turn and all their force apply,
While to the storm they give their weak complaining cry;
Or clap the sleek white pinion on the breast,
And in the restless ocean dip for rest.

—GEORGE CRABBE.

NOTE: 1. Find the lines which picture the petrel (or Mother Carey's Chicken, as it is often called); flocks of wild ducks; the sea gulls.

2. To what do these phrases refer: the troubled way; tempestuous main; restless deep; sweeping surge?

3. List the unusual words and phrases, and discuss them.

SUGGESTED QUESTIONS FOR TWO-MINUTE TALKS AND REFERENCE WORK

1. What services does mankind owe birds?

2. Would you choose a grain-eating bird for a pet or one that feeds on insects? Why?

3. What are the reasons for the periodical flight of birds?

4. Why do governments set aside reservations for birds?

5. What bird never builds a nest of its own?

6. How many miles can a carrier pigeon fly in an hour?

7. Tell how the pigeon is of service as a carrier.

8. Explain why birds are often called "the winged wardens of the farms."

9. Birds are often classified as birds of prey, creepers and climbers, fishers, sea-birds, scratchers, etc.

Find illustrations of each class named.

SOME BOOKS ABOUT BIRDS

1. "Some Common Birds in Their Relation to Agriculture." Farmers' Bulletin No. 54. U. S. Dept. of Agriculture.
A helpful booklet. Write for it.

2. "Bird Stories from John Burroughs." Houghton.
A charming book of sketches of bird-life written by a world-famous naturalist. Illustrated by Louis Fuertes.

3. "Bird Life," by Frank Chapman. Appleton.
"The Travels of Birds," by Frank Chapman. Appleton.
These books are among the best of our bird books. "Bird Life" is a guide to the study of our common birds, and is illustrated with 75 full-page colored plates and numbered drawings. "Travels" is a small, inexpensive book telling of the migrations of birds and their travel habits.

4. "Book of Birds," by Olive Thorne Miller. Houghton.
The author has also written: "True Bird Stories," "Bird Ways," "In Nesting Time." Her books have grown out of many years of patient observation.

KNOWING INSECTS

An article in a leading magazine recently was titled "The Insects Are Gaining." The writer told of many instances where insects harmful to plant and animal life had increased so greatly in number that food and clothing supplies were seriously affected by them. The coddling moth and the boll-weevil are two well-known examples. There are many others. Find out as much as you can about harmful insects and about ways in which the government is attempting to get rid of them. Much interesting material may be obtained by writing the Bureau of Agriculture, Washington, D. C., and also State Departments of Agriculture at your own State capital.

Nature has provided means of keeping the balance in insect life by the feeding of some insects upon others, and by the feeding of many birds upon insects. The study of these insect and bird friends is helpful as well as interesting. Do you know these friends? Do you protect them?

NOTE: Observe how all parts of the bodies of insects are fitted to their needs in the environment in which they must live. For example, beetles have hard wing-cases over their thin, lacy wings. Why?

BOOKS THAT WILL HELP YOU KNOW INSECTS

1. "Tiny Toilers and Their Work," by Clark Glennwood. Century. 2. "Insect Life," by A. B. and J. H. Comstock. Appleton. 3. "Social Life in the Insect World," by Jean Henri Fabre. Century. "Book of Insects," by Jean Henri Fabre. Dodd.

HOW A CRICKET MAKES ITS SOUND

Do you know how a cricket makes its sound? As you read make a note of the facts about crickets that are new to you.

"Creedle cree, cree cree, creedle, creedle, creedle, cree!"

I often wondered about the steady, unvarying sound of the cricket. Its tone never "ran down" or became flat. If a note was flat to begin with, it ended just so. I made many an effort to see the sound produced; but it was only by accident that I finally stumbled upon the performance.

One day, a cricket's *"creedle cree, cree cree"* sounded close at hand—at my very feet, in fact. On the floor in a patch of sunlight, under a shelf, sat the performer, a male cricket. Over the forepart of his body he had erected, almost vertically, a short pair of glassy, semi-transparent brown wing-covers that looked very much like wings. The color suggested the brown of smoked glass. The wing-covers vibrated in pulses, and as they trilled, the inner edges passed each other and barely perceptibly touched. Yet the rubbing of those rough edges made cricket music.

Since I had a full front view, I thought that possibly the legs, hidden from me by the erected wing-covers, played some part in producing the sound. As if in answer to my thought, the cricket turned half way round and continued his music, thus giving me a side view; then he suddenly folded his wing-covers, one overlapping the other on his back, and explored the sunny patch.

I realized that I had never been aware of wings on what I had supposed to be the hard shiny body of a cricket. Twice more during the hour I saw the cricket erect his wing-covers and trill them in song. Then he scurried away to a dark shelter.

—NINA LEUBRIE.

ON THE GRASSHOPPER AND CRICKET

The poetry of earth is never dead:
  When all the birds are faint with the hot sun,
  And hide in cooling trees, a voice will run
From hedge to hedge about the new-mown mead;
That is the Grasshopper's—he takes the lead
  In summer luxury,—he has never done
  With his delights; for when tired out with fun,
He rests at ease beneath some pleasant weed.
The poetry of earth is ceasing never:
  On a lone winter evening, when the frost
    Has wrought a silence, from the stove there shrills
The Cricket's song, in warmth increasing ever,
  And seems to one, in drowsiness half lost,
    The Grasshopper's among some grassy hills.

—JOHN KEATS.

NOTE: Notice during your vacation in the heat of summer whether grasshoppers make their sound when other outdoor voices are still.

According to the poet, when does the cricket's song seem like the grasshopper's?

THE VOICE THAT BEAUTIFIES THE LAND

(NAVAJO)

The voice that beautifies the land!
The voice above,
The voice of the thunder,
Among the dark clouds
Again and again it sounds,
The voice that beautifies the land.

II

The voice that beautifies the land!
The voice below,
The voice of the grasshopper,
Among the flowers and grasses
Again and again it sounds,
The voice that beautifies the land.

—From "American Indian Lyrics,"
selected by *Nellie Barnes.*

SOME WAYS OF STUDYING FLOWERS

> That the world may be more beautiful for all, I promise not to pluck flowers nor to destroy plants in woods and fields where they are unprotected; except such as flourish abundantly, or are in the nature of weeds. . . . All my influence shall be used to protect wild flowers from destruction by others.
>
> —WILD FLOWER PRESERVATION SOCIETY OF AMERICA.

Come down to Kew in lilac-time, in lilac-time, in lilac-time;
Come down to Kew in lilac-time (it isn't far from London);
And you shall wander hand in hand with Love in summer's wonderland.
Come down to Kew in lilac-time (it isn't far from London).

The cherry-trees are seas of bloom and soft perfume and sweet perfume,
The cherry-trees are seas of bloom (and oh, so near to London!)
And there they say, when dawn is high and all the world's a blaze of sky
The cuckoo, though he's very shy, will sing a song for London.

—ALFRED NOYES.

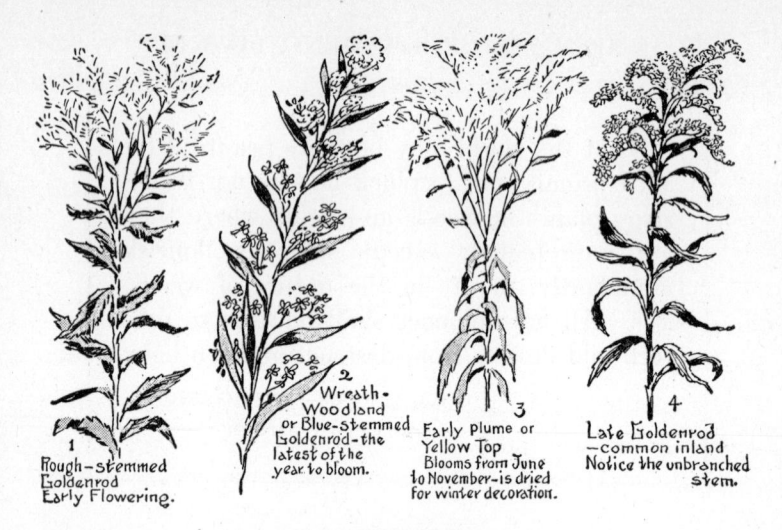

1. Rough-stemmed Goldenrod Early Flowering.
2. Wreath-Woodland or Blue-stemmed Goldenrod—the latest of the year to bloom.
3. Early plume or Yellow Top. Blooms from June to November—is dried for winter decoration.
4. Late Goldenrod—common inland. Notice the unbranched stem.

GOLDENROD

Collect different kinds of goldenrod for the class. If you get the plants in different soils, pin tags on them that you may remember which soil and plant belong together. Will you need parts of the plant other than the blossoms, to help you classify it?

Have you ever thought of the uses of the goldenrod other than that of making our fields and roadsides beautiful? Some interesting ones are told in this story.

"I just passed a field of goldenrod and I believe every bee in my hives was there working on the flowers," said Mr. Erdman, with a twinkle in his eye.

It was one of the rich years when goldenrod flared in the fields and all along the roads. The prospect of combs filled with light golden-yellow honey pleased Mr. Erdman, because he liked the wild tang of goldenrod better than the cloying sweetness of white clover or basswood.

When I went to the field to hear the hum of bees and see them work, I began to realize what a variety of goldenrod grew in our village. In that one field alone I counted five different kinds. And along the roadside and in ditches I saw others growing. It is said that there are more than eighty kinds of goldenrod native to the United States, and only three kinds native to Europe. I have seen goldenrod planted in gardens in England, where it was given a place of honor with favorite flowers. Were it not so common here, don't you think it would be grown in our gardens also?

Different kinds of goldenrod thrive in different kinds of soil. One variety likes dry soil, another thrives in swamps and peat bogs. One goldenrod prefers rocky uplands; one, rich meadows and woods. Goldenrod grows in shade and in sun, east and west, far north into Canada, and a few varieties have strayed south into Mexico.

Goldenrod varies in other ways. It may have broad leaves, or it may have narrow ones. It may have tall, stout, rough stems, or smooth, thin stems, branched or wand-like. It may have spreading flower clusters, thick, plume-like clusters, or tiny clusters all along the stem. The flowers may be pale yellow, deep golden yellow, greenish-yellow, and even white! But the white variety is better named *silver-rod*.

Not only bees feast at the goldenrod; flies, wasps, hornets, and beetles come for their share of nectar. And in winter, even when snow lies deep on the ground, the plumy seeds are food for sparrows, juncos, and other seed-eating birds. The swellings or galls that we see on the stems here and there, in summer and fall, are shelters for insects that will fly out into the world in spring.

—NINA LEUBRIE.

THINGS TO DO AND DISCUSS

1. Have an exhibit of the different kinds of goldenrod and goldenrod galls you are able to bring to school. Keep a record in drawings.

2. To what uses is goldenrod put by man? bees? hornets? flies? butterflies? other insects? birds?

3. Unusual phrases for special study. What do these mean:
wild tang of the goldenrod   *plumy seeds*
cloying sweetness of white clover or basswood
strayed south into Mexico. How can a plant stray?

CHOOSING THE RIGHT WORD TEST

What have you learned by studying goldenrod? Select the word in the parenthesis which will complete the sentence correctly.

1. Goldenrod is (always, usually) yellow.
2. Goldenrod is a (wild, cultivated) flower in our country.
3. The leaves of the various kinds of goldenrod are (all alike, different).
4. The stalks are (all alike, different).
5. The seeds of the goldenrod (roll, pop, stick to things, fly).
6. Goldenrod blossoms furnish nectar for (insects, birds, animals).
7. (Insects, birds, animals) eat the seeds.
8. Goldenrod galls are made by (men, insects, birds).

FRINGED GENTIANS

Gentians of some kinds may be found in all parts of our country. Usually, however, they are not common, and sometimes they are not even blue.

Late in September and well into October, if there is no frost, we may look for the lovely blue fringed gentians. They grow in moist places usually, in woods and meadows and hillsides. One year we may find them in a certain place, and then never see them there again. As the plants grow from seeds each year, new plants come up only where the light, hairy seeds, blown by the wind, have found moist places in which to sprout. Gentians that grow in the sun are a darker blue than those that grow in the shade.

Fringed gentians close at night and open in the sunny morning. If the day is dull, however, the gentians remain closed. But if, during a dull day, the sun suddenly shines, in a few minutes the petals of the gentians unfold. Since the flowers stay closed in dark weather, the pollen and nectar within the fringed blue cups are safe from rain.

It happens that one gentian flower needs the yellow pollen from another gentian flower in order to bear good seeds. Strangely enough, certain flying insects help scatter the pollen. The bumble bees go to gentians for sweet nectar and pollen for their young. While they gather nectar, some of the pollen sticks to them. The bees scrape most of this off and pack it on their hind legs. When they visit the next flower, a few grains of pollen that are still

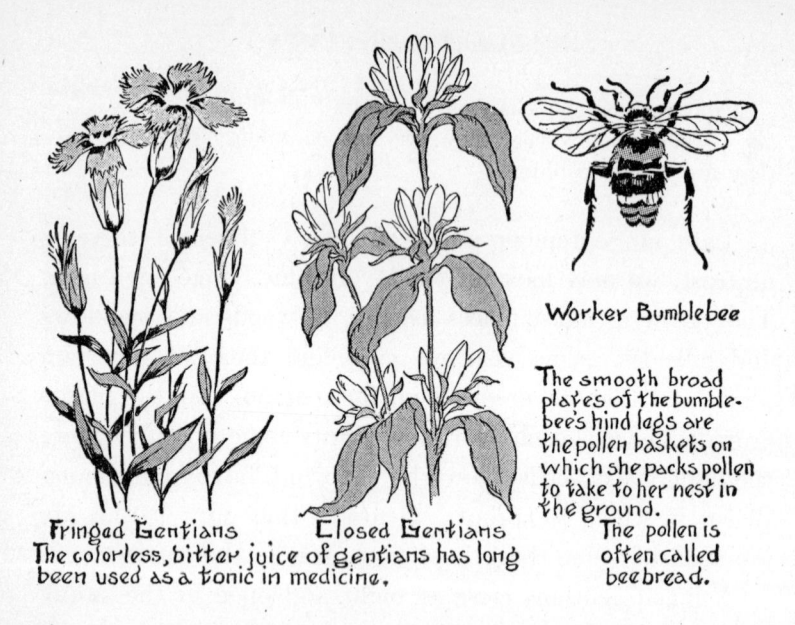

Fringed Gentians
The colorless, bitter juice of gentians has long been used as a tonic in medicine.

Closed Gentians

Worker Bumblebee
The smooth broad plates of the bumblebee's hind legs are the pollen baskets on which she packs pollen to take to her nest in the ground. The pollen is often called beebread.

left on their heads or bodies drop off and new pollen is carried away. The bees have what they came for—nectar and pollen. The plants get what they need—the exchange of pollen.

The long, delicate fringe of the gentians not only attracts insects flying by, but it prevents crawling insects from climbing up over the edge of the flower and stealing the nectar. Should they try to climb over, their feet become entangled in the fringe. It is fortunate that the nectar and pollen are saved for flying insects because crawling insects would not carry pollen well; it would be rubbed off them by the time they crawled to the next flower.

—NINA LEUBRIE.

FOR DISCUSSION

What is pollen? What is its use? In what flowers have you seen pollen? How does the fringed gentian scatter its pollen? How does the fringed gentian keep its pollen dry? How does it keep the pollen safe from crawling insects? If you ever see another flower safeguard its pollen in this manner, tell the class about it.

The fringed gentian and some of our other lovely wild flowers are in danger of being exterminated. The Wild Flower Preservation Society of America asks you to read these slogans. Discuss them in class. Help others to understand what they mean.

SLOGANS

I will learn to enjoy
And not to destroy.

What I have not sown
I must not pick.

The Flower says:

If you pick my seeds this year
I can give you no flowers next year.

Do you find the woods and fields beautiful?
Help to keep them so.

Do not pick the flowers.
Do not spoil the trees.
Keep our country beautiful.

NOTE: "The Burgess Flower Book for Children," by Thornton W. Burgess, has very good illustrations. Little, Brown.

"Fieldbook of American Wild Flowers," by F. S. Mathews, will give help in identifying flowers. Putnam.

CLOSED GENTIANS

Closed or bottle gentians like shaded, moist places. But sometimes we find them growing along roadsides in the sun. Those growing in the open are a deeper violet blue than those growing in shade. Occasionally we see a plant which bears white flowers. As a rule, however, the closed gentians are purple-blue and turn a deep reddish-purple with age.

Instead of opening with the sun and closing with the dark like the fringed gentians, the bottle gentians always remain closed. The rain cannot get in and spoil the nectar; frost cannot injure the delicate inner flower parts, nor can insect thieves easily carry off the pollen. For if once they force their way into the flower, they are trapped within the closed bottle.

In order to make healthy seeds, closed gentians need an exchange of pollen, just as fringed gentians do. And the story of how pollen is carried from one closed gentian to another is much like that we have just read. The bumblebee makes this exchange without knowing it. When she comes after nectar and pollen for food for the young bees, she forces her tongue through the overlapped tip of the flower; next she pushes her head in, then her forelegs, and a part of her body. By the time she has sipped nectar, she has rubbed off a few grains of pollen that have stuck to her from the other flowers she has visited, and she is smeared with fresh pollen. Then she backs out of the flower and with her feet scrapes off much of the pollen that she has just collected on her head and body. She packs this on her hind legs and goes off to other closed gentians. Whenever she sips nectar, she scatters and gathers pollen. Thus, without knowing it, the bumblebee pays in service for the sweets and pollen she takes.

—NINA LEUBRIE.

Note: It is very important for certain plants to have the pollen dust of one plant taken to another of the same kind. Why is this? Read carefully the manner in which this is done in gentians and be ready to tell the class.

How does the closed gentian guard against insect thieves?

JACK–IN–THE–PULPIT

Study the pictures if you haven't a real Jack-in-the-pulpit to examine. Find each part as you read about it.

Jack-in-the-pulpit is a plant of many names. It is also known as Indian turnip, wild turnip, pepper turnip, marsh turnip, brown dragon, and bog-onion. From these names you can tell something about the plant and its habits. Some early settlers knew it by still another name—*memory root*. If a person bites into the raw bulb-like root or corm, he has cause to remember that bite many a day. For merely a taste makes the tongue and throat feel as if one had swallowed hundreds of pricking needles. That memory does not soon pass. It is said that tiny needle-like crystals in the corm penetrate the tongue and throat, and cause the pricking and stinging. The Indians boiled the corm and the scarlet berries for food. They knew that the cooked or dried corm loses its sting. It then has a flat taste.

When you wish to see Jack-in-the-pulpit at its best, go to shaded, wet woods. Its colors are darker there than when it grows in open sunlight.

You can easily see why Jack is sometimes called brown *dragon*. Jack's flowers are within the hood at the base of the club-like green rod. Tiny flies and gnats slip down

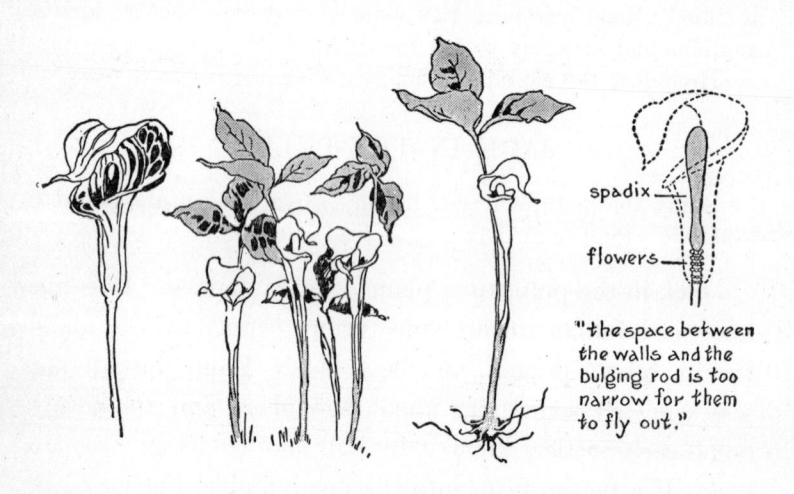

"the space between the walls and the bulging rod is too narrow for them to fly out."

into the hood for nectar and pollen. But the walls are too slippery for them to crawl out again, and the space between the walls and the bulging rod is too narrow for them to fly out. Many are imprisoned within and die there. A few, however, find their way out of the gap in the flaps of the walls, and carry pollen to the next Jack-in-the-pulpit that they visit.

FLOWER IN THE CRANNIED WALL

Flower in the crannied wall,
I pluck you out of the crannies,
I hold you here, root and all, in my hand,
Little flower—but *if* I could understand
What you are, root and all, and all in all,
I should know what God and man is.

—ALFRED, LORD TENNYSON.

NOTE: Try to express this thought in your own words.

The poem also makes an excellent oral reading exercise. Read it aloud. Be sure you enunciate each word distinctly.

BOOKS ON FLOWERS

1. "How to Know the Wild Flowers," by Frances T. Dana. Scribners.

Good illustrations and excellent description.

2. "Wonders of Plant Life," by Martin Duncan. Oxford University Press.

Six small books giving interesting points on plant life.

3. "Field, Forest, and Farm," by Henri Fabre. Century.

Another splendid book by this famous scientist.

4. "The Wayside Flowers of Summer," by Harriett L. Keeler. Scribners.

"Our Northern Summer." Scribners.
"Our Early Wild Flowers." Scribners.
"Our Garden Flowers." Scribners.

Very helpful books. Well illustrated, accurate, and entertaining.

5. "Flower Guides," by C. A. Reed. Doubleday.
"Wild Flowers East of the Rockies."
"Western Flower Guide."
Standard field books. Small size and handy to carry in the pocket. Fully illustrated.

6. "Rocky Mountain Flowers," by F. E. and E. S. Clements. H. W. Wilson Company.
A reference book.

SUN PRINTING

Read the lesson through silently. Make note of anything you do not understand. Have the way in which things are to be done and the order in which they come so clear in mind that you can help others to understand. Make yourself familiar with the working of the printing-frame.

Flower and leaf pictures can be taken without a camera. To do this you will need sunlight, a printing-frame such as photographers use, a clean glass to fit the frame, blue-print paper cut the desired size, and a supply of fresh water.

Directions: Arrange the flower with its leaf on the clean, dry glass in the frame. On this place the slightly colored side of your blue-print paper, close the frame, and put it out in the sun where the direct rays will strike the glass.

If the light is strong, in about three minutes look at your print. Do not examine it in the sunlight. Open one shutter of the frame, raise the paper and peep at the print. If the paper has a bronzed appearance it is ready to take out of the frame. If it has not bronzed, close the frame and again put it in the sun. When the print is ready, take it indoors and put it into a basin of clean water. Souse the paper face up under the water for about a minute. Whenever the water becomes yellow, put the print into fresh water, or under running water. Wash it until the blue is clear and the white parts have no yellow in them. Then put the wet print, face up, on newspaper to dry; but not where the sun will strike it. The paper will be pale and faded if it was not exposed long enough. While the print is having its final bath you can take another picture; but do not drop water on the glass or on anything in the frame.

NOTE: There are different kinds of blue-print paper. Some kinds do not bronze in the sun. You may have to experiment with several sheets of paper before you find out how long your particular kind needs to be exposed to the sun.

FOR DISCUSSION

1. If you have everything for the work but haven't the proper weather, what then? If you have the right weather and almost everything you need but the blue-print paper, what then? Where will you wash the prints? What arrangements can you make to take turns in using the basins or running water?

2. Will you be able to print at recess or after school, or during school or at home? All these things need planning.

3. While you are printing, you may wish to refer to your book for information. But now is the time to ask questions. When every one has had a chance to read the lesson and make notes of difficulties, bring your questions to class for discussion. Let some one show the class how the printing-frame works.

THE TOWN I LIVE IN

"The Town I Live In" is not greatly unlike thousands of towns in the United States except that it is near Lake Michigan, and it has a fringe of bluffs and dunes along the shore.

Every locality has its spots of interest. Every common thing in nature has a tale of magic to unfold, but only he who wonders, may read it. Many people see the sand along the shores of their lakes, but how few pick up a handful to look at it closely and wonder how, when, and where about it. The answers to our questions often lead us many miles away, and back many, many years in time. Henry David Thoreau, who lived the greater part of his life in Concord, Massachusetts, said: "I have traveled a good deal—in Concord." He looked at his neighbor's farm and enjoyed the beauty that he saw there. He said: "I retained the landscape and have annually carried off what it yielded without a wheelbarrow."

In the story which follows the writer carried off many rich prizes. Can you tell what they were? Did you ever carry off any "prize" from the town you live in? This story also shows that if you will look around the place you know best you will find much that it would be pleasant to hear more about. You will not need to travel far in order to come upon interesting sights and experiences.

I

Greenbush, a Buried Village

When you are in the town and look northward up the main road, you see a high wall of dunes about three-quarters of a mile away. This wall of sand shuts off all view of the lake. There was a time, however, about fifty years ago, when a road ran directly to the lake. In those days the place was called Greenbush, but the Greenbush post office was on the main road, where now the dune stands, and not where the town is today.

At that time a little cluster of houses stood near the shore and a pier jutted out into the lake. Nowadays only a double row of worn piles shows where the scow and the steamer took on their loads.

Greenbush was a busy enough place. Down its main road and leading to the pier a wooden railroad ran far into the back country. Noisy little cars, drawn by horses and piled with cord-wood, four feet long, rattled over the wooden rails and unloaded on the pier. All along the road, rick after rick, ten feet high, stood ready to fill the empty cars.

But where was the wood being sent? It was the time of the Chicago fire. The city had just been burned, and thousands of people were homeless. To furnish "chop-wood" and to fire the kilns then baking bricks to rebuild the city, Greenbush shipped her beech and maple.

At the same time, old Lake Michigan had its work to do. It ground stones into sand and the waves pushed the sand ashore. Then the wind blew the sand farther and farther out of the reach of the water. It piled the sand into little drifts, and then built them into little hillocks. Some of the hillocks became sandhills or dunes. The work of the water and wind never stopped. The shrubs and the tough grasses that grew on the upper beach made good places for sand to collect—starting-places for new dunes. Whenever the wind, carrying its load of sand, met any obstacle in its path—plant, or driftwood, or house—it dropped some of its load then and there. Before people in Greenbush realized what had happened, there was a line of low dunes on the shore.

But as the dunes grew larger, the woods in the back country were rapidly being thinned out. For you cannot feed a busy line of cars, year after year, with the best hardwood of a region, and still have the best hardwood left to feed it endlessly. As could have been expected, the woods dwindled away.

But if woods became thinner, farm land became cleared; and soon orchards grew where once beech and maple stood. Besides, to the north, there was much wood for shipping. "Let the axmen go there!" said the man who wanted to settle. And go they did, those who did not care to stay and farm. The steamer and scow no longer stopped at Greenbush pier, nor the neighboring piers. No longer the horse trains jangled down the road. Word had been given to move on. Greenbush village became deserted.

II

The Living Dune

Nowadays when you walk on top of the big Greenbush dune, you may know that under it several houses lie buried. A peach orchard and an apple orchard also lie beneath.

Nothing remains of Greenbush except a few fruit trees, and the old rotting piles in the lake. If you look out over the orchard country at the foot of the dune, you know that sooner or later those trees, also, will be buried.

Even when the ends of the branches are all that one can see of an apple or peach tree that the dune has covered, those ends have flowers in spring; and in autumn the arms stretching out of the sand bear fruit.

The dune moves on like a great monster. Only a few feet a year it advances, faster in high winds or when people disturb its sand; slower at other times, but always on. The townsfolk ask, "Will the dune, after centuries, reach the town?"

But they know the dune can be held in check. First it must have a covering on it to keep the sand from shifting —a covering of plants may prove the best. To begin with, the long, gentle slope and the top will need covering; then the steep sides. Brush or tangle of any kind will hold down the exposed places. If natural dune plants get a foothold and are undisturbed, in time a mat of plants will bind the dune.

But it will take constant care to keep the plants undisturbed. Burrowing animals and thoughtless persons can open up any dune to destruction. They dig a hole and the wind eats its way into the dune and destroys the plants— and the dune rolls on.

Thoughtful, earnest persons can keep the Greenbush dune from moving inland. It will be a great struggle, and it will take time and endless work; but it can be done, and it will be worth the while.

III
Indians at Greenbush

Before the town of Greenbush was thought of, Indians knew this region. We have reason to believe that Indians paddled in their canoes along this shore of the lake. There are stories of their going and coming. But we know with certainty that they tramped this country, because we find their implements.

Dunes that for years keep their secrets may suddenly give them up. The wind covers things with sand, but often in time uncovers them. Wind not only levels to the ground the dune it has taken years to build, but it hollows out places as well. When the wind scoops out a hollow, we call it a "blow-out." Now and then we find stone arrowheads, fish spear points, sharp flakes of flint, stone hammers and axes, in a sandy blow-out. Many of these tools and weapons are perfect and do not look wind or water-worn. When we find such an implement we say:

"Think of it! The last person who held this in his hand was an Indian!"

Perhaps some of the curiously bent old trees along the shore were signal trees for the Indians. Perhaps some of the trails we use were first made by them. Who can say? But when their stone arrowheads and knives and hammers and tools are uncovered year after year in one blow-out after another, we know beyond doubt that Indians once were here.

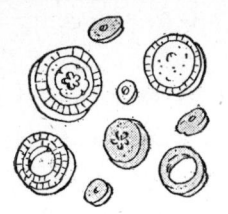

IV

Stone Beads

Along the water's edge we pick up flat round bits of stone pierced through the middle like beads. The holes are round or star-shaped. If you ask what they are, any town child will say at once: "Those are Indian beads."

It is probable that the Indians did string them and wear them; but the Indians did not make them. The story of these "beads of stone" is almost like a fairy tale.

Once upon a time there was an ocean where now there is land in the central part of the United States. The whole State of Michigan and the Great Lakes were under water. In that ocean there lived queer plants and animals. And in that salt water the one strange kind of life this story tells about looked like a plant, but was really an animal. "Crinoid" is the name we have given to it.

The crinoid grew on the ocean floor and looked like a flower, a sea lily. On its stem a flower-like head waved in the water. The rays of this sea lily opened and closed like the petals of a flower.

And what do you suppose the rays or arms of the crinoid were doing? They were feeding the mouth at the center. When tiny, tiny sea creatures floated by in the water, the waving arms of the sea lily, or crinoid, caught up the creatures and fed the mouth that was in the center of the rays. All the sea lilies lived in this way.

But there was lime in the ocean creatures that the crinoids ate, and there was lime in the ocean water that the crinoids swallowed. Gradually, as the sea lilies took in more and more lime, they became harder and harder. Yet there was a soft, live part within them which thrived on the tiny creatures in the water.

How the whole ocean bottom became a floor of rock and was gradually lifted up out of the water is a story which some day you may read. But whenever you find a "stone bead," or an "Indian bead," on the lake shore, you may know that it was once a part of a sea lily. Perhaps it was part of the crinoid's stem, or of the rays that moved in the water. Perhaps it was crushed and is no longer round. Often you will find many pieces of stems in a single stone. Thousands of years ago they were parts of curious animals living in the ocean.

Even today there are living crinoids in some ocean bottoms. Their stems are made up of joints that look much like the "beads" you find on the shore. We call these animals "sea lilies" when they are alive. When we find them imbedded in stone, we call them "stone lilies."

—NINA LEUBRIE.

CLASS PROJECT

It would be interesting to make a class book, or a book of your own on the village, or neighborhood, or city you live in. Add to it, from time to time. Will you illustrate your book?

ELLIS PARK

Little park that I pass through,
I carry off a piece of you
Every morning hurrying down
To my work day in the town;
Carry you for country there
To make the city ways more fair.

I take your trees
And your breeze,
Your greenness,
Your cleanness,
Some of your shade, some of your sky,
Some of your calm as I go by;
Your flowers to trim
The pavements grim;
Your space for room in the jostled street,
And grass for carpet to my feet.
Your fountains take and sweet bird calls
To sing me from my office walls.
All that I can see
I carry off with me.

But you never miss my theft,
So much treasure you have left.
As I find you, fresh at morning,
So I find you, home returning,

Nothing lacking from your grace.
All your riches wait in place
For me to borrow
On the morrow.

Do you hear this praise of you,
Little park that I pass through?

—HELEN HOYT.

Tell in your own way how you might feel about some place as the poet feels about Ellis Park.

AFTERNOON ON A HILL

I will be the gladdest thing
    Under the sun!
I will touch a hundred flowers
    And not pick one.

I will look at cliffs and clouds
    With quiet eyes,
Watch the wind bow down the grass,
    And the grass rise.

And when lights begin to show
    Up from the town,
I will mark which must be mine
    And then start down!

—EDNA ST. VINCENT MILLAY.

A STREET SCENE

The east is a clear violet mass
Behind the houses high;
The laborers with their kettles pass;
The carts go creaking by.

Carved out against the tender sky,
The convent gables lift;
Half way below, the old boughs lie
Heaped in a great white drift.

They tremble in the passionate air;
They part, and clean and sweet
The cherry flakes fall here, fall there;
A handful stirs the street.

The workmen look up as they go;
And one, remembering plain
How white the Irish orchards blow,
Turns back and looks again.
—LIZETTE WOODWORTH REESE.

In the first of these three poems, there is not one clear picture—is there? In the second, there are two. Find them. In the third, there are seven or eight. Find them.

A poem without any pictures may be as good as one that is full of pictures if the words in it make you remember things you have seen yourself.

STOPPING BY WOODS ON A SNOWY EVENING

Whose woods these are I think I know,
His house is in the village though;
He will not see me stopping here
To watch his woods fill up with snow.

The little horse must think it queer
To stop without a farmhouse near
Between the woods and frozen lake
The darkest evening of the year.

He gives his harness bells a shake
To ask if there is some mistake,
The only other sound's the sweep
Of easy wind and downy flake.

The woods are lovely dark and deep,
But I have promises to keep,
And miles to go before I sleep,
And miles to go before I sleep.

—ROBERT FROST.

TEWKESBURY ROAD

It is good to be out on the road, and going one knows not where,
  Going through meadow and village, one knows not whither nor why;

Through the grey light drift of the dust, in the keen cool rush of the air,
    Under the flying white clouds, and the broad blue lift of the sky;
And to halt at the chattering brook, in the tall green fern at the brink
    Where the harebell grows, and the gorse, and the foxgloves purple and white;
Where the shy-eyed delicate deer troop down to the pools to drink,
    When the stars are mellow and large at the coming on of the night.

O! to feel the warmth of the rain, and the homely smell of the earth,
    Is a tune of the blood to jig to, a joy past power of words;
And the blessed green comely meadows seem all a-ripple with mirth,
    At the lilt of the shifting feet, and the dear wild cry of the birds. —JOHN MASEFIELD.

In the three following poems, notice how each poet characterizes the season he writes about.

APRIL

The roofs are shining from the rain,
    The sparrows twitter as they fly,
And with a windy April grace
    The little clouds go by.

Yet the back-yards are bare and brown
    With only one unchanging tree—
I could not be so sure of Spring
    Save that it sings in me.   —SARA TEASDALE.

SUMMER EVENING

The sandy cat by the Farmer's chair
Mews at his knee for dainty fare;
Old Rover in his moss-greened house
Mumbles a bone, and barks at a mouse;
In the dewy fields the cattle lie
Chewing a cud 'neath a fading sky;
Dobbin at manger pulls his hay;
Gone is another summer's day.

—WALTER DE LA MARE.

AUTUMN

The morns are meeker than they were,
    The nuts are getting brown;
The berry's cheek is plumper,
    The rose is out of town.

The maple wears a gayer scarf,
    The field a scarlet gown.
Lest I should be old-fashioned,
    I'll put a trinket on.   —EMILY DICKINSON.

What other poems of seasons can you add to these?

THE EIGHTH PSALM

O Lord our Lord, how excellent is thy name in all the earth! who hast set thy glory above the heavens.

When I consider thy heavens, the work of thy fingers, the moon and the stars, which thou hast ordained;

What is man, that thou art mindful of him? and the son of man, that thou visitest him?

For thou hast made him a little lower than the angels, and hast crowned him with glory and honor.

Thou madest him to have dominion over the works of thy hands; thou hast put all things under his feet:

All sheep and oxen, yea, and the beasts of the field;

The fowl of the air, and the fish of the seas, and whatsoever passeth through the paths of the seas.

O Lord our Lord, how excellent is thy name in all the earth.

NEARER THAN THE STARS

Our nearest neighbor out in the vast spaces beyond our earth is the moon. Beyond the moon, but nearer than the stars, are the planets: Mercury, Venus, Mars, Jupiter, Saturn, Uranus, and Neptune. The moon—although it is always changing in appearance—seems like an old friend that we look upon with close interest. When we become acquainted with the planets, they too become as friends we delight to look for.

Now and then on clear nights, we see streaks of light shoot across the sky like rockets. Sometimes we say they are falling stars. But that is not true. Stars never come near the earth. What we see are meteorites (mē'tĕ-ŏr-īts), small bits of matter from the vast spaces beyond the earth. As they strike our atmosphere, they are heated by friction to the burning point. Usually these small particles hurl themselves into our atmosphere, flare up, and burn to gases. Sometimes, however, they are large enough to reach the earth. You may have seen some of them which have been found and placed in a museum.

Away out in space beyond the path of Mars hundreds of small bodies called asteroids (ăs'tĕr-oids) revolve about the sun. They range in diameter from about twenty to four hundred miles. Most of them keep within the vast space between Mars and Jupiter. At times, however, one of them comes within 14,000,000 miles of the earth.

The following pages tell of the moon, and something about the planets.

THE MOON

This selection will give you many interesting facts. Read it silently and rapidly the first time. Then go back over it and make a complete outline of it:

a. Choose a good heading for each paragraph.
b. List all important points in the paragraph under it.

Try to answer each question in the selection.
It will aid your reading and save time to make sure of the following words before you begin to read:

origin	craters	satellite
telescope	impact	gravity
chasms	serenely	orbit

After you have read this account of what the moon is really like, you may be interested to read a story by H. G. Wells called "The First Men in the Moon." In this the author uses scientific knowledge to make life on the moon seem possible.

Two hundred and forty thousand miles from us, the moon serenely moves in her path around the earth. It might help us to form some idea of the tremendous distance of our nearest neighbor in space, if we considered how long it would take an aeroplane, flying in a straight line at the rate of one hundred miles an hour without stopping (if that were possible), to reach the moon. Such a thing as this flight to the moon, of course, is absurd for the reason that beyond a few miles from the earth's surface there is no air to support an aeroplane.

Compared with the earth, the moon is quite small. Its whole area is less than that of Asia. One writer states that if the waters of the Pacific could be rolled into a globe, their bulk would be just about the size of the moon. The diameter of the moon is about 2,163 miles, which is only a little more than one-fourth the diameter of the earth.

Because the moon is comparatively near to us, its surface has been carefully studied through the telescope. Many details have been discovered. In fact, we now know more about the surface of the moon than we do about some parts of the earth. There are, for instance, some parts of Alaska where there are great forests and lakes and mountains and valleys about which little is yet known. Vast tracts of the polar regions and much of Asia and Africa have yet to be explored. But on the side of the moon nearest the earth there is no area of any size that has not been photographed and mapped many times.

The telescope shows us that the surface of the moon is much more rugged than that of the earth. There are many lofty mountains and numerous ranges. Two of the mountains are 25,000 feet high and seventy are over 18,000 feet. This seems very strange and almost unbelievable when we consider that the moon is so much smaller than the earth. You may wonder how the height of mountains on the moon can be determined. It is done by measuring the shadows which they cast; just as the height of buildings and of trees on the earth can be measured by their shadows.

There are also flat areas which correspond to our plains.

One strange feature of the surface are numerous deep, narrow chasms or "clefts" which run for hundreds of miles in fairly straight lines through mountains and across plains.

Photographs and the telescope show prominent markings called "craters" because they look like the craters of our volcanoes. These huge, saucer-like dents are from a mile to one hundred and thirty miles in diameter, with walls thousands of feet high. Sometimes they have a volcanic-like cone in the middle. There are various theories regarding the origin of the moon's "craters." One

Courtesy of the American Museum of Natural History.
LUNAR LANDSCAPE.
From a painting by Howard R. Butler.

is that they are of volcanic origin. Another theory is that before the moon became our satellite, and revolved about the earth, it followed a path where now the asteroids are; at that time it was struck repeatedly by satellites; the impacts caused the dents, as well as the mountains of the moon. Later, the earth, by its superior gravity, attracted the moon —captured it—and held it in its present path. Both of these, however, are theories only.

It is now believed that there is no air or water on the

surface of the moon, unless it be in very small quantities—too meager to support life as we know it. Clouds are never observed, even with the aid of the telescope. There can be no weather, such as we have. It is probable that there is little soil; possibly none. Do you see how the lack of air and water explains the jagged roughness of the mountains and the absence of soil?

Did you ever realize that the same side of the moon is always turned toward the earth? No one on earth has ever seen the other half of the moon. What it is like we can only imagine. The reason for this strange fact is that the moon takes as much time to turn on its own axis as it does to go on its path around the earth — about twenty-eight days. It rotates on its own axis once for each revolution in its orbit about the earth.

To understand this, let one pupil play he is the earth and another pupil the moon. While the earth child turns round and round, the moon child, *always facing inward*, circles slowly around the earth. For every twenty-seven and one-third complete rotations the earth child makes, the moon child, always facing the earth, makes but one.

Because of the absence of air and water on the surface of the moon, there is nothing to shield it from the intense heat of the sun in the long day there. Our atmosphere, clouds, and immense bodies of water on the surface of the earth absorb an enormous amount of the sun's heat. Then, too, we have a change from day to night about every twelve hours on the average. But on the moon, the sunshine is continuous at any one place for almost half of our month. The night, which is about fourteen of our days and nights, is pitilessly cold, as there is no atmosphere to retain the sun's heat. In a year of our time, then, we may think of the moon as having somewhat more than twelve and a half of its long, burning days, and twelve and a half of its long, freezing nights. It is probable that during the period of sunshine the rocks become heated to such a temperature that all life as we know it would burn; and during the long night the surface becomes colder than any cold we know on earth.

The moon gives off no light of its own. It "shines" only from the side on which the sun shines. The opposite side is in utter darkness—the deepest and blackest darkness. Moonlight is reflected light. When we look at the shining moon, we really see sunlight reflected from the moon's surface. And that reflected light traveling through space and the earth's atmosphere with unthinkable speed reaches us one and one-fourth seconds after it leaves the moon. There is very little heat in it, and that is absorbed by our atmosphere before it reaches the earth.

Of considerable interest are the shadows we see upon the surface of the moon. They are very deep and black and are caused by the high mountain ranges. The unusual intensity of these shadows is one proof that there is no atmosphere on the moon. It is the appearance of the shadows which gives us the idea of the man's face on the moon, and gave rise to the stories about "The Man in the Moon."

Have you ever thought how our earth would look, if it were possible for an intelligent being to be on the moon? The earth reflects sunlight. It is called earth-shine. To a person on the moon, the earth would look to be about four times as large as the moon appears to us. It would show changes of form just as the moon does to us. Because of our atmosphere, water, and vegetation, the earth-shine would appear a bit different. The polar regions would be very bright and the tropical regions would present a greenish tinge. Why? The same part would change appearance with the weather. Why? The land areas would look different from the sea. Why?

Another interesting fact about the moon is the weight of objects on its surface. The weight of an object there is about one-sixth what it would be on the earth. A boy who weighs one hundred pounds here would weigh only sixteen and two-thirds pounds there. He could throw a baseball six times as far. The same effort to jump three feet high here would lift the boy eighteen feet high there. It would be very foolish for earth boys to try to compete with moon boys in a field meet by radio! See if you can find out the reason for these facts.

An account of the moon would be incomplete without reference to the superstitions which have grown up about it. From earliest times the moon has been looked upon with feelings of wonder.

Primitive man[1] looked upon it with fear and reverence.

[1] primitive man: the earliest people.

He was frightened by eclipses. He worshipped it as a god. Even the Romans had a goddess of the moon, whom they named Luna. In later times as well, many superstitions grew up in popular belief. It was believed that certain crops must be planted by the moon, some in the light and some in the dark of it, if they were to do well. One common belief was that sleeping in moonlight affected the mind. Many superstitions regarding the mysterious powers of the moon still exist, but with the increase of scientific knowledge such beliefs are rapidly disappearing.

FOR DISCUSSION

1. Compare the distance of the moon from the earth with the distance around the earth at the equator.
2. What would go into a picture of the surface of the moon, if you were drawing one?
3. If you were on the moon and wished to get to earth for Christmas dinner, traveling by aeroplane at the rate of one hundred miles per hour in a non-stop flight, in what month would you have to start?

NOTE: Make a list of all points in the supposed conditions of this question which are really absurd.

4. What have air and water to do with weather?
5. When is dawn? When is there twilight? Is the sun to be seen at those times? Why can there be no dawn or twilight where there is no atmosphere?
6. Make a list of all the superstitions you know and can find about the moon and bring them to class for discussion.
7. Explain: "No creature on earth has ever seen the other side of the moon."

8. Try to find out the reason why objects weigh less on the moon than on the earth.

9. Can you show how under modern civilization we do not need to depend upon the moon as earlier peoples did?

REFERENCE WORK

Look up in your geography and other books:

a. How the moon is the chief cause of tides.

b. How it affects the earth's magnetism.

BOOKS TO READ

Our knowledge in astronomy is always changing. What is accepted today in astronomy is proved false tomorrow. Wherever it is possible, therefore, consult the most recent books on astronomy.

1. "Astronomy for Young Folks," by Isabel Lewis. Duffield.
   A book with good descriptions, diagrams, pictures, and stories.
2. "The Friendly Stars," by Martha E. Martin. Harpers.
   The descriptions in this book are clear and simple.
3. "The Book of Stars," by A. F. Collins. Appleton.
   This book gives practical directions for identifying the stars and constellations, for telling time by sun and moon, and for finding one's direction by the stars.
4. "Book of Stars," by W. T. Olcott. Putnam.
   Illustrated. This book describes the constellations visible each season and gives the meaning of star names.
5. "Astronomy for Everybody," by Simon B. Newcomb. Doubleday.
   A good reference book for the teacher. It contains good illustrations of the planets, and tells much about the solar system.

6. "Starland," by Sir R. S. Ball. Ginn.

A new edition by the Director of the Observatory of Cambridge University. Illustrated. Simple in style and scientifically accurate.

FULL MOON

One night as Dick lay half asleep,
   Into his drowsy eyes
A great still light began to creep
   From out the silent skies.

It was the lovely moon's, for when
   He raised his dreamy head,
Her surge of silver filled the pane
   And streamed across his bed.

So, for a while, each gazed at each—
   Dick and the solemn moon—
Till, climbing slowly on her way,
   She vanished and was gone.

—WALTER DE LA MARE.

FOR DISCUSSION

Have you ever had the experience described in the poem? What were you thinking about the moon while it happened?

If you were writing a poem about the moon, what should you put into it?

The heavens declare the glory of God; and the firmament sheweth his handywork.

Day unto day uttereth speech, and night unto night showeth knowledge.
— *Psalm xix, 1, 2.*

THE PLANETS

The word *planet* comes from a Greek word meaning *wanderer*. Stars do not seem to move in relation to one another but the planets seem to be now in one part of a constellation,[1] now in another part. The watcher of stars in ancient times thought that planets were stars which wandered in and out of constellations, and that other stars were fixed and could not move.

Now we know that stars are suns of tremendous size, and far away from us; but planets are bodies more or less like our earth, so near to us that they are in our own solar system revolving about our sun. They are not at all near the constellations; they cannot pass through them as they seem to do.

Perhaps you have been in a fast-moving train and have noticed that from the car window the telegraph-poles or trees, or objects that are near, seem to rush by with great speed, and the very distant trees and objects seem to stand still. So it is with the planets, which are comparatively near, and the stars, which are far away.

---

[1] constellation (kŏn″stĕl-lā′shŭn): a group of fixed stars having a special name. For example: Cassiopeia (kăs″ĭ-ŏ-pē′yȧ): a constellation near the north polar star; also known as the Lady in the Chair. Also Ursa Major, the Great Bear, the most prominent of the northern constellations, containing the seven stars that form the great dipper.

SPIRAL NEBULA OF ANDROMEDA.

It is perhaps because the planets are so near the earth that our interest in them is so keen. Then, too, the earth is a planet and their origin or beginning was the same as that of our earth; they are controlled by the same sun, and by the same laws as the earth; and it is possible they will all have the same end.

The sun controls the motion of all the planets; yet each planet pulls at the others according to its size and distance, and so makes the others vary from their path around the sun.

Taken in the order of their nearness to the sun, the planets are Mercury, Venus, the Earth, Mars, Jupiter, Saturn, Uranus, Neptune. With the exception of Mercury, however, the earth is nearer to the planets than the sun is. The nearest planet to us, Venus, is three light minutes[1]

[1] light minute: the distance light travels in one minute, which is 186,000 miles.

from us. Neptune, the farthest planet, is over four light hours from the Earth.

Uranus and Neptune are so far away that we can see them only with the aid of a telescope.

THE SOLAR SYSTEM

When we speak of the solar system, we mean the sun and the planets which revolve about it with their moons or satellites.

There are many theories on the origin of the solar system. One theory is that the sun and the planets once formed a great spiral nebula.[1] Gradually the gases condensed, the more solid center formed the sun, and the more gaseous bodies thrown off became the planets. Another theory, known as the "capture theory," is that the sun, by its superior gravity,[2] attracted the planets at some far time, when they came near enough to be "caught"; and the planets in turn attracted or "captured" the smaller bodies which now revolve about them, and which we call their moons or satellites.

Because, then, of the huge bulk and greater gravity of the sun, it continues to attract the planets; they all revolve about the sun in different orbits,[3] at different distances, and

---

[1] spiral nebula: a light-giving (luminous) formation of gases in the heavens, resembling a patch of haze or cloud in the form of a great spiral, located at enormous distance from the earth. (See p. 403 for picture of a spiral nebula.)

[2] gravity: force or power to attract.

[3] orbit: the path in which a planet, comet, or other heavenly body moves in space about its center of attraction.

at different speeds. They are all opaque bodies and shine with light reflected from the sun; the amount of light we see depending upon the size of the planet, its distance from us, and its reflecting power.

In order that we may better appreciate how far the moon, sun, and planets are from the earth, some one has worked out the distances in this way:

If it were possible to travel through the thin air of our outer atmosphere, and through space beyond that, an aeroplane or a dirigible traveling at a speed of one mile a minute would pass the moon on the one hundred and sixty-sixth day; and continuing at that speed, would arrive at the sun in one hundred and seventy-seven years. From the earth to Jupiter, it would take seven hundred and forty years, at a mile a minute, and to get to Saturn it would take about fifteen hundred years.

OUR SOLAR SYSTEM IN A MODEL OF THE UNIVERSE

Let us imagine that, in a model of the universe, the earth on which we live is represented by a grain of mustard-seed. The moon will then be a particle about one-fourth the diameter of the grain, placed at a distance of an inch from the earth. The sun will be represented by a large apple, placed at a distance of forty feet. Other planets, ranging in size from an invisible particle to a pea, must be imagined at distances from the sun varying from ten feet to a quarter of a mile. We must then imagine all these little objects to be slowly moving around the sun at their respective distances, in times varying from three months to 160 years. As the mustard-seed performs its revolution in the course of a year we must imagine the moon to accompany it, making a revolution around it every month.

On this scale, a plan of the whole solar system can be laid down in a field half a mile square. Outside this field we should find a tract broader than the whole continent of America without a visible object in it, unless perhaps comets scattered around its border. Far beyond the limit of the American continent we should find the nearest star, which, like our sun, might be represented by a large apple. At still greater distances, in every direction, would be other stars, but, in the general average, they would be separated from each other as widely as the nearest star is from the sun. A region of the little model as large as the whole earth might contain only two or three stars.

*—From "Astronomy for Everybody,"
by Simon B. Newcomb.*

See Leon Barrit's "Monthly Evening Sky Maps." They are sold at 15 cents a copy; $1.50 a year. Address 367 Fulton Street, Brooklyn, N. Y.

With the aid of these maps you can locate the planets, stars, and constellations with the accuracy that you can locate cities, states, and groups of states on a map in your geography.

Identifying Planets

There are ways by which you may recognize the different planets without a telescope. If you see a heavenly body which you think is a planet and you do not know its name, read the following questions. Which one describes the heavenly body that you see?

1. Does it twinkle when it is not near the horizon? Then it is not a planet.
2. Is it very bright and silvery? It is Venus.
3. Is it very solid-looking and bright and pinkish? It is Jupiter.
4. Is it yellow, large, but not brilliant? It is Saturn.
5. Is it very bright and red? It is Mars as seen from the earth when it is directly opposite the sun. It might be called "full Mars," just as we say "full moon."
6. Is it not bright, but small and rosy? It is Mars about to pass between the sun and the earth; or Mars when it is on the further side of the sun.
7. Is it more than forty-five degrees from the sun or more than three hours after sunset? Then it is not Mercury or Venus, and must be Mars, Jupiter, or Saturn. But at times Mars, Jupiter, Saturn, Venus, and Mercury may all be nearer the sun than forty-five degrees.

When the planets are near the horizon they are difficult to distinguish, because the atmosphere makes them all look large and it may intensify their color. They twinkle a little then because they are seen through a dense atmosphere with moving dust particles in it.

Astronomical Units of Measure

Astronomical distances are so great that earth distances cannot very well be used for measuring stars.

The sun is ninety-three million miles from the earth. This distance is called an astronomical unit and is used to measure the distance of planets.

Now the stars are so far away that so small a distance as ninety-three million miles is not used. Instead, we say a star is four or five or seven light-years from us or another star. Light, you remember, travels at the rate of one hundred and eighty-six thousand miles a second. At that speed, light traveling for one year gives the unit by which we measure star distances. Thus: Alpha Centauri, our nearest star, is three and a half light years from the earth.

As no planet is a light-year from us or from any member of the solar system, we do not use this unit in speaking of planet distances. Our nearest planet is three light-minutes from us. The farthest is four light-hours away. The sun is eight light-minutes from the earth; the moon one and a fourth light-seconds from us.

FOR CLASS REPORTS

1. How many stars do you know by name and location? Make a list of them, and be ready to tell how to find them.
2. What constellations do you know and can locate?
3. Learn the names of the planets in their order from the sun. What is the distinguishing characteristic of each?

THE SPACIOUS FIRMAMENT ON HIGH

The spacious firmament on high,
With all the blue ethereal sky,
And spangled heavens, a shining frame,
Their great Original proclaim.
The unwearied sun from day to day
Does his Creator's power display,
And publishes to every land
The work of an Almighty hand.

Soon as the evening shades prevail,
The moon takes up the wondrous tale,
And nightly to the listening earth
Repeats the story of her birth;
Whilst all the stars that round her burn,
And all the planets in their turn
Confirm the tidings as they roll,
And spread the truth from pole to pole.

What though in solemn silence, all
Move round this dark, terrestrial ball?
What though no real voice nor sound
Amidst their radiant orbs be found?
In Reason's ear they all rejoice,
And utter forth a glorious voice,
Forever singing as they shine:
"The hand that made us is divine!"

—JOSEPH ADDISON.

NATURE, SCIENCE, AND INVENTION

Have you ever thought how wonderful Nature is? And how she refuses to tell her secrets to her children until they are ready to make good use of them? And how her children must study her ways and question her again and again before she will give them the knowledge and power they seek?

From the beginning of things, millions and millions of years ago, nature has carried on the work of the Great Creator, never ceasing, never neglecting even the smallest things. Sometimes she has been severe but mostly generous, provident, and abundantly good. When she is severe there is some reason for it. We do not always understand her ways.

The secrets she has told her children (plants, animals, and human beings) make an interesting story. Some of them you have learned; others are yet in store for you. You know some of her faithful servants: Heat, Cold, Water, Gravity, Magnetism, Electricity, Sound, Light, and Mechanical Forces. But you have only begun to know them. If you were to live to be a hundred years old, you could never learn all their secrets, so many and great they are!

Mother Nature in her wisdom gave something to mankind which was denied to plants and animals—namely, the ability to use Science and Invention. These were to be the means by which she intended her human children to win her secrets from her. How man has used this ability to think and create and use the gifts of Nature is a marvelous story.

MR. GROUND-HOG AND HIS SHADOW

It is important to know how to find specific points of information quickly. To do so, one must read rapidly and pass over the facts of the article not wanted. This is called "skimming" to find desired information. Try it on this selection as follows:

Read silently and rapidly to find:
1. When the ground-hog goes to bed?
2. What awakens him?
3. What the Weather Bureau reports show?
4. What records and old diaries show?
5. Why February weather varies?

After skimming the article for these facts, go back over it carefully to get other important details. Then write out a brief statement explaining:
a. What the ground-hog has to do with the weather.
b. How the weather "averages up."

The woodchuck, like the bear, is a "meat-packer." People talk about him more or less in February. His other name is "ground-hog" and his shadow is quite as famous as he is. But what is there in that old weather saying? You see, it's like this: Mr. Ground-Hog goes to bed very early in the fall—long before the cold weather sets in—and so he is up very early the next spring; long before the snow is gone, and, as it is with the other all-winter sleepers, a little extra warmth may wake him up. Toward morning, you know, we all begin to stir in our beds and get half awake. So in addition to the fact that it is nearly daybreak for him—that is to say, springtime—let there come a bright warm day in February—the second is as good as any other—and Mr. Ground-Hog is likely to come out of his hole. And, if he does, of course, he will see his shadow, after which there will probably be quite a lot of cold weather.

How Weather Averages Up

Not that his shadow makes any difference, but the point is that if you have much warm weather *early* in February you are likely to have colder weather *later* and running on into March. It's the law of averages, that's all. You see it running through the year—this averaging up of weather; it sways back and forth like a pendulum. Take it in any storm of rain or snow; first the clear sky, then the clouds, then the downfall, and after that the clear sky again. Take any month as a whole, or a year as a whole, and it's the same; you get about so much rain, so much sunshine, so much heat and cold. The United States Weather Bureau from the records once classified the storms for the last thirty years, and they found that about fifteen storms each year start over the region of the West Gulf States, twelve begin over the mountains of Colorado, forty cross the country from the North Pacific by way of Washington and Oregon; and so on, just about so many from each region each year.

And records and old diaries, going back a hundred years, show that the longer the period you examine for weather facts, the closer the average. The weather for one ten-year period will be almost as much like any other ten-year period, as the peas in a pod are like one another.

Coming back to the subject of February weather, we find in the diary of an old resident of Philadelphia in 1779: "The Winter was mild, and particularly the month of February, when trees were in bloom." He doesn't say anything about the ground-hog, but there is this to be said of the sharper changes of February and March, that at this season the earth is getting more and more warmed up and yet the cold winds from the North don't go; so there is a constant wrestling-match, and it is the wrestling of the winds one way and another that brings the changes of the weather. So if the South Winds get the best of it early in February, the North Winds, with their cold weather, are likely to win later in the month, and vice versa. Moreover, if you believe in the ground-hog proverb you are apt to notice the warm days (or cold days, as the case may be) for the next six weeks after February 2, and you won't notice so much the weather that doesn't fit your proverb! It's a way we all have; seeing the things that go to prove what we believe and overlooking the things that don't.

— From "The Adventures of a Grain of Dust,"
by Hallam Hawksworth.

FOR CLASS DISCUSSION

1. What proverbs about the weather do you know?
2. Are they real or merely superstitions?

NOTE: You will need to think clearly on this point. Do not jump at conclusions.

3. See if you can cite cases where the weather averages up.

4. It will be interesting to keep a Weather Calendar for a month and then compare it with one for the next month.

5. If you keep a Weather Calendar, note in how many cases the Weather Forecasts come true.

6. See if you can find out something about the United States Weather Bureau.

BOOKS TO READ

The author of this selection, Hallam Hawksworth, has two interesting books you would enjoy reading:
1. "The Adventures of a Grain of Dust."
2. "The Strange Adventures of a Pebble."

Both of these books have excellent illustrations.

THE WORK OF THE WINDS

Have you ever wondered about the wind—whence it comes and whither it goes, and what it really does while on the way? That is an interesting story, for the wind is one of Nature's most useful workers. It never seems to cease in its labors, but works here or there incessantly. The poet Wordsworth speaks of

". . . the busy winds
That kept no intervals of rest."

One interesting thing about the wind is its temper or disposition; sometimes gentle, sometimes boisterous, sometimes furious. But no matter what may be the mood, it is always at work.

In the following pages we shall speak of the wind as "the winds." See if you can discover why. You will learn of some of the work the winds do, and perhaps think of several other things about their work not mentioned in the selection.

Read silently and rapidly to get the main thought of each paragraph. When you have finished a section see if you can give a complete answer to the questions which follow. If you cannot, read again carefully, for you have missed the important thought.

FERTILE FIELDS THAT RODE ON THE WIND.
The winds that now help grow the corn and wheat on these broad fields by carrying the pollen from one plant to another, also brought the soil on which they grew. These are the loess plains of Nebraska. There are 42,000 acres of them.

WHAT THE WINDS DO WITH DUST

Not only do winds help plant the trees of the forest, sow the fields with grass and flowers, and water them with rain, but they make and carry soil all over the world. Besides, rock is weathered away into dust by the winds.

March leads the procession of the dusty months because the warming up of the land, as the sun advances from the south, brings the colder and heavier winds down from the north. These winds seem to have a wrestling match with the southern winds and with each other, and among them they raise a tremendous dust, because there's so much of it lying around loose; for the snows have gone, the rainy season hasn't begun, and the fields are bare.

Most people think March winds a great nuisance because dust grains are apt to get into their eyes; but dust in the eye is only the right thing in the wrong place. Just think of the amount of dust going about in March that *doesn't* get into your eyes; and how nice and fine it is, and how mixed with all the magic stuff of different kinds of soil, thus brought together from everywhere.

An English writer on farming says he thinks that English farms have done their work so well for so many centuries because the March winds have brought world-traveled dust-grains from other parts of the globe.

And the wind is a good friend to the good farmer, but no friend to the poor one; for it carries away dust, all nicely ground, from the fields of the farmer who doesn't protect his soil, and carries it to farmers who have wood lots and good pastures and winter wheat, and leaves it there; for woods and pastures and sown fields hold the soil they have, as well as the fresh, new soil the winds bring to them.

Most of the fine prairie soils in our Western States owe not a little of their richness to wind-borne dust. In western Missouri, southwestern Iowa, and southeastern Nebraska are deep deposits of yellowish-brown soil, the gift of the winds. And what apples it raises! It is in this soil that many of the best apple orchards of these States are located. And now, of course, the apple growers see to it that this soil stays at home.

But there's another kind of dust that deserves special mention, and that's the kind of dust that comes from volcanoes. Volcanoes make a very valuable kind of soil material, often called "volcanic ash." It isn't ashes, really. It's the very fine dust made by the explosion of the steam in the rocks thrown out by the volcano. The pores of the rocks, deep-buried in the earth, are filled with water, and when these rocks get into a volcanic explosion, this water turns to steam, and the steam not only blows out through the crater of the volcano, but the rocks themselves are blown to dust. This dust the winds catch and distribute far and wide. Sometimes the dust of a volcanic explosion is carried around the world. In the eruption of Krakatoa, in 1883, its dust was carried around the earth, not once but many times. The progress of this dust was recorded by the brilliant sunsets it caused. It is probable that every place on the earth has dust brought by the wind from every other place.

TO SEE IF YOU HAVE THE CENTRAL THOUGHT

Paragraph 1. How do the winds help plant trees, grass, and flowers?

Paragraph 2. Why is March likely to be the most dusty month? Name three reasons.

Paragraph 3. What is the main thought in this paragraph?

Paragraph 4. What did the English writer say about English farms and why?

Paragraph 5. Why and how do winds favor the farmer?

Paragraph 6. What point is made about certain soils in Iowa, Missouri, and Nebraska?

Paragraph 7. How is volcanic dust made? How far is it carried?

HOW DUST HELPS MAKE RAIN

NOTE: Prepare this selection for an oral class report. Find the main points in it. Fix them in mind for your report.

You remember how you can "see your breath," as we say, on a cold morning? Well, that's because the moisture in your breath is condensed by the cold. Now as the waters of the earth—the seas, lakes, rivers, and ponds—are warmed by the sun, the air above them is filled with moisture, for the heating of the air causes it to expand and draw in moisture from the water like a sponge. Expansion makes it lighter also, and it rises. Rising, it turns cooler, and the moisture condenses and comes down as rain. Mountains usually have clouds around them because moist air striking the mountainside is driven up the slope, cooling as it rises. So rain and snow often fall in mountain regions, and that's why so many rivers rise in mountains. The moist air is also condensed when it meets other and cooler air currents. But here it is that the work of the dust comes in. For to make rain you've got to have clouds, and clouds are caused by this moisture collecting around the little particles of dust of which the air is full. When these little motes of matter become cooler than the air that touches them the moisture in the air condenses into a film of water around them. Fairy worlds with fairy oceans floating in the sky!

Each of these cloud worlds is falling toward the big world below. They fall very slowly, only a few feet a day. Even if nothing else happened it might be months—yes, years—before each would come to the ground, even in still air. But when the air is very thick with moisture the water films on these dust particles grow rapidly, and thus increasing in weight, they fall faster and faster, and finally strike the earth as raindrops.

On the way down, two or more raindrops, falling in with each other, will go into partnership—melt into one—and then they hurry down so much the faster. That's why the sky grows darker and darker just before a rain, and why the lower part of a rain cloud is the darkest; the little raindrops are forming into bigger raindrops as they fall.

—From "The Adventures of a Grain of Dust," by Hallam Hawksworth.

FOR GENERAL DISCUSSION

1. In this section about the winds you have had five main topics presented to you. See if you can name them from memory. Write them down as if making a *Table of Contents*.

2. Write out a brief statement from memory about each topic. Read them in class and have the class choose the best ones. Use your own words; do not copy from the book.

3. Make a list of things you have learned about the **wind** which you did not know before. Which have been most interesting and impressive to you?

4. It might be interesting to make up a play or pageant about The Winds at Work, as follows: Let one pupil be Mother Nature who is holding court to hear reports of Wind and his helpers. Wind could have his sons and daughters tell what they have done—North Wind, East Wind, South Wind, West Wind. Also his assistants, Sun, Frost, Water, could tell of their work. **Dust** could come in with a story of real adventure.

REFERENCE WORK

If you are interested, you may wish to look up in the encyclopedia more about winds. Ask your librarian about books on winds, rain, storms, clouds, weather, and so on.

Here are two poems about the wind. Read them silently and prepare to read them orally. If there is any point or reference you do not understand, bring it to class for discussion.

THE WIND

I saw you toss the kites on high
And blow the birds about the sky;
And all around I heard you pass,
Like ladies' skirts across the grass—
  O wind, a-blowing all day long,
  O wind, that sings so loud a song!

I saw the different things you did,
But always you yourself you hid,
I felt you push, I heard you call,
I could not see yourself at all—
  O wind, a-blowing all day long,
  O wind, that sings so loud a song!

O you that are so strong and cold,
O blower, are you young or old?
Are you a beast of field and tree
Or just a stronger child than me?
  O wind, a-blowing all day long,
  O wind, that sings so loud a song!

—ROBERT LOUIS STEVENSON.

THE WINDY NIGHT

   Alow and aloof,
   Over the roof,
How the midnight tempests howl!
 With a dreary voice, like the dismal tune
 Of wolves that bay at the desert moon;—
   Or whistle and shriek
   Through limbs that creak,
   "Tu-who! tu-whit!"
   They cry and flit,
"Tu-whit! tu-who!" like the solemn owl!

   Alow and aloof,
   Over the roof,
Sweep the moaning winds amain,
   And wildly dash
   The elm and ash,
Clattering on the window-sash,
   With a clatter and patter,
   Like hail and rain
   That well nigh shatter
   The dusky pane!

   Alow and aloof,
   Over the roof,
How the tempests swell and roar!
   Though no foot is astir,
   Though the cat and the cur
Lie dozing along the kitchen floor,
   There are feet of air
   On every stair!
   Through every hall—
   Through each gusty door,
  There's a jostle and bustle,
   With a silken rustle,
Like the meeting of guests at a festival!

   Alow and aloof,
   Over the roof,
How the stormy tempests swell!
   And make the vane
   On the spire complain—
They heave at the steeple with might and main
   And burst and sweep
Into the belfry, on the bell!
They smite it so hard, and they smite it so well,
That the sexton tosses his arms in sleep,
And dreams he is ringing a funeral knell!

     —THOMAS BUCHANAN READ.

HOW MEN LEARNED TO FLY

John T. Trowbridge, an American poet, lived from 1827 to 1916. Early in his day the idea of man's traveling in the air was considered by most persons as a good joke. Trowbridge wrote a popular poem which you may enjoy reading. "Darius Green and His Flying Machine." It used to be in school readers and it amused those who read it. The poem says:

> "Darius was clearly of the opinion
> That the air was also man's dominion,
> And that, with paddle or fin or pinion,
> We soon or late should navigate
> The azure as now we sail the sea.
> The thing looks simple enough to me;
> And if you doubt it,
> Hear how Darius reasoned about it:"

At the end of the poem, when Darius at his first effort in flying falls to earth with a crash, the poet adds a little moral:

> "And this is the moral—stick to your sphere;
> Or, if you insist, as you have the right,
> On spreading your wings for a loftier flight,
> The moral is, Take care how you light."

HOW MEN LEARNED TO FLY

I

The ancient Greeks had a story about a man who made a pair of wings by which he could fly. They were fastened to his shoulders by wax. One day his son Icarus (Ĭk′àr ŭs) thought he would like to try them. He flew too high and the heat of the sun melted the wax by which the wings were held. Down tumbled Icarus into the sea and was drowned.

For centuries men have longed to be able to move about in the air. All over the world there are stories of magicians who could fly. But as men began to study science, they wondered whether it might not be possible to do this.

Roger Bacon, who died before 1300, after a life given to the study of science and philosophy, declared that men could make machines that would fly through the air, but he did not tell how to make them. In 1670, Francisco Lano sketched the first airship. It was like a boat, to be navigated with oars and sails and kept afloat by four copper globes from which the air had been exhausted. This would have been a kind of balloon, but unfortunately the copper globes were too thin and would have collapsed.

Nearly two centuries before that, the great artist, Leonardo da Vinci, who was also an engineer, studied the flight of birds and dreamed that men might learn to fly as they do. He drew sketches of wings to be fitted to the arms and legs; but he did not find a practicable way to fly.

The first balloon ascent took place in Paris, in 1783.

It was watched by our own inventor, Benjamin Franklin, who saw great possibilities in it when a way had been found by which the balloon could be steered.

Franklin's description of the balloon makes us wonder how any one had the courage to go up in it:

"Its bottom was open and in the middle of the opening was fixed a kind of basket grate, in which faggots and sheaves of straw were burnt. The air, rarefied in passing through this flame, rose in the balloon, swelled out its sides, and filled it. The persons, who were placed in the gallery made of wicker and attached to the outside near the bottom, had each of them a port through which they could pass sheaves of straw into the grate to keep up the flame and thereby keep the balloon full. . . ."

In this frail vessel the inventor and a friend rose above Paris to a height of five hundred feet and traveled a short distance, managing to keep in the air until they found a place where it would be safe to land. One of them told Franklin later that "they lit gently, without the least shock, and the balloon was very little damaged."

Since then, the balloon has been greatly improved, but, it was always at the mercy of the winds and more or less unmanageable. Men saw that it was not by improving balloons that the problem of flight in the air would be solved.

II

The first machine that would really fly, built on the plan of imitating the bird, was made by Samuel Pierpont

Langley. The small model that he built, which was about sixteen feet long and weighed about thirty pounds, and had two sets of wings, was launched on the Potomac River, May 6, 1896, and flew half a mile in a minute and a half. This is the first successful flight ever made by a machine heavier than air. The next problem was to make one large enough to carry people. The government provided money for experiment and Langley set to work in 1898.

It is interesting to read his own account of how the idea for his machine came to him:

"Nature has made her flying machine in the bird, which is nearly a thousand times as heavy as the air its bulk displaces. . . . I well remember how, as a child, when lying in a New England pasture, I watched a hawk soaring far up in the blue, and sailing for a long time without any motion of its wings, as though it needed no work to sustain it, but was kept up there by some miracle. . . . How wonderfully easy, too, was its flight! There was not a flutter of its pinions as it swept over the field, in a motion which seemed as effortless as that of its shadow. After many years and in mature life, I was brought to think of these things again, and to ask myself whether the problem of artificial flight was as hopeless and as absurd as it was then thought to be."

Langley was more than fifty years old when he began his experiments with airplanes. For seven years he had been a civil engineer and an architect; then for twenty years he had been an astronomer; by 1887, he had made such a reputation as an astronomer that he was appointed secretary of the Smithsonian Institution, the position held long before by Joseph Henry, who first got the idea for a telegraph.

After making nearly forty models, Langley got a machine light enough to fly, but at first he could not balance it. It was five years more before he ventured upon the first flight on the Potomac River.

Six months after the first success, another model was launched and flew for a short time at a speed of thirty miles an hour. Encouraged by this, Langley and his assistant, Charles M. Manly, set to work to make an engine that should be at once light enough and strong enough. They wrote to all the great builders of automobile engines in the United States and in Europe, but could find none who would undertake to furnish such an engine as was needed. A builder in New York attempted to do so, but failed after several trials. Finally Manly undertook to build the engine in the Smithsonian shops, and succeeded in constructing a powerful gasoline motor that weighed only 124 pounds, and actually gave 52 horse power. This was the lightest engine ever built until 1917.

In October, 1903, a flying machine was launched over the Potomac River, but this time it carried a passenger, the maker of its engine. Then happened a tragedy. The machine was launched from the roof of a house boat; but by a defect in the launching apparatus, the plane was caught and damaged before it got into the air at all, so that it plunged into the river. The pilot cleared himself from the wreckage and was rescued by men in a boat. A few days later the experiment was tried again, and again the launching apparatus failed to work. Again Manly went down in the river—this time to the very bottom, but he was ready to try once more. But the newspapers made fun of the experiment, the Government refused more money for the work, and Langley soon after died of a broken heart.

III

In 1914, Glenn Curtiss, long after airplanes of many kinds were flying, and long after the death of Langley, took the original machine with the original engine and flew with perfect success on Lake Keuka. In this way he proved that the first successful flying machine, notwithstanding the disastrous accident in the launching, had both the power and the proper construction to fly in October, 1903.

On December 17, 1903, the Wright brothers made the first successful flight with a machine carrying a man; and after that there was no question that men could fly. The Wrights, who had always been interested in mechanics, and who had experimented with bicycles, by 1900 were experimenting with gliders. After learning how to balance and control the gliders, they introduced a light engine into one and accomplished the first successful flight.

The next step in the development of the airplane was to make one that could also be propelled in the water—the flying boat. This was the invention of Glenn Curtiss, who in 1900, like the Wrights, was the owner of a bicycle shop. In 1911, the first flying boat was shown at an aviation meet in Chicago.

The War hastened the improvement of means of flying and machines of all types were turned out in the factories of Europe and of America. And immediately after the

THE FIRST FLIGHT WITH A MOTOR-DRIVEN HEAVIER-THAN-AIR MACHINE AT KITTY HAWK, NORTH CAROLINA, DECEMBER 17, 1903.
Orville Wright in the machine, Wilbur running alongside of it.

War, the first long flights across the ocean were made. The NC4, built in the Navy Department, left Newfoundland May 16, 1919, and twelve hours later arrived at the Azores, more than a thousand miles away. On May 27, the NC4 left the Azores and arrived at Lisbon nine hours later. On May 30, the NC4 left Lisbon and arrived at Plymouth, England, in ten hours and twenty minutes. In November, 1919, Captain Sir Ross Smith undertook to fly from England to Australia in thirty days, and made the trip in less than twenty-eight.

Side by side with experiments in flying with planes, other experiments were being carried on with dirigible balloons. Notwithstanding bad accidents, these became more and more successful, until finally on July 2, 1919, the British R34, in charge of Major G. H. Scott, left Scotland, arrived at New York, July 6, and made the return trip in seventy-five hours.

Commercial use soon began to be made of the results of these experiments. The first mail service by airplane was established between Washington and New York before the end of the War. Soon after, a transcontinental service was begun and a line was established between Key West and Havana. A regular service between Paris and London, carrying both passengers and mail, was soon under way. Here and there, all over the world, companies were formed for developing this new means of transportation.

But experimentation went on. Soon men were practicing in machines that used the currents of the air to fly like birds. When this method of flying has been perfected, the dream of Leonardo da Vinci, in the fifteenth century, and of Samuel Langley, in the nineteenth century, that men would one day be able to fly like birds, will be completely realized.

The realization of this dream was hastened, in May, 1927, by Charles A. Lindbergh, a young man in his early twenties, who alone made the first non-stop flight across the Atlantic from New York to Paris. In his monoplane, "The Spirit of St. Louis," he flew through fog, sleet, and storms, making the journey in thirty-three and a half hours. His modesty, courage, and skill so appealed to the whole world that he was received in Europe and the United States with the highest honors.

THINGS TO DO

1. Bring clippings, pictures, and magazines to class and give short talks about flying.
2. Make a list of celebrated flights since 1919 with planes and airships to show what wonderful progress is being made.

REFERENCE WORK

1. Who will volunteer to look up some interesting facts about: Roger Bacon, Leonardo da Vinci, Samuel Langley, Glenn Curtiss, Wilbur and Orville Wright? A research group might work together to do this.
2. Others might look up facts about our Air Mail Service.
3. It would also be interesting to have reports on the following: The First Flight Across the Atlantic; The First Flight Around the World; The Flight of "The Norge" Over the Pole; Captain Byrd and His Airplane Flight to the Pole.

BOOKS FOR READING

C. R. Gibson, in his book on "Great Inventions," gives a good account of balloons and aeroplanes.

Another interesting book is by H. E. Maule, "Book of New Inventions."

There are many recent good magazine articles. Ask your librarian to help find some for you.

In "Air-Craft of Today," by Turner, there is a vivid description of the sensations one feels during ballooning, pp. 152-155.

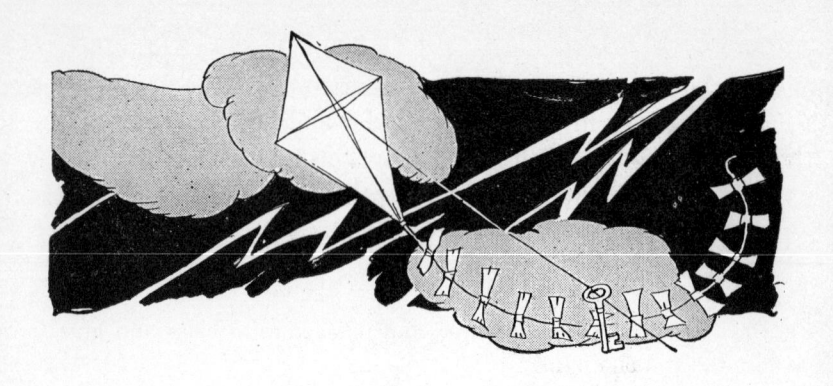

HOW MEN LEARNED TO USE ELECTRICITY

Have you ever thought how much we depend upon electricity in our daily lives? Just think of the number of uses to which it is put in home and community. Imagine, if you can, what we should do now without it. There would be no telegraph or telephone, no radio, no electric cars and trains, no electric bells, no electric motors, no electric lights! Many other inventions in common daily use would be impossible without electricity. We use it so much and in so many ways that our industry, transportation, and communication would be hopelessly ruined if our electrical equipment were to be put out of use.

The following account will tell you some of the main points in the story of man's effort to learn about and control the most powerful force on the earth. Many interesting discoveries and inventions are necessarily left out here. You will learn of them later if you continue in school. Some of you may desire to look them up immediately in the books listed at the end of the account. That will be good reference work.

Nearly every topic presented here will furnish facts and ideas for discussion, questions, and reference work. For this reason the account will be interesting to read in class, one topic at a time. Read carefully and note for discussion points not clear to you.

In books on electricity, encyclopedias, and magazines, you can find good illustrations of many points, and additional facts to make them clear. There are always some boys particularly interested in electricity. Here is a good opportunity for them to help the class. To do this they may need to use pictures or make sketches on the board, and to explain in their own words the parts that are not clear to the class.

AIDS TO READING: As you read this account do these things:

1. Note the main idea in each paragraph.
2. If some question comes to your mind when reading, jot it down to ask in discussion.
3. Bring in good pictures or illustrations you may find.
4. Read as many references as you can.

HOW MEN LEARNED TO USE ELECTRICITY

THE BEGINNING

The story of electricity is a long one. As much as two thousand years ago, the Greeks had observed that amber[1] and several minerals, when rubbed, have a strange power to attract other light substances, such as bits of lint or feathers. You can produce the same effect by rubbing a stick of dry sealing-wax with a piece of dry flannel or fur and then touching it to bits of dry paper, or ravelings from common white wrapping string. A stick of ebonite or a large black rubber comb will give even a better result.

---

[1] amber (ăm'bĕr): a yellowish, mineral-like resin, which the ancient Greeks named electron (ē-lĕk'trŏn). From this name we have our word electricity, because rubbing amber was the first known way to produce the strange force we now know as electricity.

The materials must be dry. This is called making electricity by friction.

The ancient Greeks knew also of a certain kind of stone, a peculiar kind of iron ore, that would attract small particles of iron and hold them firmly. This peculiar stone was found in different parts of Greece and Asia Minor. We now know it as magnetic iron ore. The small pieces of it which they used were natural magnets. But the Greeks made little use of the facts they observed, except to show how the strange force acted. Many exciting stories were told about it. There was one story about a shepherd named Magnes, who lived on the island of Crete. One day while tending his sheep on Mount Ida he noticed that his iron-tipped staff was so strongly drawn to earth that he could hardly pull it away. Looking down to see what was the matter, he discovered it was resting on a peculiar stone, which had a strange power of attraction. Another story tells of a powerful magnetic mountain which pulled the nails out of ships, even when they were at considerable distance from it. These stories show how unusual occurrences in nature stirred the imaginations of men in the far-off days.

The first step toward the knowledge and use of electricity was taken when men learned something about magnets and their force (called magnetic force or magnetism) and found that a strange force could be produced by rubbing (friction) different substances. They could not explain it and they did not know how to use it.

About Magnets

As you have now learned, magnets probably were first known to the European nations through the discovery of natural magnetic iron by the Greeks. The region about Magnesia became well known for this peculiar stone. From it (Magnesia) the name *magnet* was taken. Some early writers say the name was taken from the shepherd Magnes. At any rate, the word *magnet* probably was taken from a Greek name.

Real knowledge about magnets grew very slowly. It was more than a thousand years from the first we knew of magnets before much practical information about them was gained. The first man to bring together the facts about magnets and their action was William Gilbert, a famous physician who lived in the days of Queen Elizabeth. He was appointed by Elizabeth to be her chief physician. All the time he could spare from his professional duties, he devoted to the study of nature. In the year 1600, he published a book called "On the Magnet," in which he put the results of eighteen years of study and experiments with magnets. This shows how long and patiently men have had to work, to know anything about nature.

Dr. Gilbert learned many things about magnets and their force, which led to later discoveries and inventions. He believed the earth itself to be a great magnet, as we know is true. His work made a new starting point for other men, from which they could carry on the never-ending search for truth.

About Electricity

From the time of Thales (600 B. C.), one of the seven wise men of Greece, little more real knowledge of electricity had been gained until the time of Dr. Gilbert, a thousand years later! This tireless and ever-questioning experimenter made valuable discoveries about electrical force. He found that many other substances besides amber can be electrified by rubbing, and that some conditions are more favorable than others for making electricity by friction. But he did not know how to make electricity in large quantities, nor how to store it when made. In fact no one before the time of our Benjamin Franklin (more than one hundred and fifty years later) had been able to store and make successful use of electricity in the daily life of men. It was only a strange thing which provoked men to ask questions about it.

So you see the simple beginning of one of the greatest powers in our daily lives. It is a story of wonderful interest. There is a great deal more to learn about it. When you think of this brief sketch, do you not wonder at the great progress we have made in recent years? A day now brings forth more than was discovered in a hundred years in early times.

The Telegraph

The telegraph instrument was one of the most marvelous inventions of the first half of the nineteenth century. In 1830 many men, both in Europe and America, were experimenting with electricity. Joseph Henry, the inventor of the electro-magnet, knew that experiments were being made to discover how electricity might be used for signaling. In 1831, he strung a mile of fine wire between an electric battery and a bell, the clapper of which was connected to an electro-magnet. The experiment succeeded. You can see how it worked by examining a small electric bell. The diagram will show you the parts of it. This experiment made Henry feel sure that it would be possible to make an instrument by which messages could be sent long distances.

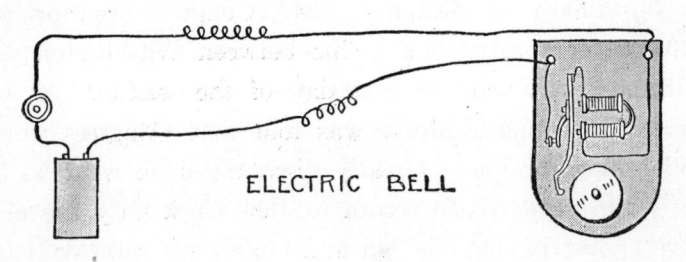

ELECTRIC BELL

Henry did not try to invent a practicable telegraph, but he gave the idea to Samuel F. B. Morse, who set to work on it in 1832. It is difficult for us to realize what a task it was for Morse to make progress with his work. He could not buy the things he needed for they were not to be had at any price. Electro-magnets were not for sale. There was no insulated copper wire.

Even bare copper could be purchased only in small quantities and at a very high price. It was a discouraging undertaking. Many persons made fun of the idea, just as many did of Columbus and other pioneers of discovery and invention. Finally Morse was able to interest friends and secure money to carry on his plans.

After eight years of hard work, the United States Government issued a patent to Morse. By this time (1840) he had done all that he could without more help. He wished Congress to grant him money for constructing a telegraph line. Some of the leaders in Congress were interested; others ridiculed the idea. The Postmaster-General said it would be unwise to throw money away on such a foolish idea. Many declared it could never be a paying success.

But finally on March 4, 1843, Congress appropriated $30,000 for constructing a line between Washington and Baltimore. It was the last day of the session. At ten o'clock that night, Morse was told that Congress would do nothing for him. Greatly discouraged he went to his hotel and prepared to return to New York City the next day. After paying his bill and buying his railway ticket he had only thirty-seven cents left! Then came the good news that at the last moment the money had been granted. He went to work with new courage. And on May 24, 1844, the first message, "What hath God wrought," was sent from the Supreme Court room in Washington to Baltimore.

The invention of the telegraph illustrates what courage and patience and hard work were required of men to learn how to use electricity. It is a wonderful story of a great success from small beginnings. Think how news is gathered from the ends of the earth, how trains are moved over our great railway systems, and how industry and commerce have been aided by the telegraph!

The Telephone

Alexander Graham Bell (1847–1922) conceived a different idea for the use of electricity. He thought it might be made to carry the sound of the human voice along wires, so that people could talk to one another from a distance. Inventors both in Europe and America were working on the

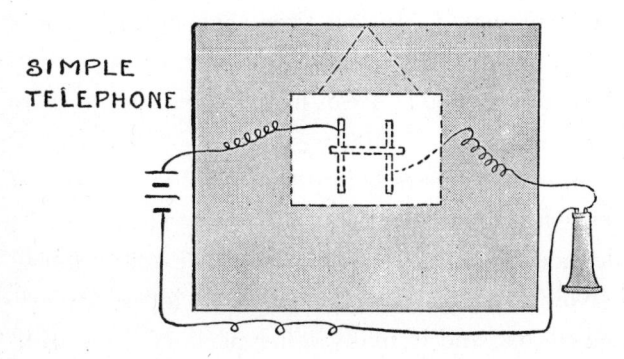

SIMPLE TELEPHONE

idea. When he was about twenty-eight years old, Mr. Bell took his idea and plans to Joseph Henry, who was then secretary of the Smithsonian Institution[1] at Washington, D. C. You will remember Mr. Henry as the man who invented the electro-magnet. Mr. Henry listened to Bell's plan with great interest and encouraged him by saying he thought "it was the germ of a great invention."

"I don't know enough about electricity," said Bell.

---

[1] Smithsonian Institution: an institution endowed by James Smithson, and founded in Washington, D. C., in 1846, for research work and the diffusion of knowledge.

"You can learn," replied Henry. "If you don't have the knowledge, get it." And Bell got it. He went back to Boston where he had been living, rented a room, and studied electricity by day and by night. One of his friends, Thomas Watson, came to help him. After much hard work and many failures, at last they succeeded. They had strung wires from a second-story room to the basement. On March 10, 1876, Bell sent Watson to the basement. Then speaking into the instrument, Bell said: "Watson, come here; I want you." In less time than he ever made it before, Watson ran up the three flights of stairs, shouting excitedly: "I can hear you! I can hear the words!" The telephone was the result.

It was a number of years before the telephone was perfected and men were interested to put money into it. In 1881, the Bell Telephone Company was organized with $6,000,000 behind it. Now the Bell Telephone is used in every part of the United States, and in many other parts of the world. More messages are sent in a day by telephone than by telegraph and letter combined. It is easy to talk from New York to San Francisco. And, too, we can talk across the ocean. It can now be done by the aid of radio broadcasting. The wireless phone or radio-phone will no doubt be perfected in the near future. Think of the changes brought about by the telephone in fifty years! Here is something which we all know and use in our homes, something which has become so necessary a part of our lives that we do not often stop to think how wonderful it is.

The Radio

It is marvelous how man has conquered the electrical forces of the earth and is putting them at work for himself. Probably the most wonderful of all electrical inventions is the radio, which developed out of experiments with wireless telegraphy. We are all so familiar with the radio-receiver in our homes that we almost think of it as if it had always been here. But there is a long story back of it. To Guglielmo Marconi, an Italian scientist, belongs the credit for the first practical start toward radio. His first success came in 1896, when he sent a wireless message across the English Channel to France, a distance of thirty-two miles. In 1901, he succeeded in getting a message from the coast of England to St. John's, Newfoundland, a distance of more than three thousand miles.

Since 1901, many scientists and inventors have worked on the radio. Americans have led the world in its development. Radio broadcasting is familiar to all of us. The next step is the perfection of the radio-phone.

So you have the high points in the story of how men learned to use electricity. Many other points of interest have been purposely omitted, like the experiments of Franklin, who in his memorable experiment with the kite in the clouds proved lightning to be identical with electricity. Many inventions and uses of recent days you know about.

Just think of it! In the far-off days when lightning flashed, men trembled in terror for fear of the fire from heaven. It was to them the wrath of the gods. Ages passed. Little by little, the fire of heaven was found to be sleeping in the earth—in every earthly object. Little by little man learned to awaken it and control it for his use. Now it is doing a large part of the work of the world. By its use, each of us has willing, obedient, useful servants at his command! And the end is not yet.

AFTERWORD

So often in life the end is only the beginning. You have reached the end of GOOD READING and you are only at the beginning of good reading. You can go on with good reading all your lives if you wish. And however much you read there will be always more good books waiting for you —books which rest and interest you when you are tired, amuse you when you are sad, encourage you when you are discouraged, give you companionship when you are lonely. Good books contain the best of the thoughts and experiences of great men and women on all subjects that people think and talk about.

Since this is true, it is strange that there are people in the world who are always looking for something to help them "pass away the time." No one who has learned the joy of the companionship of books is ever at a loss what to do with spare time.

But it is very important to read wisely. Newspapers and magazines tell you what is going on in the world and offer you both information and amusement; but they are made up so as to interest as many people as possible. Each number contains things that interest some people and bore others; yet many people who pick up a newspaper or a magazine think that they must read it all, and so spend a great deal of their time which might be used with far more pleasure and profit in another way.

This waste of time you can easily avoid. You have been learning how to look up, in different kinds of reference books, information that you need and how to pass over what you do not need; you have learned how to read the newspapers by the headlines and to skip the columns that are not interesting to you; and you have learned how to find your way about libraries, and, with the aid of librarians, to choose among many books on the subject those which are best. You have begun to enjoy reading. You have made a beginning in learning what, as you grow older, you will find out to be one of the most important aids to successful and happy living—what to read and how to read it.

The ability to read wisely is a key that unlocks all the treasures of learning and wisdom. The great founders of our nation and those who maintained its unity—such men as Washington, Franklin, Jefferson, and Lincoln—had no more school education than is now given in a good high school, but all of them had learned to read wisely and all by wise reading and deep thought achieved lasting fame for themselves and the benefits of liberty and security for us. Habits of wise reading and honest thinking will help you, too, to live lives honorable to yourselves and useful to your fellow men.

WORD LIST

In reading this book, if you do not understand what a word means or how it should be pronounced, look for it in the list. The diacritical marks over the vowels tell you which of the vowel sounds is the right one to use. The vowel sounds are given together at the head of the list.

ā, as in fāte
â, as in câre
ă, as in ădd
ä, as in ärm
à, as in àsk

ē, as in ēve
ĕ, as in ĕnd
ī, as in īce
ĭ, as in ĭll
ō, as in ōld

ô, as in ôr, all (ôl)
ŏ, as in nŏt
oi, as in oil
o͞o, as in mo͞on
o͝o, as in fo͝ot

ou, as in out
ū, as in ūse
û, as in ûrn
ŭ, as in ŭp
', as e in shovel

A

abashed, embarrassed.
adversary (ăd'vûr-sâ-rĭ), enemy.
adverse (ăd-vûrs'), unfavorable.
alkali (ăl'kà-lī), *here* desert, so-called because the earth is full of alkali or soda ash.
aloe (ăl'ō), a gay-flowered tropical plant.
Alpha Centauri (ăl'fä sen-tô're).
alternative (àl-tûr'nà-tĭv), choice of two things.
amphitheater (ăm''fē-thē'à-tûr), *here* a piece of level ground surrounded by hills.
appalling (ăp-pôl'ĭng), filling with dismay.
arid (ăr'ĭd), very dry.
aroma (à-rō'mà), pleasant smell.
aslope, slanting.

B

baffle, stop a person by puzzling him.
basalt (bà-sôlt'), a dark volcanic rock.
beaker, a large wide-mouthed cup.
beset (bē-sĕt'), hemmed in.
black-prowed (proud), with bows painted black.
blunderbuss (blŭn'dûr-bŭs), a short gun with a large opening (no longer used).
Boer (bo͞or), a South African of Dutch ancestry.
boom (bo͞om), a long beam projecting from a derrick.
brawn, an old-fashioned English Christmas dish of boiled pork, chopped and seasoned, and pressed into a loaf.
brunt, shock.
butte (būt), a steep hill standing apart from others.

C

cable-drum, a barrel-shaped piece of machinery on which a rope is wound and unwound.
cairn (kârn), a heap of stones raised as a landmark.
capacious (kà-pā'shŭs), able to contain much.
carronade (kăr''rō-nād'), a cannon used on board ship.
cauldron (kôl'drŏn), a large kettle.
cavalcade (kăv'ăl-kād''), a procession on horseback.
chapping, *Scotch for* knocking.
cinch, girth tightly.
cloying, deadening the sense of taste.
combustible (kŭm-bŭs'tĭb'l), able to burn.
confederate (cŏn-fĕd'ûr-āt), partner.
confront (cŏn-frŭnt'), face.
constancy (kŏn'stăn-sĭ), steadiness.
contemplate (kŏn'tĕm-plāt), view with continued attention.
corps (kōr), an organized body of persons.
corral (kŏrräl'), an enclosure for keeping animals in.
corslet (kôrs'lĕt), metal breastplate and backplate (especially sixteenth century).
coulee (ko͞o-lā'), the deep bed of a stream, even when dry.
coyote ((kī-ō'tē), the prairie wolf.
craggy (krăg'ĭ), rocky.
craven, cowardly.
creosote (krē'ō-sōt), a dark, oily liquid made from wood tar.
crevasse (krĕ-văs'), a deep, narrow split in a glacier.
crinoid (krī'noid), a plant-like sea animal.
crossbow, a bow set crosswise on a stock.

445

croup (kroop), the part of a horse's back behind the saddle.
curlicue (kûr'lĭ-kū), a flourish, as in writing.

D

debouch (dē-bouch'), open out into.
defective, lacking.
Dekanakwidah (dĕk″à-nà-kwē'dà).
deliberation, *here* slowness.
demotic (dē-mŏt'ĭk), literally, belonging to the common people.
demur (dē-mûr'), object.
depraved, made bad.
diacritical (dī″à-krĭt'ĭ-kăl), used to show differences in pronunciation.
dimity, a thin cotton material with thread-like stripes.
dirigible (dĭr'ĭ-jĭb'l), that can be steered (used especially of a balloon).
disputant (dĭs'pu-tant), a person engaged in arguing.
disputatious (dĭs″pū-tā'shŭs), inclined to argue.
divide, a watershed.
Duke Humphrey, dine with, have nothing to eat.

E

ebonite (ĕb'ŏn-īt), a black kind of hard rubber.
emaciated (ē-mā'sē-ā″tĕd), very thin.
embattled, drawn up in battle order.
enjoin, command.
equipment, *here* engine and train together.
equivalent (ē-quĭv'àl-ĕnt), equal in worth.
ewer (yū'ûr), a wide-mouthed pitcher.
excavate (ĕx'kà-vāt), dig out.
exile (ĕg'zīl), forced separation from one's country.
expostulate (ĕx-pŏs'tū-lāt), argue with some one against a course of action.
exterminate (ĕx-tûr'mĭn-āt), destroy.
extremity, the end of strength or endurance.

F

fall, the part of a rope to which the power is applied in hoisting.
fawning (fôn'ĭng), courting favor by trying to please.
ferment (fûr-mĕnt'), *here* become irritated.
ferocious (fē-rō'shŭs), fierce.
fiord (fyôrd), a narrow bay (Norwegian word).
flagon (flăg'ŏn), a large vessel with a handle and a spout.
floe (flō), a low, flat mass of floating ice.
forestall (fôr-stôl'), get ahead of.

formidable (for'mĭd-à-b'l), difficult enough to frighten.
Francisco Lano (frän-chĭs'kō lä'nō).
frigate (frĭg'āt), a kind of sailing vessel.
frontiersman (frŏn-tērz'măn), a man who lives on the edge of inhabited country.
frumenty (froo'mĕn-tĭ), wheat boiled with milk, sugar, and raisins.
full-bottomed wig, a large wig of long hair, worn in the eighteenth century.
furtive, sneaking.

G

girder, steel beam laid horizontally to bear weight.
goatskin, a bottle made of a goatskin.
good-e'en, good evening.
gorge, a narrow valley between steep mountains.
granary (grăn'à-rĭ), a storehouse for grain.
grape and canister: canister is a cluster of bullets in a case fired from a cannon and scattering when they come out; **grape**, larger balls also fired as a group.
Guglielmo Marconi (gūl-yĕl'mō mär-kō'nē).
guttural (gŭt'tûr-ăl), pronounced in the throat).

H

hardtack, hard biscuit taken on long voyages because they keep a long time.
harpy, in mythology, a monstrous bird with the head of a woman.
hatch, *here* make a network of lines.
head, the beginning of a stream.
hieroglyphics (hī″ûr-ō-glĭ'fĭks), the name given to one kind of Egyptian writing.
high seas, the ocean miles away from land.
hireling, a person who is hired.
hold, lowest part of the inside of a ship.
hurdle, a movable frame of twigs woven together, used for enclosing.

I

igloo (ĭg'loo), an Eskimo hut.
ignoble (ĭg-nō'b'l), dishonorable.
illimitable (ĭl-lĭm'ĭt-à-b'l), boundless.
immemorial (ĭm″mĕ-mō'rĭ-ăl), going back beyond memory.
impassive, not showing emotion.
imperative (ĭm-pĕr'à-tĭv), urgent.
imperishable (ĭm-pĕr'ĭsh-à-b'l), lasting forever.
impulse, *here* thrust.
incalculable (ĭn-kăl'kū-là-b'l), not to be measured.
inhospitable (ĭn-hŏs'pĭ-tà-b'l), *here* desolate.